Eat London³

Eat London³

All about food
Peter Prescott &
Terence Conran

Photography by Lisa Linder

conran
OCTOPUS

Authors' Acknowledgements
I've got to say a huge congratulations and thank you to Lisa Linder, our wonderful photographer. I've worked with many different photographers over the years and none has been able to capture the essence of a place, a recipe or a person – usually a chef or sommelier, bar staff or a waiter/ess – like Lisa. I would also say that Lisa did it with great efficiency and often in particularly difficult conditions. I'd like to offer equal praise to David Hawkins, our superlative graphic designer/art director, who has brought all three editions of *Eat London* to life. We've worked together for over a decade now, so he should also know a thing or two about restaurants.

And, not to be forgotten, Irene Lentsch, who helped me coordinate everything on this latest edition of *EL* and has also worked with us for a number of years – Irene is a restaurant marketing specialist and passionate about all things restaurants.
Peter Prescott

An Hachette UK Company
www.hachette.co.uk

Third edition published in 2017
by Conran Octopus Ltd,
a division of Octopus Publishing Group Ltd
Carmelite House
50 Victoria Embankment
London EC4Y 0DZ
www.octopusbooks.co.uk

ISBN 978 1 84091 746 8

A CIP catalogue record for this book is available from the British Library.

Printed and bound in China

10 9 8 7 6 5 4 3 2 1

Publisher: Alison Starling
Managing Editor: Sybella Stephens
Creative Director: Jonathan Christie
Art Direction and Design: Untitled
Photographer: Lisa Linder
Photographer's Assistant: Dominika Stanczyk
Map Illustrations: David Bray
Senior Production Manager: Katherine Hockley

Where a view is expressed by a particular author, this is denoted by (PP) for Peter Prescott and (TC) for Terence Conran.

The majority of the research for this book was completed in 2016. Forgive us if some of the facts have changed by the time you read the book.

Contents

Introduction

Terence Conran and Peter Prescott

Above **Peter Prescott (left) and Terence Conran.** Opposite **Lunch at Parabola at The Design Museum on bespoke plates by 1882 Ltd.**

London is the dining-out capital of the world! This third edition of *Eat London* aims to provide the key evidence to prove this absolute fact and convince any wavering mind. London is the place that any great chef or restaurateur wants to be. It is home to the most diverse selection of food and drink destinations any city can offer. It is a melting pot of creative talent and a place to enjoy everything from a deconstructed kebab to Taiwanese steamed buns. From super high-end dining to snacking on a budget, from mono-ingredient food trucks and market stalls to some of the most over-the-top menus on the planet: the diversity and the quality are nonpareil.

While we are obviously keen to promote the talents and drive of fellow friends and colleagues in this, the most addictive form of employment, we think a large part of our success is due to our customers. It seems to us that chefs and restaurateurs are pushed to ever-higher heights due to the insatiable demand of the restaurant-going public in London. Our great city is hungry for new tastes and thirsty for a great night out. Thankfully, we are blessed with the most open-minded and quality-hungry clientele, a populace that is willing to endure everything from queuing (something that is becoming the essential mark of a new opening, but also something that we really do not want to do) or an arduous booking process, or sky-high prices to down-at-heel locations, just to sate their desire for a tasty morsel. Of course, they also enjoy some of the most cossetted and brilliantly designed environments and some of the most professional service standards you can ever dream of. There is also a sense of informality, fun and enjoyment that is now such a distinguishing component of the London food and drink scene.

We also think London's food and drink suppliers need to be mentioned. We might not have a great central market or anything close to the magnificent Rungis on the outskirts of Paris, but our multitude of supplier networks is world-class. Whatever is needed at whatever time of day you can usually get in a London kitchen, something that hasn't gone unnoticed by the great chefs of the world. Plus, we are now rightly proud of our fantastic home-grown produce and it is gracing the finest kitchens and impressing an international audience new to the charms of our amazing cheeses, fish and shellfish and rare-breed meats. Even English sparkling wines are the toast of leading sommeliers.

While London can never be accused of being inexpensive, we do also think that one of the reasons for our pre-eminence in the restaurant field is the value for money that can be enjoyed, especially if you know where to look. London has become great in many other areas, but these are often at the top end of the financial stakes — we're thinking about property, fashion, luxury brands and the like. Unlike these sectors, we think the more in-vogue strands of the food world in London are at the more affordable end of the market. We also think the intense competition that comes with a plethora of operators also helps keep the prices reasonable. We don't have any statistics to back up this statement, but we genuinely think that average restaurant prices are the same today as they were eight to ten years ago. Compare this to other things and we don't think the results would be the same. Plus, look at the cost of the restaurant in the top Michelin restaurants in Paris and New York and you will soon see that a comparable London list is far more reasonable — but perhaps this isn't the best example of value for money.

Many around the world will think our statement about the quality and appeal of London restaurants is wildly inaccurate. In the case of many, perhaps (mostly) elderly French people, just the idea of our statement is ludicrous. London has transformed from a culinary joke to an exemplar of great food and drink experiences. It is an epicentre for excellent cafés, restaurants, bars, bakeries, cheese shops, butchers, food markets, food pop-ups, ethnic street food, for everything from breakfast to late-night pizza, and every other type of food and drink need. In the previous edition, we commented that there had been a restaurant revolution. This is still valid, and we would further venture that the revolution continues at a pace, and the restaurant scene is almost constantly evolving.

This change has happened very, very quickly and it is this speed of change that typifies the restaurant world. It is ten years since the first edition of *Eat London* was published, and looking back, it is palpable how much has changed in a relatively short period of time. Tastes are changing, new ideas are emerging and new standards are expected. Plus, young and talented people are drawn to the food and drink world like never before. This has brought great change and in our opinion a much wider view as to what dining out is all about. The spectrum of what is defined as a restaurant is being stretched to ever-wider points. In fact, we are getting to a position where perhaps even the word restaurant might not be enough, or is possibly becoming dated. I was reminded of this recently when a (really excellent) tapas bar with no tables, just counter dining, won restaurant of the year for two consecutive years.

Dining out is now such an everyday must-do activity. This mindset has fuelled new styles of food or different concepts and formats; it has helped to welcome young start-ups, food and drink entrepreneurs with small budgets but big ideas. The extent and range of offerings are widening all the time. This polarizing of ideas – from stripped-back tiny spaces to huge multi-million-pound dining rooms, is making London the envy of the world.

This new edition of *Eat London* tries to demonstrate that eating out and enjoying delicious food in London can involve anything from a café in a converted railway arch in Hackney to an opulent fine dining establishment in Mayfair. In this new edition, we've included more bars that also happen to serve great food. Over recent years, there's been a re-emergence of the wine bar, whether specializing in natural and biodynamic wines (mostly in East London) or *grands vins*, decanted, thanks to the help of the new-fangled Coravin system. And London is now blessed with fantastic cocktail bars.

It is certainly evident that the centre of gravity has swung from the west to the east; it was previously the case that the most exciting openings were almost always in West End locations. Now, we are all looking east. It started in Shoreditch, then came Dalston, now there is much to enjoy and relish in deepest Hackney and beyond. Saying all that, given the constantly swelling number of restaurants, this edition has focused more on central London locations and sadly had to drop a few local residential neighbourhood places.

Also new to this book is a short list of out-of-London restaurants. These are day-trip destinations where you can enjoy great food and service. However, away from London there is a shorter supply of decent places to eat and drink – the revolution is yet to happen, and we see nothing that is likely to change in the near term, but happen it will, and central London rents and rates will help make the change.

Above **The elegant interior at Spring at Somerset House.**

Right **Fine dining at Texture.**

Left **One of the brilliant cheese retailers at Maltby Street Market.**

Our own little collection of cafés, restaurants and food stores has also grown in the past four years and we are proud to include most of them in this edition. However, we want to stress that our main objective with this book is to highlight and promote the idea that London is the best place to eat in the world. Restaurateurs are friendly and happy people, we hope. Yes, we might be in great competition with our neighbouring eateries, but in our mind there is a bigger issue to be concerned with. We all want to be successful and see London at the pinnacle of all things food and drink.

Peter Prescott's own circumstances have changed, substantially, since the last edition. He says, 'I'm now happily married and have the joy of a young son, and a daughter due in 2017. This has brought a number of new perspectives on dining out, which I have tried to incorporate within my comments. It is interesting to experience first-hand how restaurateurs deal with young children and their parents. Family-friendly cafés and restaurants can be very special places, with a wonderful bonhomie. I would also say that nights out without our son demand more. It's made me more selective when deciding on the destination for a good night out; I've applied this focus on the list of entries in this new book.'

'I'm a Londoner and a restaurateur,' writes Peter, 'and this book is very much a personal view on the restaurant world, shared by Terence. Of course, it is also an insider's view and it certainly isn't always objective. I'd like to think that I'm well informed when it comes to what's happening, who's opening or closing or refurbishing or relaunching or changing chefs or managers.'

We learn a lot from visiting other restaurants and sometimes even more from interviewing other chefs and managers. It's an addictive world and something that is also rather gossipy. There is now great spirit among restaurateurs – rewind 10 to 15 years and we didn't really engage with each other, but now there is a fraternal atmosphere. We have inevitably included a few restaurants and bars belonging to friends and former colleagues, but would add that we pay for all of our meals, unless stated to the contrary, and we never say in advance that we are visiting a particular restaurant. We're not pretending or trying to be a replacement for your favourite restaurant guide. Perhaps we are steering you in the direction of a particular place or potentially putting you off somewhere. The restaurant world is all about people, and people have good and bad days. Restaurants can be scintillating one day and terrible the next. If fact, you can have good and bad experiences on tables immediately next to each other on the same day at the same time. This book is about capturing a moment, a particular element or a unique experience. It might go out of date very quickly and you might also find that some of the comments are still relevant in years to come. With the emergence of social media, online restaurant-booking platforms and feedback forums, we are all restaurant critics now. So, don't take our word for anything – see what others are also saying. We are both very positive in regard to what social media has brought to the restaurant world, particularly Instagram, but there are faults – TripAdvisor springs to mind. If you really want to get an objective view, we would refer you to the generally excellent *Time Out*.

Great praise and best wishes to all in the restaurant world, and happy eating and drinking to everybody else.

June 2017

Below **Lunch at Bibendum Oyster Bar.**

If you're thinking of starting up a new restaurant, café or bar, first make up your mind about what sort of place you want. Then search the property market in the area you have selected for something you can afford, and remember that most rents escalate upward every five years, so what may seem reasonable and affordable may not be so next year. Check with your local authority that the property has permission to be used for catering with alcohol.

Having found your property, start to make your business plan, and remember that to construct a medium-size restaurant costs approximately £1 million, with the kitchen being roughly a quarter of that total. Professional kitchens are very different from domestic kitchens – they have to suffer a huge amount of wear and a lot of tear. Of course, a café can cost much less but even so a good coffee machine is very expensive. I give this advice as I have seen many optimistic restaurateurs get into financial trouble because the costs of opening their place have exceeded their estimates. And remember, once the restaurant has been fitted out, there are still staff to train, rent to pay and stocks of food and wine and spirits to buy. Suppliers are unlikely to give you much credit until they see how successful you are. I say all of this because I have designed well over 100 restaurants, cafés and bars and owned quite a few of them, the first of which were my soup kitchens in 1953.

Now for something a bit more constructive – the big problem of what type of restaurant or café. Get to know the area that your property is in and form an opinion of what is missing. Eat at every restaurant in the area and take notes of the quality of the service and the price of main dishes, the wines and the overall bill – it's a good idea to take your manager with you if you have appointed one by this stage. Also, go to the cafés in your area and have a cup of coffee or a drink, again noting details and prices. Try to make a decision about whether to have a formal or an informal atmosphere, then visit local supermarkets or food shops to try to work out what the locals are buying. M&S is a good food store with quality products, as is Waitrose. If there is a preponderance of discount supermarkets such as Aldi and Lidl, then this is a sign that you will have to be very competitive with your prices.

Hopefully by now you have come to a decision on the type of restaurant or café or bar you plan to open and if any nation's food is to be emulated, for example, French, Italian, American or even British. Then try very hard to find something original, which is difficult, as London is so full of new restaurants that almost every nation is represented, so a formula like Burger & Lobster may be the only solution.

Once you have your idea and have talked about it with enthusiasm, this is the time to appoint your designer. Look at their work closely and, even more important, be sure that you can work with them from a personal point of view. Try to find a designer who has worked on restaurants or cafés before, as there is a lot of technical detail required in producing a successful project. You will also probably need a separate kitchen designer and supplier. If, by now, you have found a chef, he or she should get involved in the design of the kitchen so they can't complain that it isn't right for them.

Now brief your designer. First the budget: use very strong words and a letter to explain that it must not be exceeded. Then ask for detailed drawings of the site that indicate the position of drains, water, gas and power supplies, as these

How to Design a Restaurant

Terence Conran

will, to an extent, indicate where the kitchen and lavatories are situated. Also, you will need a secondary means of escape – important because there are often fires in kitchens. Now sit down with your designer and discuss the general layout of the restaurant, remembering that the waiting staff have to take hot food and drink to the customers, and dirty plates, cutlery and glasses back to the wash up. So they need space not only to collect the dirties, but also to house the technology that tells the kitchen what has been ordered, and at what price. This information is stored so a final bill can be produced that lists everything that has been consumed, plus it calculates VAT and shows the service charge. This technology is expensive but essential in any modern establishment.

Next comes the joyful part of the project – how is it going to look, does it have any theme? Modern and slick, or rustic and comfortable? Is the look related to the menu and nationality of the food you serve? Do you expect a mainly young audience or an older, richer one? Is it in a city or large town or in the country? All this has to be discussed with your designer, plus, of course, the colours and materials, especially the floor, which takes a lot of wear and has to be easily cleaned. Consider the quality of light and its ability to be dimmed to soft and mellow, and also the acoustics – a textured ceiling helps, likewise a carpet and fabric on seats and banquettes and space between tables. What's on the walls? Perhaps you can find young artists living or working in your area and you become something of a local gallery, selling their work from your walls – provided, of course, that you like it and your customers do as well. Don't forget the graphic design of your menus, wine lists and so on – this is very important, as you will undoubtedly use social media to market your project and a strong graphic style helps.

At the end of the day this is your project and it needs to be as personal as possible and your character should be clearly visible and evident in every area of your place. Make sure you taste every dish before it joins the menu, and taste all wines before you buy them. Good luck!

11

Above **Graham Blower's Launceston lamb pie with kidneys, sweetbreads and a wonderful suet pastry crust.**
Left **A corner of the atrium at the new Design Museum, featuring part of the hyperbolic paraboloid roof and a view to the second-floor restaurant overlooking Holland Park.**

Balham
Battersea
Brixton
Clapham
Dulwich

The recent character of Brixton has been shaped by the arrival of what became known as the Windrush generation – the first wave of immigrants from Jamaica, on board it in 1948. They sought employment in the nearest Labour Exchange, on Coldharbour Lane, and then found accommodation nearby. Most ended up settling for good, and the new British African-Caribbean community opened market stalls and stores along Electric Avenue – so-called because it was the first London street to be lit electrically. This was one of the first parts of London to sell sweet potatoes, yams and mangoes – and it is still one of the cheapest places to buy them. But the demographic of the area is rapidly changing. The covered Caribbean market that was the Granville Arcade is barely recognizable now it has been rebranded as Brixton Village. A community project successfully fought off redevelopment attempts in 2009, and the market was Grade II listed because of its cultural significance – although, if not physically, it was to change visually beyond all recognition by 2011. In an effort to revive what was becoming a disused and depressed shopping arcade, a scheme offered local entrepreneurs a free lease for a few months if they opened a new business there. The result was a flourishing day and night market, with independent restaurants, shops and even a Champagne bar. Brixton Village has been criticized in recent times because it caters noticeably less for the Caribbean community that once inhabited it. However, it is undeniably popular with locals, and for the first time, north Londoners head to Brixton in search of supper options. It certainly goes some way to bridge the culinary gap between Brixton and its neighbours Clapham, Battersea and Balham.

Anyone visiting Brixton might do a double take at the sight of a windmill, Ashby's Mill. This working mill is celebrating its 200th birthday, and you can buy excellent Brixton-ground flour inside.

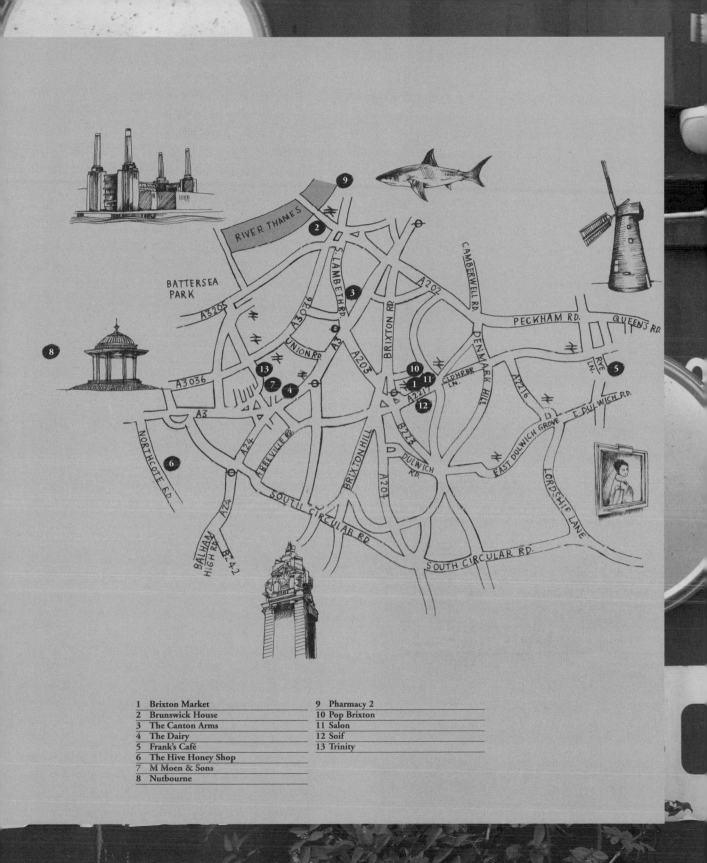

1 Brixton Market
2 Brunswick House
3 The Canton Arms
4 The Dairy
5 Frank's Café
6 The Hive Honey Shop
7 M Moen & Sons
8 Nutbourne

9 Pharmacy 2
10 Pop Brixton
11 Salon
12 Soif
13 Trinity

Left **The always-vibrant Brixton street market.** Right **Smoked mackerel.**

14

Brixton Market Electric Avenue, SW9 8XJ

www.brixtonmarket.net

In April 2010, the then Secretary of State for Culture overturned a previous decision and confirmed the market's importance by giving it a Grade II listing. The listing was granted not so much for its architecture as for its cultural importance, not to mention the community benefit. Over the years, this cluster of arcades and street markets incoporating Brixton Village and Market Row has become the epicentre of many positive things, while also being the symbolic soul of black Britain. Best known as an African/Caribbean centre, it actually offers much, much more. Electric Avenue, the street immortalized by Eddy Grant's chart hit, is home to all manner of butchers, fishmongers and greengrocers, plus an excellent supermarket selling Asian produce. The huge displays of fish on ice, the vegetables and fruit from far-flung places and the esoteric meats – think tripe, trotters, tails and tongues – might not be the finest of produce, and there is certainly still a whiff of illegal substances, but it is colourful and full of character. This is a vibrant and multicultural hub that says a lot about today's London. Certainly, Brixton Market is far more genuine than Borough Market and equally appealing for Londoners and visitors from beyond our shores.

To get the most from your trip, check the opening hours and what is actually going on the day that you are planning to visit. They have all sorts of different market days, from flea markets to makers' markets and even a market day devoted to bakers and cake makers. The farmers' market in Brixton Station Road on Sunday is one of the best in town, and Saturday afternoon can get very lively. This is a place to really soak up the wonderful atmosphere.

Mark Dobbie

"

Carioca in Brixton Market is a regular haunt for me. They do Brazilian breakfast maize muffins, chorizo, poached eggs and avocado – I can't go past it.

Chef patron, Som Saa

Right **You can be assured of a wide range of ethnic and mainstream ingredients at Brixton Market.**

Below **Scenes from around Brixton Market.**

Brunswick House 30 Wandsworth Road, SW8 2LG

020 7720 2926   www.brunswickhouse.co

This has to be one of the most quirky and different dining and party destinations in London. Having started out as the business headquarters of antique emporium LASSCO, an architectural salvage yard set within a near derelict, crumbling Georgian mansion that was originally built for the Duke of Brunswick in 1758, it is now one of the most distinctive restaurants in the capital. Being surrounded by a bus station and some of London's most unattractive architecture also adds to the experience, in a perverse manner. Inside, it is a warren of rooms all dressed in a mismatch of furniture, antiques and oddities. Alone, all of that would be enough to draw people to this location, but when you add inventive food from the amazingly talented Jackson Boxer, you have a real treat on your hands.

The Canton Arms 177 South Lambeth Road, SW8 1XP

020 7582 8710   www.cantonarms.com

The British Sunday lunch is a long-held tradition that should never be lost. However, despite its eternal popularity, the number of places where you can enjoy a solid example of this very enjoyable meal are rapidly reducing. In my view, The Canton Arms offers one of the best versions available in London. It is also very good value for money, with their Bloody Mary, the quintessential pre-lunch Sunday drink, at just over £5. This is a pub setting so you don't want anything pricey, instead you want earnest and generous stuff, which The Canton Arms delivers. The menu is appropriately straightforward, with first courses, mains and puddings – no messing around with small tapas-style dishes and creative headings for their food. However, the utterly fantastic sharing dishes do deserve a special mention. Many of the dishes serve three or four, and they've also recently had a seven-hour-roasted salt marsh lamb shoulder that served five or more. Plus, you've got to try their roasties – another key constituent of a proper Sunday lunch. As you would expect, it is going to be very busy (tables are first come, first served), but go early and stay late. It is well worth the trek to this rather uninspiring corner of London (PP).

Right **Perhaps there is less regard for modern food hygiene standards at this corner of Brixton Market.**

Venison, Burnt Plums and Parsley Root

Serves 4

For the venison

1 star anise
10g (¼oz) juniper
10g (¼oz) black peppercorns
1 beetroot, finely chopped
100g (3½oz) coarse sea salt
100g (3½oz) dark brown sugar
300g (10½oz) venison loin
a few fresh cobnuts, to serve

For the parsley root purée

200ml (7fl oz) chicken stock, reduced to 100g
200g (7oz) parsley root (fresh, not dried)
30g (1oz) cultured cream or crème fraîche
30g (1oz) coconut butter
sea salt flakes

For the burnt plums

20g (¾oz) fine sea salt
100g (3½oz) dark brown sugar
2 seasonal plums
20g (¾oz) cider vinegar
10g (¼oz) black treacle

You will also need a sous-vide machine

Start with the venison. Lightly toast all the spices in a dry frying pan over a medium heat, until they turn a shade darker and smell aromatic. Tip into a spice grinder and grind to a powder. Purée the beetroot in a food processor or blender, and mix it with the ground spices, salt and sugar. Rub this cure all over the venison loin, then set a timer and wait for 8 minutes. After that time, briefly rinse off the cure. Place the venison on a large plate lined with a clean all-purpose cloth, put another clean cloth on top, and leave in the fridge to dry for 1–2 hours.

To make the parsley root purée, pour the stock into a saucepan, place over a medium heat and reduce until it has halved in volume.

Scrub the parsley root vigorously to remove all the dirt. Slice it into even thin discs on a mandoline or using a sharp knife. Spread out in a large vacuum-pack food bag to form a single, even layer and seal the bag with no air. Cook in a sous-vide machine at 100°C (212°F) for 15 minutes, or until it has broken down. Blend the cooked parsley root with the cream and coconut butter, gradually adding the reduced chicken stock until you have a smooth, velvety textured purée. Taste and season with salt.

For the plums, mix the salt with half the sugar in a dish. Cut the plums in half, remove the pits and roll them in the sugar mix, making sure the cut sides are well coated, packing it on slightly. Place the plums, cut sides down, in a cold saucepan, set it over a medium-high heat and let the sugar caramelize. Once caramelized, turn them over, add the remaining sugar and mix with a splash of water. Now, make the sugar mixture and juices into a caramel in the pan, taking the mixture to 135°C (275°F) on a sugar thermometer without stirring; swirl the pan if you want, from time to time. Remove the plums if they are breaking down too much. Once the caramel has been achieved, add the vinegar and treacle and bring it all together.

Now cook the venison. We cook it over charcoal, turning, until the internal temperature is 52°C (126°F) on a meat probe thermometer. Feel free to cook it as you prefer, but whatever way you choose, allow to rest for 15 minutes before serving.

Gently reheat the parsley root purée and the plums in their liquor. Carve the venison and serve it with the purée, plums and some cobnuts.

Robin Gill

"

Maltby Street Market and that entire area near Bermondsey has to be the best kept foodie secret; we have some of the best breweries, some incredible foodie stalls where you can buy anything from amazing charcuterie to bao, and 40 Maltby Street is one of my favourite places to sit, eat, drink and people watch.

Chef patron, The Dairy

Opposite **A traditional milk churn, now used as a prop at The Dairy.**

The Dairy 15 The Pavement, SW4 0HY
020 7622 4165 www.the-dairy.co.uk

The massively experienced, but still very young, Robin Gill brings more than a dollop of east London cool to this otherwise very straight, some might say boring or worse, corner of south-west London. All the usual Hackney-esque dining room accoutrements are present: reclaimed and recycled furniture, salvaged factory lights, a hotchpotch of vintage cutlery, odd-shaped plates, whipped butter presented on a rock, and too-cool-for-school staff. Predictably, the menu is based on small plates and a tasting menu: nothing so gauche as a conventional menu with first courses, mains and desserts. Instead, on the day I visited, with a good mate from the wine industry who treated me to an excellent new-wave pinot noir from a natural wine maker in Burgundy, we ordered food listed under headings of Garden, Sea and Land. Looking for a solid meal and not just a spew of micro ingredients on tiny plates, we ordered everything on the menu, though we did have to ask a few questions about the fish dish descriptions, which included soused 'Willy's' mackerel and 'Lady Hamilton' cod. We were made to feel stupid not knowing that Willy and Lady Hamilton were, of course, the boats that brought home the catch. After this, things got a lot better, in fact, close to perfect and certainly a demonstration that the kitchen is about more than just a few modern clichés. We had a really delicious lunch and the service, which started on a low note, proved they were passionate about what they were doing and exceptionally well informed in regard to the various foods served. The Dairy team also have a couple more ventures in the area and the highly rated Paradise Garage, in Bethnal Green (PP).

Frank's Café Peckham Multistorey Carpark, 133 Rye Lane, SE15 4ST
www.frankscafe.org.uk

Located on the tenth floor of a crappy old car park, Frank's is an odd blend of experimental architectural project, evolving art installation and an ultra relaxed – read very basic and a bit grimy – bar and café. However, its hugely redeeming feature is the spectacular view, especially on balmy summer's evening. They welcome dogs and children and it is only open in the summer months.

The Hive Honey Shop 93 Northcote Road, SW11 6PL
0207 9246 233   www.thehivehoneyshop.co.uk

The tiny store houses a 1.5-m (5-ft)-high glass-fronted hive with 20,000 bees, and James Hamill, the owner and fourth generation beekeeper (his family has been keeping bees since 1924), produces unpasteurized honey from his own Surrey Bee Heaven Farm, and various other UK locations. This must-visit little shop has been open since 1992 and now boasts the largest selection of English and international honeys in the country. You can also find beekeeping equipment, protective clothing, beeswax, honeycombs, royal jelly and much more here.

M Moen & Sons 24 The Pavement, SW4 0JA
020 7622 1624   www.moen.co.uk

This excellent butcher's shop has a noteworthy history, but more importantly has moved with the times: modern and forward-thinking, it also offers cheeses, store-cupboard essentials, marinades for barbecues, potted things, oils, chutneys and much more. An essential resource for local households.

Nutbourne 35–7 Parkgate Road, SW11 4NP
020 7350 0555   www.nutbourne-restaurant.com

Named after the Gladwin family's farm in Sussex, this is a sister to their excellent restaurant Rabbit across the river in smarter Chelsea (see page 155) and The Shed in Notting Hill. All three specialize in the lovely concept of farm-to-fork, with a focus on quality meat and fresh fish cooked over a charcoal grill.

Best for...
rooftop bars

Everybody is heading upward, to a place where the food and drink almost touch the sky.

| Boundary Rooftop |
| Coq d'Argent |
| Frank's Café |
| Radio Rooftop Bar at the ME |
| Sushisamba |

This page **Pop Brixton includes more than 50 different independent young businesses.**

Above **Recycled shipping containers at Pop Brixton.** Left and below **A wide variety of dining and drinking destinations and the Pop Brixton community initiative.**

Pharmacy 2 Newport Street, SE11 6AJ

020 3141 9333 www.pharmacyrestaurant.com

The original Pharmacy restaurant, located in Notting Hill, has gone down in the world of restaurant folklore for many reasons. It originally opened in 1998 and was backed by Damien Hirst and PR guru Matthew Freud and immediately became one of the most fashionable restaurants in London. It had a fantastic party atmosphere but it certainly wasn't the place to get a good meal. Instead, it was all about the groundbreaking design – made to look like the inside of an actual pharmacy, with wonderfully controversial art by Hirst. It was constantly in the gossip columns and news – just what every restaurant needs, but to sustain interest it also needs good food and service. There were all sorts of rumours about the place and the risqué antics that the celebrity clientele got up to. There was also a high-profile dispute about the name, which was breaching the Medicines Act 1968. The restaurant closed in 2003, but managed to achieve further notoriety when the art, which was reputed to have been loaned to the restaurant by Damien Hirst, was reportedly sold for £11 million.

Pharmacy 2 is certainly less newsworthy, but no less interesting in terms of the design and art. It is a collaboration between Hirst and food personality Mark Hix. Hirst and Hix seem like two peas from the same pod and it all seems to work in a light-hearted and fun kind of way. The menu isn't anything to write home about, but it is what you want to eat in this type of setting. Go at the weekend – start with a tour of the adjoining Newport Street Gallery, then head to the restaurant for a bloody good bloody Mary and a no-nonsense Brit brunch.

The staff are also super friendly – we visited on a busy Sunday afternoon when our young son was being particularly boisterous and they were especially patient and accommodating of his demands while offering us a lovely smile (PP).

Pop Brixton 49 Brixton Station Road, SW9 8PQ

020 3879 8410 www.popbrixton.org

This is a very worthy community initiative set up on a disused plot of land by Lambeth Council as a temporary home for over 50 different independent young businesses, including quite a few restaurants and street food traders, plus retailers, offices for young creatives and various entrepreneurial groups. They also host all manner of events, from music gigs to Zumba classes. Like Boxpark in Shoreditch, they use recycled shipping containers as their homes. It is currently planned to be in situ until Autumn 2018 – let's see if it stays for longer. In the meantime, it includes a few notable eateries, including Zoe's Ghana Kitchen and Duck Duck Goose (a modern Cantonese canteen). While there is a lot going on at Pop Brixton, we suggest that you visit on a day when also touring nearby Brixton Market.

Salon 18 Market Row, SW9 8LD

020 7501 9152 www.salonbrixton.co.uk

There are lots of interesting little dining spots in and around Brixton Market, but one of the most ambitious is Salon. They offer a more ingredient-focused and modern take on British food with an emphasis on vegetables, although it certainly isn't a veggie restaurant. In the evening, the restaurant above the deli downstairs focuses on a fixed set menu, a trend that is increasingly popular, but it won't be liked by everybody. The weekend is different and far more accessible.

Soif 27 Battersea Rise, SW11 1HG

020 7223 1112 www.soif.co

You'd be very happy if you lived within easy walking distance of Soif (French for 'thirst') and equally pleased if you travelled across London for one of their excellent lunches or suppers. It is the archetypal local bistro with the added attraction of an exceptional wine list – they also do off-sales for all of the wines. Soif is part-owned by Les Caves de Pyrene, a pioneering wine merchant that specializes in natural wines so you can expect a strong bias toward wines that can be more than a little funky, a word that the wine industry uses to describe these sometimes volatile and sometimes brilliant wines. It is a noisy and rustic place, but it has some charming features, such as the zinc-topped bar and the quirky wine-related art. A seat on the small outside terrace in the summer is a joy, especially when accompanied by a tray of oysters, charcuterie and cheese.

Trinity 4 The Polygon, SW4 0JG

020 7622 1199 www.trinityrestaurant.co.uk

Adam Byatt, the chef patron behind this excellent multi-faceted dining destination, is more than a local hero. Over the past ten years, he has mastered the art of an upmarket neighbourhood restaurant. Initially humble in their intentions, they've gone on to achieve greatness and a Michelin star for their efforts. At heart, Byatt is a cook and restaurateur with an innate talent. The business has expanded and matured into a glamorous addition for the area. It is especially enjoyable on a summer's afternoon when you can enjoy a post-prandial walk around Clapham Common.

A day trip out of London

London offers an excessive wealth of quality restaurants, but outside the capital the situation is very different. There are very few decent places to enjoy a high-quality meal, especially one without irritating fuss, froth and pretension. Here is a short list of places that you might want to visit for a trip out of the capital.

The Ethicurean
Barley Wood Walled Garden,
Long Lane, Wrington, Bristol BS40 5SA
01934 863713 www.theethicurean.com
Perfect on a summer's day. You can dine inside the old potting sheds or outside overlooking the extensive fruit and vegetable gardens with the valley and rolling hills in the distance. All the ingredients are sourced locally, if not from their own gardens. The menu is seriously inventive without being formal or pretentious. They also make their own tinctures and a wonderful vermouth called The Collector.

The Hand and Flowers
126 West Street, Marlow SL7 2BP
01628 482277 www.thehandandflowers.co.uk
This is the only pub in the UK to garner two Michelin stars, for telly chef Tom Kerridge. It is particularly difficult to snag a table so you might also like to try The Coach, in the centre of Marlow, Tom's other place, where you can just walk in and wait for a table.

The Hind's Head
High Street, Bray, Maidenhead SL6 2AB
01628 626151 www.hindsheadbray.com
Bray is a tiny village on the upper reaches of the River Thames, just outside Maidenhead, that is bizarrely home to a clutch of excellent restaurants in the form of Heston Blumenthal's world-renowned Fat Duck, plus The Waterside Inn, which also has three Michelin stars, plus Caldesi in Campagna and my personal favourite The Hind's Head – Heston's answer to upmarket British pub food.

Le Manoir aux Quat'Saisons
Church Road, Great Milton, Oxford OX44 7PD
01844 278881 www.belmond.com/
le-manoir-aux-quat-saisons-oxfordshire
The long-standing home to Raymond Blanc's two-star restaurant, kitchen garden and hotel.

The Sportsman
Faversham Road, Seasalter, Whitstable CT5 4BP
01227 273370
www.thesportsmanseasalter.co.uk
At the time of writing, I still haven't managed to dine at this much-admired restaurant, which is wildly frustrating, especially as many of my friends in the restaurant business rate it so highly. Since 1999 it has been run by bon viveur Stephen Harris (also consulting on the menu at Noble Rot – see page 116) and has retained a Michelin star since 2008. They specialize in food from the region, which inevitably includes great oysters from the Thames Estuary, fish from the North Sea, plus meat and game from nearby and the salt marshes (PP).

'Nduja Croquettes, with Aïoli and Pickled Cucumber

Serves 5 (makes about 20 croquettes)

For the croquettes

60g (2¼oz) unsalted butter
60g (2¼oz) plain flour, plus 40g (1½oz) extra for coating
100ml (3½fl oz) ham stock
100ml (3½fl oz) double cream
25g (1oz) strong Cheddar cheese, finely grated
100g (3½oz) smoked pig's cheek (guanciale) or salami ends and rinds, finely chopped
100g 3½oz) 'nduja
50g (1¾oz) sobrasada (soft, spreadable chorizo)
pinch of sea salt flakes
¼–½ teaspoon chilli powder, to taste
¼–½ teaspoon paprika, to taste
2–3 eggs, lightly beaten
40g (1½oz) panko breadcrumbs
vegetable oil, to deep-fry

Melt the butter gently in a heavy-based saucepan. Stir in the 60g (2¼oz) of flour and cook, stirring, for 1 minute. Gradually stir in the stock, stirring after each addition, to make a thick sauce, then add the cream in the same way. Bring to the boil, then reduce the heat and simmer gently, stirring occasionally, for 4 minutes. Stir in the cheese, then turn off the heat.

Place a heavy-based frying pan over a medium heat and add the pig's cheek or salami ends. Cook, stirring, until browned on all sides. (Reserve the rendered fat; it's great for cooking pork chops and so on.) Put the browned pig's cheeks or salami in a bowl and mix in the 'nduja, sobrasada and the creamy sauce. Season with the salt, and chilli and paprika to taste, then chill the mixture to firm it up (overnight is best).

Form the mixture into 20g (¾oz) balls. Place the 40g (1½oz) of flour in a shallow dish, the eggs in a second dish, and the breadcrumbs in a third. Roll the balls first in the flour, then in the egg, and finally in the crumbs, to coat. Set on a plate, cover and chill again, if you have time; this will allow the crumb coating to adhere more closely.

Fill a deep-fat fryer, or a large saucepan, with oil (if using a saucepan, fill it up to one-third of the way up the sides). Heat over a medium-high heat until the temperature reaches 180°C (350°F). If you don't have a thermometer, throw in a breadcrumb: if it sizzles immediately the oil is ready for cooking.

Deep-fry the croquettes, in batches, for 2–3 minutes, turning, until golden brown all over. Remove with a metal slotted spoon and place on kitchen paper to absorb excess oil while you quickly fry the rest. Serve hot, with aïoli and pickled cucumbers (see right).

For the aïoli

6–8 garlic cloves, plus 2–3 extra garlic cloves, finely grated, to taste
flavourless vegetable oil, for poaching, plus an extra 300ml (½ pint)
4 egg yolks
Dijon mustard, to taste
150ml (¼ pint) olive oil
juice of 1 lemon
pinch of sea salt flakes

Put the 6–8 whole garlic cloves in a heavy-based saucepan, cover with the oil, and place over a medium heat. Bring to a simmer, then reduce the heat to as low as it will go. Poach for about 45 minutes, until the garlic is soft, but not falling apart. Remove these confit garlic cloves with a metal slotted spoon. (You may as well make a lot of this; they are delicious and will get eaten, and you can cover them with the oil in a jar; they will keep for weeks.)

Put the confit garlic cloves in a blender with the grated garlic, egg yolks and mustard, and blend to a smooth paste. Slowly trickle in the 300ml (½ pint) of vegetable oil, then the olive oil, still blending, until emulsified, thick and glossy. Taste and season with extra mustard, lemon juice and salt.

For the pickled cucumbers

12 cucumbers
12 shallots
fine sea salt
750ml (1¼ pints) cider vinegar
750g (1lb 10oz) granulated sugar
750ml (1¼ pints) water
1 teaspoon caraway seeds
1 teaspoon mustard seeds
1 teaspoon ground turmeric

Start making these the day before you want to eat them. Cut the cucumbers in half lengthways, scoop out the seeds with a teaspoon and slice thinly into half moons. Peel the shallots and slice into half moons the same thickness as the cucumbers. Weigh the shallots and cucumbers together, make a note of the weight, then tip them into a large bowl. Add 1.5 per cent of their total weight in salt and mix again. Leave to salt overnight in a colander in the sink, weighted down with a plate and a couple of tin cans, so the water is extracted.

Next day, make the brine: mix the vinegar, sugar and measured water in a large, heavy-based saucepan and bring to the boil, adding the spices. Add the cucumbers and shallots, return to the boil, then immediately remove from the heat. Transfer to sterilized jars or containers and seal. This makes more than you need for this recipe, but they keep well and are good with all cured meats, some cheeses, patés, in salads and with burgers.

More places to visit in the area

Art & Craft
2a Streatham High Road, SW16 1DB
52 Knights Hill, SE27 0JD
www.artandcraft.london
This tiny specialist beer shop, from the independent Inkspot Brewery, stocks more than 500 bottled craft beers, many of which are brewed locally in south London.

Bistro Union
40 Abbeville Road, SW4 9NG
020 7042 6400   www.bistrounion.co.uk
A sister to the excellent Trinity (see page 20). Open all day every day serving neighbourhood bistro food.

The Butchery
49 London Road, SE23 3TY
020 8291 4219   www.thebutcheryltd.com
Run by Aussies, and specializing in native-breed, free-range, pasture-fed and dry-aged meat. You can also find them at a few different markets across south-east London, including as part of the Spa Terminus group in Bermondsey.

Moxon's
Clapham South Underground Station,
Nightingale Lane, SW4 9AE
020 8675 2468
149 Lordship Lane, SE22 8HX
020 8299 1559
www.moxonsfreshfish.com
Run by former restaurateur Robin Moxon, this fishmonger stocks a wide selection of fresh fish, seafood and award-winning fish cakes.

Toasted
36–8 Lordship Lane, SE22 8HJ
020 8693 9021   www.toastdulwich.co.uk
Backed by the same people as Soif (see page 20) and with a similar ethos, but they've also managed to retain plenty of individuality.

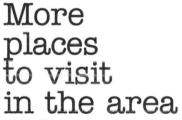

Above **Inside the brilliant Trinity in Clapham, and Adam Byatt's take on** *iles flottante.*

Barnes
Chiswick
Hammersmith
Wandsworth

For those driving in from the home counties west of London, the site of the Ark in Hammersmith is a sign they've arrived. The 1980s office building, designed to resemble an ocean liner, sits on the A4 flyover – a locally hated stretch of elevated road, completed in 1961, which cleaved the centre of Hammersmith in two, and carries about 90,000 cars a day into London. One of the first roadways of its kind, the A4 effectively ended any claims Hammersmith would ever have to prettiness or character – but there is now some suggestion it could be replaced with an underground tunnel, restoring the town centre (if not the St Paul's Church graveyard, which it destroyed). While the construction of the A4 flyover has been called an 'act of the vandalism' by architects hoping to dismantle it forever, the length of the Thames that runs a short distance south of it is a London gem. Ravenscourt Park is probably the best in the local area, and from Hammersmith to Putney and beyond are riverside pubs, theatres and perfect vantage points for the annual Boat Race. JMW Turner, who knew a bit about scenery, chose Hammersmith as his home, and submitted *Apollo and Python* to the Royal Academy while he lived here by the river. William Morris, who lived at Kelmscott House right on the river for the last 18 years of his life, described the place as 'certainly the prettiest in London'. His wisteria-draped home is now open to the public, and full of the artist's wallpapers, watercolour designs, a selection of textiles and a view of the river that illustrates exactly what he meant. Within the borough, Shepherd's Bush market is worth a visit, and contrasts in every possible way with the massive American-style Westfield shopping mall nearby. For us, the only real reason to venture to this quarter of London is for The River Café, possibly the best restaurant in the capital.

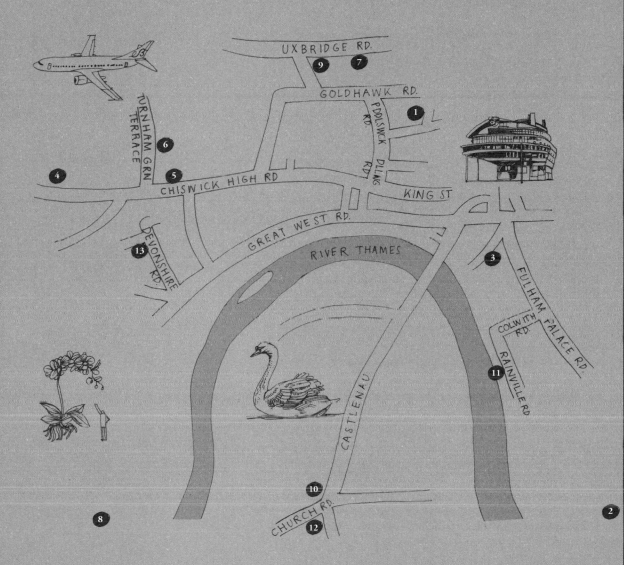

UXBRIDGE RD.

9 7

GOLDHAWK RD.

1

PDDLSWCK RD.

DLLNG RD.

TURNHAM GRN TERRACE

6

4

5

CHISWICK HIGH RD.

KING ST

GREAT WEST RD.

13

DEVONSHIRE RD.

RIVER THAMES

3

FULHAM PALACE RD.

COLWITH RD.

RAINVILLE RD.

11

CASTLENAU

8

10

CHURCH RD.

12

2

1	Anglesea Arms	9	Princess Victoria
2	Chez Bruce	10	Riva
3	The Gate	11	The River Café
4	Hedone	12	Sonny's Kitchen
5	High Road Brasserie	13	La Trompette
6	Natoora		
7	The Nutcase		
8	Petersham Nurseries Café and Teahouse		

Right **Red Breme onions** are grown in the clay soil of a dried-up river bed.

RED BREME ONION
— BREME , ITALY —

Anglesea Arms 35 Wingate Road, W6 OUR

020 8749 1291 www.angleseaarmspub.co.uk

Given the choice, we'd prefer a restaurant to a pub, but we also recognize that in the right hands a good public house can serve some very enjoyable food and drink – often better than the over-garnished and fussy food to be found in many restaurants. This excellent example of the type calls on proven classic dishes and earthy ingredients. Go for a pint of real ale and a slow-cooked pork belly.

Opposite
Natoora provide many of London's top restaurants, and they also have a flagship shop at Turnham Green.

Chez Bruce 2 Bellevue Road, SW17 7EG

020 8672 0114 www.chezbruce.co.uk

In the past, this restaurant has been voted the best restaurant in the whole of London, eclipsing the once unbeatable Ivy, Gordon Ramsay, Jason Atherton and all other celebrity chefs. Yet most Londoners wouldn't be able to name its chef and it doesn't have a fancy concept or particular USP. Instead, its main features seem to be consistent quality at a modest level, and always being professional.

Bruce Poole (an alumnus of Bibendum in its heyday) and Nigel Platts-Martin have been the restaurant's owners since 1995, and you can therefore expect a copious wine list. Although principally a neighbourhood restaurant, it is virtually impossible to just call in; reservations need to be made some time in advance.

The food is based on classic and regional French cuisine, with a few Spanish and Italian excursions, but all modern and relevant. The cheese board is a delight. The dining room has a lovely herringbone timber floor, slender chairs and simple tableware, and the close proximity of the tables helps to relax the atmosphere.

The Gate 51 Queen Caroline Street, W6 9QL

020 8748 6932 www.thegaterestaurants.com

The Gate is considered by many to be one of the best vegetarian restaurants in London. We're probably not best qualified to judge, but the menu certainly includes some delicious ingredients, and the kitchen serves up a wide range of textures, colours and flavours that would satisfy any hungry visitor. They also have recently opened sister restaurants in Islington and Marylebone so they must be doing something right.

Hedone 301–303 Chiswick High Road, W4 4HH
020 8747 0377 www.hedonerestaurant.com

I've only been to Hedone once and that was before their change to a tasting-menu-only format, but I remember being impressed by the clarity of the tastes and the creativity shown by the kitchen, without it showing up as fussiness on the plate – and the bread, which I now consider to be the benchmark ever since I tasted it (PP).

Hedone is all about one person, the hugely impressive Mikael Jonsson, the former Swedish lawyer turned chef. The restaurant has limited opening hours so that as much of the food as possible can be personally prepared by Mikael. His menus change daily and often two or three times in the day due to the limited availability of the high-quality produce that he works with.

High Road Brasserie 162–170 Chiswick High Road, W4 1PR
020 8742 7474 www.highroadbrasserie.co.uk

Part of Nick Jones' über-cool Soho House Group and open to non-members, the Brasserie at High Road House is great for a long, lazy weekend breakfast or brunch, with newspapers, strong coffee, a croque monsieur, eggs Benedict or perhaps some waffles with blueberries and crème fraîche. The design by Ilse Crawford is very agreeable, especially the zinc bar, the patchwork-style floor tiles and the light fittings. If you get a chance, try to visit other parts of this boutique hotel: given the space restrictions and the miniature bedrooms, the finished work is very comfortable in a summer-beach-house-meets-Shaker manner.

Natoora 35 Turnham Green Terrace, W4 1RG
020 8742 8111 www.natoora.co.uk

The Natoora story is certainly an interesting one; they've very quickly become the modern-day greengrocer of choice. Starting out in 2005 as an internet start-up distributing other people's produce and not holding any stock of their own, they are now one of the UK's best fruit and vegetable suppliers, both to the restaurant trade and direct to the public. There is, of course, a certain charm associated with a longstanding and historic family merchant or tradesman, but sometimes progress is needed. As far as the restaurant world is concerned, until recently, most fruit and veg produce arrived in London at the two main wholesale-orientated markets at New Covent Garden and New Spitalfields, near Leyton in East London. Unlike the beautiful markets on the Continent, the London markets are over-refrigerated horrid places, in my view, and I've witnessed a surfeit of tired and several-day-old flaccid fruit and vegetables. The people behind Natoora spotted this problem and stopped buying from the markets and instead went direct to the farmers and growers, from across Europe and the British Isles. Very often these are specialists in their own right, whether they grow carrots in sand or rhubarb in the dark; Natoora focus on some of the rarest and best examples in their class. They also work with foragers and those in far-flung places producing the oddest and most distinctive ingredients, something that chefs crave. Of course, they have seasonality at their heart and also taste, possibly more so than business objectives. Anyway, they've survived and prospered, and the good people of Chiswick have a world-class greengrocer on the doorstep, lucky them (PP).

Far left and left
Al fresco dining at Petersham Nurseries.
Right **Globe artichokes growing at Petersham Nurseries.**

The Nutcase 352 Uxbridge Road, W12 7LL

020 8743 0336

This very unusual shop specializes in Arabic nuts (raw and dry-roasted, some of them on the premises) and sweets and fruits. Everything, from mulberries to lupin and pumpkin seeds, plus baklava and Turkish jellies, is to be found here, alongside a range of coffees from North Africa, which they will grind for you while you wait.

Petersham Nurseries Café and Teahouse

Church Lane, Petersham Road, Richmond TW10 7AG

020 8940 5232   www.petershamnurseries.com

Take the day off for this one. Jump on the train at Waterloo Station, and within 20 minutes you will be at Richmond Station. Then walk to the Arcadia that is Richmond Hill, down the hill towards the meandering Thames and across Petersham Meadows in the full glare of the grazing cattle. For a townie, this is already bucolic bliss. And when you reach Petersham Nurseries, it just gets better. Everything here – and we mean everything – has been done with an enormous helping of panache. Like no other garden centre (hardly the *mot juste* when it comes to Petersham), this is a botanical experience that far surpasses the paradigm.

For eight years Skye Gyngell (now at Spring, see page 203) was the head chef and achieved a Michelin star in 2011, while also producing several admirable cookbooks, writing on food for a national newspaper and generally being elevated to become one of the top food personalities in London. And it's all amply deserved. Quite simply, Skye put Petersham Nurseries on the culinary map, which was a massive achievement given the restaurant's location. But times change. Skye was reported to have said that she was tired of guests complaining about the setting, having being led to believe by Michelin that it was a rather fancy place. This resulted in her departure. Since then there have been a few ups and downs, but it remains a decent place for lunch on a sunny afternoon of escapism. Various events take place in summer, from wine tastings to set-menu candlelit supper clubs.

Below **Tour the nurseries after a delicious lunch.**

Princess Victoria 217 Uxbridge Road, W12 9DH

020 8749 5886 www.princessvictoria.co.uk

Overseas visitors to London (especially Americans) often ask their hotel concierge to recommend an archetypal British pub. Well, it's not so easy these days. There are now many different variants on the once omnipresent corner ale house; classic examples are closing at a rapid pace and new formats are emerging. The era of the (ugly named) gastropub is well and truly with us; then you also find full-on restaurants in pubs, and pubs with pizzerias and Thai food, to mention only a couple of the differing styles. Unless you are well informed, it is all very perplexing. We have given much thought to our criteria for inclusion in *Eat London,* particularly when it comes to pubs. In general, a pub must demonstrate something that separates it from others or gives a reason for the tourist or hardened foodie to travel to an odd location to warrant inclusion. We were keen to include the Princess Victoria, a former gin palace dating back to 1829, on the strength of a number of interesting features, including its massive wine list with lots of quirky entries and illustrations, wine shop, its gin list and over 40 different gin cocktails, and its charming garden – not to mention its food. However, I certainly wouldn't say that it is the archetypal pub.

Riva 169 Church Road, SW13 9HR

020 8748 0434

A small and basic dining room, probably with fewer than 40 seats, which also manages to be romantic, with purposeful Italian food that attracts celebrities and bigwigs who have all heard about this discreet restaurant's excellent reputation. Andrea Riva, the owner, hails from Lombardy, and the food follows a northern Italian style. While the room and table settings appear simple, and a little tired at the edges, the food is world-class. The qualities of this place are not always obvious, but on reflection you will realize that some of the best culinary treats in London are to be found here. Possibly one of the biggest compliments we can give to this restaurant, and possibly to any other, is that it was a long-time favourite of the irreplaceable late AA Gill, a legendary restaurant critic.

Above **The meandering River Thames.**
Right and far right **Enjoying strawberry granita among the flora at Petersham Nurseries.**

The River Café Thames Wharf, Rainville Road, W6 9HA

020 7386 4200   www.rivercafe.co.uk

What started out mainly as a canteen for a neighbouring architectural practice is now one of London's most admired restaurants. This was no ordinary architect's office, however: it was that of Lord Rogers, and the shell of the building was a 19th-century warehouse on the north bank of the Thames. Since those early days in 1987, The River Café has set the bar for modern Italian cooking in London. This is the kitchen where Jamie Oliver was first spotted, and where Hugh Fearnley-Whittingstall worked before his television career took off. Now it has a waiting list of chefs willing to work there for virtually no pay.

After well over 25 years of supreme consistency, The River Café has experienced some flux over recent years. A fire that started one Saturday night in early April 2008 closed the restaurant until the autumn of that year. During this time, it was reported that all the staff were retained and sent on training to enable them to immerse themselves in Italian food culture, so that the reopened restaurant would further strengthen its commitment to quality at every level. When it did reopen, we were treated to several improvements on the already excellent design. The wood oven is now more prominent – painted a shocking pink – a cheese room has been added, along with a private dining room, and the state-of-the-art kitchen is now fully open and visible. It's a triumph on every level, from the complementary colours to the industrial light fittings, the gently vaulted ceiling and the herbs and salad leaves in the garden outside. All make this a treat for both the fan of high design and the layperson alike.

The second major event came in early 2010 with the very sad loss to cancer of co-founder Rose Gray. Ruth Rogers now continues the passionate search for the finest ingredients, especially from Italy – a continual and tireless effort that has helped earn the kitchen universal respect across the industry. The phenomenal success of The River Café cookbooks means their style of cooking has gained global renown. The River Café chocolate nemesis has entered chefs' vernacular and become a byword for flourless chocolate cake (even when the recipe in their cook book doesn't always work). Another much-copied dish is their squid with chilli and rocket: somehow, others don't seem to deliver quite the same level of excellence. Menus always start with the *aperitivo* of the day, in the form of a variation on a Bellini made with Prosecco, with Charentais melon, pomegranate, strawberries, pear, blood orange or grapefruit sometimes substituted for the white peaches that usually form the core ingredient. The all-Italian wine list follows the same earnest sourcing policies and is passionately promoted by the eloquent young staff, and service is impeccable.

Fans and critics alike often comment on the high menu prices. But while the style might be *cucina povera,* the ingredients are far from 'poor kitchen'. Whatever the case, the diaries remain busy, and it's always difficult to get a table at short notice. Speaking for ourselves, we trust that the proprietors apply the same margins as other restaurants, and believe that the management would find cupidity vulgar. The high prices must surely be due to the quality of ingredients (and the generous portions) and the normal costs of running a high-quality restaurant. Quite simply, The River Café experience is perfect in every way, without any faults or flaws. It is the best restaurant in our view in the whole of London and has been for quite some time.

Ruth Rogers

"I love going to Granger & Co. in Notting Hill, or The Wolseley – if I'm lucky, I'll see my friend Jeremy King.

Chef patron, The River Café

Above **The shocking pink-coloured wood oven at The River Café.** Right **Amalfi lemons, just one of the quality ingredients sourced by The River Café.**

Right **Roast
baby beetroots.**

Above **Broad beans for the vignole (spring vegetable stew).**
Left **Good olive oil and Parmesan in plentiful supply at The River Café.**

Right **Grissini to start every good Italian meal.**

Left **The River Café lemon tart.**

Above **The massive open kitchen at The River Café.**

Right **Sian Wyn Owen, head chef at The River Café.**

Left **Brown crab.**

Sonny's Kitchen 94 Church Road, SW13 0DG

020 8748 0393   www.sonnyskitchen.co.uk

A Barnes staple for more than 20 years, Sonny's still feels fresh, modern and relevant. The whole enterprise was given a fillip a few years back with the introduction of two Michelin star chef Phil Howard as a partner to help give another portion of pedigree. The menu consistently offers the good, solid and satisfying food that we all want to eat. The dining room is pleasant, and has interesting artworks on the walls. Local residents are lucky to have assets such as this restaurant and the adjoining food shop on their doorstep. If you're not a local, go for Sunday lunch before a saunter through Barnes village and along the river.

La Trompette 3–7 Devonshire Road, W4 2EU

020 8747 1836   www.latrompette.co.uk

Owned by Nigel Platts-Martin, master of high-quality neighbourhood restaurants, and Bruce Poole, the maestro at Chez Bruce in Wandsworth, La Trompette was destined to become the leading high-quality restaurant in Chiswick. You need only look at the chef's CV to see quality; Rob Weston has worked with Marco Pierre White, Guy Savoy and at Le Gavroche, and before his current berth he was with Phil Howard as sous chef for 15 years. In 2013, the whole place was given a makeover with everything lifted to an even higher level. La Trompette is not exactly an-every-other-evening or call-in-for-a-drink type place, but more of a destination for a celebration or special treat.

Best for...
all-time
favourites

None of these are what you might call fine dining – they are much better than that! Places to enjoy proper delicious food, friendly service and a great atmosphere.

Bistrotheque
Moro
The River Café
Rochelle Canteen
St John

Left **Some of the artwork at Sonny's Kitchen.** Right **Some of the traiteur items on sale in Sonny's Kitchen Foodstore.**

More places to visit in the area

The Glasshouse
14 Station Parade, Kew TW9 3PZ
020 8940 6777
www.glasshouserestaurant.co.uk
Another consistently excellent restaurant from Bruce Poole and Nigel Platts-Martin.

Macken Bros
44 Turnham Green Terrace, W4 1QP
020 8994 2646 www.mackenbros.co.uk
If you buy your fish from Covent Garden Fishmongers, your meat course must come, after lengthy discussion, from butcher Rodney Macken.

Mortimer & Bennett
33 Turnham Green Terrace, W4 1RG
020 8995 4145
www.mortimerandbennett.co.uk
A leading delicatessen and fine-food store with first-rate products from around the globe.

R Chocolate London
10 Paved Court, TW9 1LZ
020 8332 3002 www.rchocolatelondon.co.uk
Heaven for a chocoholic.

Rick Stein
Tideway Yard, 125 Mortlake High Street, SW14 8SN
0208 878 9462 www.rickstein.com
Recently opened, this is Rick's only London outpost of his brilliant fish and seafood menu.

Above **Cattle in the meadow alongside the Thames, below Richmond Hill.**

Bayswater
Kensington
Notting Hill

Since Richard Curtis made us all howl with laughter at the notion that a travel bookseller could afford a villa in Notting Hill, the area has lost, if none of its beauty, then a little of its edge. It's a charming place to spend time – houses, cafés and shops are painted in ice-cream shades, all the better to take an Instagram snap in front of, and there are an abundance of pretty mews to get lost in. But commercial rents in the area are so extortionate that enterprising start-ups and young restaurateurs couldn't hope to open here – and the dining and shopping scene is the loser. Old favourites like The Cow are enduringly, and justifiably, popular – but it's hard to imagine a street food market like Dalston's Street Feast or Lewisham's Model Market opening here. Instead, this is an area that is now host to seriously high-end restaurants like The Ledbury.

It is only on market days, when produce sellers and vintage fashion collectors line the streets, that the area's original bohemian spirit is revived a little. And, of course, during the carnival weekend, when even the smartest town houses start charging for the use of their loo. Looking at the plush high street down the road at Kensington, it's hard to believe it was once a mecca for punks and hippies. The market, where Freddie Mercury once had a stall with Roger Taylor, has been replaced with a building that houses PC World. But there is a reason that most of the French community in London choose to make it their home – the borough is beautiful, green, superbly well kept and full of excellent restaurants.

In November 2016, Kensington High Street experienced a seismic awakening – the new Design Museum opened. Located in the former Commonwealth Institute and transformed by über minimalist architect John Pawson, the new space houses a bar and restaurant overlooking Holland Park.

Left **Thierry Tomasin at Angelus, his wine-orientated restaurant.**

Angelus 4 Bathurst Street, W2 2SD

020 7402 0083   www.angelusrestaurant.co.uk

A pleasant eccentricity runs through this small 'brasserie de luxe', from its art nouveau-styled interiors to the patron himself. Thierry Tomasin, from Gascony, was schooled at Le Gavroche and has achieved many accolades for his expertise in wine. He drives the service brigade toward excellence with passion and (some say) ferocity. The signature dish is foie gras crème brûlée – sounds weird but again seems to work, like so many other aspects of Thierry's French refuge.

Assaggi 39 Chepstow Place, W2 4TS

020 7792 5501   www.assaggi.co.uk

Although chef Nino Sassu is from Sardinia, the food at this discreet and special restaurant features food from all over Italy. The portions are generous and the flavours full on. If you are not clear about any items on the menu, you can be assured that the delightful and knowledgeable staff can eloquently explain exactly how each dish is prepared and the component ingredients. Don't expect an over-designed dining room: the charm of this place is that it is simply a room with bright colours above a half-decent pub. It's also reassuringly expensive.

Books for Cooks 4 Blenheim Crescent, W11 1NN

020 7221 1992   www.booksforcooks.com

If, as Janet Street-Porter once claimed, cookery books are the new porn for the socially ambitious, then this is a hard-core sex shop. At the rear of the shop is a small café where you can enjoy a simple lunch or cake while perusing your purchase.

Bruno Loubet

I adore The Ledbury. I first met Brett Graham (the head chef) years ago when I lived in Australia. When I finally visited The Ledbury I was instantly in love with it – Brett's food is so distinctive and has such a strong sense of identity.

Chef patron, Grain Store

Casa Cruz 123 Clarendon Road, W11 4JG

020 3321 5400   www.casacruz.london

Rare evenings out with my wife have to be special to justify the journey, the babysitter and our time, among other things. So, it was with this backdrop that we recently ventured to a Notting Hill backstreet to try out Casa Cruz, and I can confidently say that we had a great evening together. We enjoyed some very special service, thanks to a friend who is the manager here, and a very chic setting, with good lighting and waiters in white dinner jackets. The menu is full of really delicious, but not cheap, food – think premium jamon, truffles, fine steaks, langoustines, wild fish and so on. It's all very upmarket Latin America and all super stylishly done. For me, it was a chance to enjoy a few glasses of Argentina's best chardonnays and malbecs (PP).

Clarke's 124 Kensington Church Street, W8 4BH

020 7221 9225   www.sallyclarke.com

Following a four-year stint in California, where she became friends with Alice Waters at the seminal Chez Panisse, Sally Clarke returned to London in 1984 and established Clarke's. In 1988 Sally opened the adjoining shop, which has flourished ever since. The bakery is renowned across London, with many leading delis, hotels and restaurants serving its breads and pastries. The shop stocks an extensive range of excellent fruit, vegetables, larder essentials, sauces, salads and much more. It also offers a seasonal menu (changing twice weekly) of sweet and savoury cakes and tarts, from apricot clafoutis and bitter chocolate cake to tarts of oven-dried tomato, goats' cheese and basil, and asparagus, leek and Parmesan.

C Lidgate 110 Holland Park Avenue, W11 4UA

020 7727 8243   www.lidgates.com

David Lidgate runs this fourth-generation family butcher's with his son, and together they understand customer service at its best, with nothing being too much trouble. They sell excellent quality meats, some from royal estates, poultry, game in season, sausages, shepherd's and cottage pies made on the premises and much more. If you want heather-fed Shetland lamb, a haunch of wild boar or teal and other wild duck, this is the place to come.

The Cow 89 Westbourne Park Road, W2 5QH

020 7221 0021   www.thecowlondon.co.uk

The Cow is a Notting Hill institution and helped fashion the original and best format of the gastropub movement, while the landlord, Tom Conran, is the evergreen local champion. Downstairs is a great boozer, or saloon bar, with proper ales, plus bottled British and continental beers, and much more. The short-order kitchen on the ground floor is perfect for lunch. The menu includes fish stew, moules marinière, beef and Guinness pie, sausages braised in beer and onions; or maybe a pint of prawns or a plate of oysters will hit the spot. It's all good and the prices are very reasonable.

Upstairs, the small dining room serves some of the best food in Notting Hill. That doesn't mean that it is striving to chase stars; it simply has an attentively planned menu and first-rate cooks in the kitchen, while the ingredients are highly seasonal and come from the finest sources.

Right **The inspiring Sally Clarke at her eponymous restaurant, shop and bakery on Kensington Church Street.**

Crazy Homies 125 Westbourne Park Road, W2 5QL

020 7727 6771   www.crazyhomieslondon.co.uk

Inspired by the street vendors and taquerias of Mexico, Tom Conran and his crew have created a neighbourhood hangout where you can really let your hair down. The small tequila bar on the ground floor has cosy corners in which to enjoy your totopos corn chips with salsa or a taquitos-rolled tortilla. The menu in the subterranean dining space extends to burros, enchiladas, light salads and shrimp cocktails. Every meal ends with churros (doughnuts) with chocolate.

Dock Kitchen Portobello Docks, 342–344 Ladbroke Grove, W10 5BU

020 8962 1610   www.dockkitchen.co.uk

After spells at the magnificent River Café, Moro and Petersham Nurseries (possibly the best training grounds for any chef), this is where the fantastic Stevie Parle burst onto the London restaurant scene. Before Dock Kitchen, she ran something called Moveable Kitchen, and the idea was developed and adapted to fit this permanent home for the recipes and ideas that Stevie collects while travelling the world in search of new and unusual ingredients. Now, each month, they run special feasts or supper-club style events that might be all about the food of a particular country or region, a particular ingredient or just an idea that inspires them – they call it an experimental kitchen, and it is indeed a fascinating idea to bring constant evolution to a restaurant. Try to attend one of their events if you can. Also home to a Tom Dixon studio and shop, alongside the Grand Union Canal in a converted Victorian wharf, this far corner of Ladbroke Grove is worth journeying to for a daytime visit.

E&O 14 Blenheim Crescent, W11 1NN

020 7229 5454 www.rickerrestaurants.com

This is another celebrity hotspot by restaurateur Will Ricker, serving great Eastern and Oriental (E&O) pan-Asian food and cocktails in glamorous and sometimes noisy surroundings.

Electric Diner 191 Portobello Road, W11 2ED

020 7908 9696 www.electricdiner.com

The Electric is an essential part of modern Notting Hill life. The landmark building includes an ornate cinema that is operated in a thoroughly up-to-date manner, with large and comfortable armchairs, footstools and side tables, where you can also get proper food and drinks before the movie. The ground-floor French-American diner forms the epicentre of cool Notting Hill. Open for breakfast, lunch and dinner seven days a week, it has a menu that includes dishes like duck confit hash, steak frites and plenty of burgers and 'dog' options. Upstairs is a private members' club, as in other Soho House outposts.

Above and right **The barrel-vaulted ceiling at the Electric Diner on Portobello Road.**

Left **The two-seater dining booths as you enter Hereford Road.** Right **Hereford Road was formerly a Victorian butcher's.**

Geales 2 Farmer Street, W8 7SN

020 7727 7528 www.geales.com

Geales first opened in 1939, and in 2007 it was given a refit that confirmed its position as the original, proudly swanky chip shop. Expect battered fish from the top drawer. The menu includes much more, from oysters and shellfish to classics like fish pie, lobster and Dover sole, but don't bother about all of that and opt for some posh fish and chips. The wine list is also pretty chichi, all to be followed by traditional old-school puddings.

Hereford Road 3 Hereford Road, W2 4AB

020 7727 1144 www.herefordroad.org

If you order from the midweek set lunch menu at this restaurant, you will experience some of the best-value dining in London. At the time of writing, the price for three really excellent courses is just £15.50 – exceptionally good value for cooking of this standard. The à la carte menu is also attractive and keenly priced. Everything about this restaurant shouts honesty and sincerity. Seasonal fare and a wide knowledge of delicious and often underused ingredients are also conspicuous features, and the portions are generous without being daunting.

Tom Pemberton, an alumnus of St John Bread and Wine, is the chef patron, and much of the menu at Hereford Road echoes the St John idiom. With the kitchen at the entrance of this former Victorian butcher's shop, Tom has a perfect vantage point to offer his guests an enthusiastic welcome and bids sincere thanks and farewells while at the same time preparing all the food. A beautiful example of a neighbourhood restaurant.

Terence Conran

" Fish and chip shops have universal appeal in British society.

Restaurateur, Albion, Boundary, Lutyens & Parabola at The Design Musem

Whole Grilled Plaice with Brown Shrimps, Nettles, Ramsons and Ramps

Serves 1

1 whole fresh plaice, trimmed
25 g (1 oz) butter
1 garlic clove, finely chopped
handful of cooked peeled brown shrimps
1 bunch of nettles, blanched by plunging into
boiling water for 1 minute
small handful of ramps (wild leeks),
finely chopped
small handful of ramsons (wild garlic),
finely chopped
extra virgin olive oil
lemon juice, to dress
salt and freshly ground black pepper
a little grated nutmeg, to serve

Season the plaice with salt and pepper and place dark-skin-side up, in an ovenproof frying pan. Dot a little of the butter on top and place under a preheated hot grill. When the skin has browned and crisped nicely, turn over, dot with a little more butter and grill briefly until light golden in colour. Transfer the fish from the pan to a serving plate and set aside to keep warm.

Take the fish pan with its juices, add the remaining butter and the garlic, and sauté the brown shrimps over a medium heat until hot. Add the blanched nettles, ramps and ramsons to the pan and wilt down, stirring lightly or as necessary for a couple of minutes.

Serve the greens and shrimps with the fish. Dress with extra virgin olive oil and freshly squeezed lemon juice, and season with salt, freshly ground black pepper and grated nutmeg.

Hummingbird Bakery 133 Portobello Road, W11 2DY

020 7851 1795 www.hummingbirdbakery.com

A high-quality American home-baking shop, the Hummingbird Bakery specializes in cupcakes, brownies, New York-style cheesecake, apple pie, pecan pie, key lime pie, Mississippi mud pie, banana bread, sweet and savoury muffins and great cookies. Drop in and try the cupcake special of the day on your way to Portobello Market.

Kitchen W8 11–13 Abingdon Road, W8 6AH

020 7937 0120 www.kitchenw8.com

If you live locally to this restaurant, you'd be very happy for two reasons; first, it is a very grown-up and elegant area that isn't exactly inexpensive and second, this restaurant perfectly complements the neighbourhood. There is a calmness and friendliness about the service, which is led by the very experienced David Chevalier (brilliant name) and it is also professional and efficient. Combine this with a very confident menu and on-point cooking, and you can see why the restaurant secured a Michelin star in 2011 and has retained it ever since. This place has integrity at its heart. If you want a proper Sunday lunch, increasingly rare to find, this is a good restaurant to choose.

The Ledbury 127 Ledbury Road, W11 2AQ

020 7792 9090 www.theledbury.com

Once relatively rundown, Notting Hill is now home to City bankers, high-flying lawyers and successful entrepreneurs, all generously represented among the habitués of the Ledbury.

Having trained under Philip Howard at The Square in Mayfair, chef Brett Graham opened The Ledbury kitchens in 2005 and has already scooped a string of awards, not least the Michelin Man's approval.

The menu is very modern haute cuisine, perhaps a little too architectural and precise for my liking, with all manner of endless ingredients crowding onto every plate.This appears to be the style favoured by young chefs and Michelin inspectors, as the Ledbury is now one of the most admired restaurants in London. The wine list is comprehensive, and the restaurant is known to host more fine wine events than any other in London.

Above **Playful and fun coloured cupcakes from Hummingbird Bakery.**

Brett Graham

"

I love Ottolenghi on Ledbury Road. They sell great pastries and their croissants are some of the best you can find in London.

Head chef, The Ledbury

Above **A young customer enjoying lunch at Malabar.**

Lucky 7 127 Westbourne Park Road, W2 5QL
020 7727 6771 www.lucky7london.co.uk

The classic hamburger is at the heart of Lucky 7, but it also delivers so much more. The patty is 100 per cent aged organic Aberdeen Angus, the bun is baked locally to a special recipe, the red onions, tomatoes and pickles are chosen for flavour and are sliced by hand. It seems simple, but so many 'hamburger joints' don't offer these essential basics.

Tom Conran has created this bijou, authentic but modern East Coast-style diner with sensitivity. Booth seating, an open kitchen, authentically eclectic 1950s-style fittings and diner tableware have all been fused with irreverent artwork to create a snugly informal environment. Lucky 7 bridges the gap between a café and a restaurant, with fast service and cool music making the perfect all-day all-comers' destination.

Jumbo Wally (pickled dill cucumbers), 'homeslaw', spicy black beans, beer-battered onion rings and tasty French fries complement the extensive choice of burgers. The milk shakes are the best – try the five-dollar shake.

The Magazine Restaurant Kensington Gardens, W Carriage Drive, W2 2AR
020 7298 7552 www.magazine-restaurant.co.uk

On the two occasions that I've been to this restaurant it has been very, very quiet – this is mainly because it is in possibly one of the most difficult restaurant locations in the whole of London. On a sunny day, the prospect of a lovely walk through the park to the restaurant is appealing, but it isn't exactly a first choice for dining out. This is all a bit of a shame because the space is actually unique. Designed by the late Dame Zaha Hadid, it is all organic forms and wavy flowing surfaces, not a straight line or angle in sight. For fans of Zaha's work, this is a must-visit location, especially as there are very few examples of her work in London. I would also say that the food isn't too bad either (PP).

Malabar 27 Uxbridge Street, W8 7TQ
020 7727 8800 www.malabar-restaurant.co.uk

When visiting Malabar, I was immediately taken by the array of metal tabletop equipment. The food is served in traditional Indian fashion on metal thalis, and beakers, platters, coffee pots and other items are all in stainless steel. Speaking from experience, the cost of buying and replacing operating equipment from plates to glassware is uncertain and expensive, but everything here is unbreakable and, I suppose, less desirable to the petty thief. I find this utilitarian approach certainly works in this setting, and everything seems to looks even better once it has acquired a dimpled surface and attractive patina. It appears that the restaurant owners are kindly passing on the cost savings, providing delicious Indian food at modest prices. On Sunday lunchtimes, children eat for free, and there is a buffet with a variety of curries and tandoori dishes, as well as multicoloured aniseed sweets rounding off all meals (PP).

Marianne 104 Chepstow Road, W2 5QS

020 3675 7750 www.mariannerestaurant.com

The fact that Marianne (Lumb) herself is larger than life with oodles of enthusiasm and energy magnifies the diminutive size of her micro restaurant. With just 14 seats it's a cosy and intimate setting, but somewhere with big promise. Set up in 2014 after Marianne established her reputation being runner-up to the much-hyped *MasterChef: The Professionals* title, the restaurant has gone on to win numerous awards, accolades and special achievements. Bagging a table is quite tricky so this is certainly somewhere to remember when planning a special occasion. Like many of the best chefs, Marianne has done her time cooking in private service all around the world. This must surely be one of the most difficult things to do in the culinary career world and is most certainly a sign of somebody with true cooking ability.

Melt 59 Ledbury Road, W11 2AA

020 7727 5030 www.meltchocolates.com

Chocolate contains phenylethylamine, a chemical related to amphetamines, which has been shown to make us feel more alert, and at the same time imparts feelings of contentment. Phenylethylamine is also known as the 'love drug'; it mimics the chemistry of our brains when we are in love, which is why chocolate has a reputation as an aphrodisiac. So go to Melt to get your phenylethylamine levels high!

The all-white minimalist open-plan kitchen inside the shop allows the team to pour large quantities of chocolate onto the counter in front of shoppers who can watch them at work, filling the air with a strong chocolate hit.

The range and choice at this excellent chocolate boutique are exceptional. It should also be said that the creativity and integrity of the management are also highly praiseworthy.

Right **Create your own style in chocolate.**

This page **Chocolate figures and lollipop-making classes at Melt.**

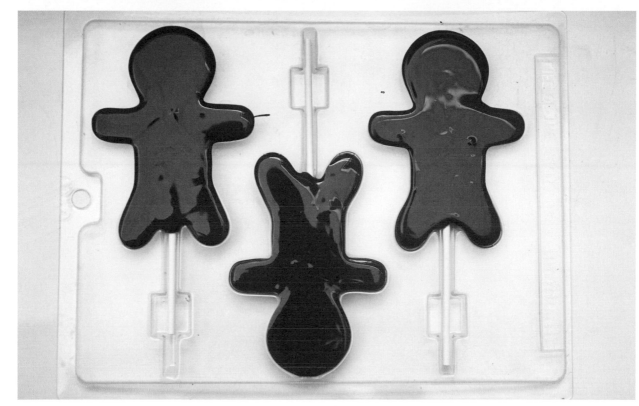

Louise Nason

"

I always make a delicious meal when I buy fish from this great fish shop attached to Kensington Place Restaurant. Park outside on the double yellow – but watch out for a ticket! They deliver, which is very useful when preparing for a party.

Founder, Melt

Negozio Classica 283 Westbourne Grove, W11 2QA

020 7034 0005   www.negozioclassica.co.uk

This small store, bar and lounge is devoted to Italian high-end style, and sells a range of exclusive products, including knives from Tuscany, *balsamico* from Modena, buffalo cheese, pesto and wildflower honey. Or you can just call in for a cappuccino, a glass of wine or a grappa.

Right **Children from six years old upward can join the one-hour chocolate masterclasses, which include the story of chocolate, a tasting – obviously – and how to make small chocolate figures.**

48

Parabola at The Design Museum 224–238 Kensington High Street, W8 6AG
020 7940 8795   www.parabola.london

On Thursday 24 November 2016, just about the time of writing this updated
version of *Eat London*, we opened our latest restaurant. Parabola, named after
the famous hyperbolic paraboloid roof at the new Design Museum, formerly
the Commonwealth Institute on Kensington High Street, has a dual
personality. During the day, it offers fantastic views over Holland Park together
with an informal and contemporary all-day menu, starting with brunch, then
moving to lunch followed by afternoon tea, all designed to complement a visit
to the stunning new John Pawson-designed museum. In the evening, Parabola
is transformed into an exciting destination for a regularly changing programme
of culinary talent as part of its Guest Chef Series – becoming home to some of
the UK's most exciting and leading chefs, cookbook writers and food
personalities. Each chef designs a unique supper-club-style menu, giving the
diner the opportunity to enjoy something that isn't normally available in
London and at an affordable price. The series was launched by Rowley Leigh,
one of London's most intelligent and renowned cooks and food writers. Other
big names from the food world who are planning menus for Parabola include
Stéphane Reynaud, Claude Bosi, Valentine Warner, Oliver Rowe, Marianne
Lumb, Shaun Hill, Jeremy Lee – quite a list.

Above **Parabola, the
restaurant at the new
Design Museum,
overlooks Holland
Park on one side and
the John Pawson-
designed atrium
under the hyperbolic
paraboloid roof on
the other.**

Right **Bramley apple
pies at Parabola.**

This page **All food from the Parabola opening menu in November 2017.**
Left **Partridge with pearl barley and roast vegetables.**
Right **Beetroot and horseradish-cured salmon.**
Below **Baked aubergine with harissa and pomegranate.**

Royal China 13 Queensway, W2 4QJ

020 7221 2535 www.royalchinagroup.co.uk

This is the original restaurant of probably the most highly rated and most reputable traditional Chinese restaurant group in London, with five other branches around the capital. The two distinct black-and-gold dining rooms seat about 200 people, yet you can still expect queues for the strictly authentic dim sum at the weekend. The dim sum chef works from 8am to 5pm, so don't go after this time if you want the real thing – although the main menu is also very good.

Six Portland Road 6 Portland Road, W11 4LA

020 7229 3130 www.sixportlandroad.com

There's an appealing modesty and confidence about this place, something that is seemingly evident in everything that they do, from the room and endearing service to the menu size and format. On the website, it rather amusingly says that the kitchen is staffed by a team of two, so you can be assured of a very personal experience. I would also say that you can drink at modest prices thanks to a patron who knows more than a few things about wines and how to create a lovely list. As a result, this is an enormously well-liked place (PP).

The Spice Shop 1 Blenheim Crescent, W11 2EE

020 7221 4448 www.thespiceshop.co.uk

In 1990, while studying for an international business degree, Birgit Erath started a small weekend stall on the Portobello Road Market. The weekend project soon became a serious business, and in 1995 she opened a shop on Blenheim Crescent, a stone's throw from the original stall, which has now become one of the most inimitable spice stores in the UK. Birgit now travels the world to find new spices, creating blends and mixes that are often based on ancient traditions. If you want to get serious about cooking dishes from the subcontinent or Asia, this is your starting point. Or you can simply call in for seasonings, as they stock a huge range of salts, from Maldon and *fleur de sel* to Diamant de Sel, a naturally formed and mined salt from Kashmir.

Tom Conran

" I would much rather shop in a specialist food store than a supermarket – although you may have a broader choice in the bigger shops, the actual experience can leave you cold.
If I had to choose one shop as an all-time favourite, it would have to be R Garcia & Sons on Portobello Road.
Owner, The Cow and Crazy Homies

Left **Outside the must-visit and one-of-a-kind The Spice Shop.**

Saturday in Notting Hill

A great way to explore the best of Notting Hill in a day.

Start with breakfast or early brunch at Granger & Co

Do a little shopping on Westbourne Grove – it's just like New Bond Street, so be prepared

Call in at Melt to see a chocolate demo and try the finest truffles

Admire the stunning food displays at Ottolenghi

Head to The Cow for oysters and a Guinness

Brave the crowds and head to Portobello Market (avoid buying overpriced junk)

Read a few chapters at Books for Cooks with a strong espresso

Pick up some rare delights at the Spice Shop or Garcia & Sons

Take in a film: relax in the leather armchairs at the Electric Cinema

For those with more stamina, carry on to E&O for an Asian-inspired martini

Finish with a swanky dinner, fine wine and professional service at The Ledbury

Summerill & Bishop 100 Portland Road, W11 4LQ

020 7221 4566 www.summerillandbishop.com

If you're planning a very special dinner party and want the most exquisite tablecloths, dinner service, cruets and the like, you'd be wise to visit this flawlessly styled shop. However, be prepared – it is very chichi and that generally comes at not a modest price. They've also got a small space where they have a range of classes from cookery techniques to flower arranging and how to plan a perfect event. If you are visiting the area for the first time, do allow yourself a little time to explore, including a wander around Holland Park – both a beautiful park and possibly the most exclusive neighbourhood in all of London.

Whole Foods 63–97 Kensington High Street, W8 5SE

020 7368 4500 www.wholefoodsmarket.com

Whole Foods Market is huge in America, but its arrival in London has been less successful than might have been hoped. Newspaper stories about the project's massive investment and ambitious aims soon gave way to reports of unimaginable financial losses.

But what is Whole Foods really like? There is much to be impressed by, and some elements that are still disappointing – though much less so now than when it first opened. On balance, it's definitely worth a visit. The hot foods and salads on the ground floor still need attention, and it would be nice to see more genuine experts on the shop floor. On a recent visit to the cheese room, we encountered little enthusiasm from the person behind the counter; there was none of the information or opportunities to sample that are second nature at Neal's Yard Dairy (see page 295) or La Fromagerie (see page 245).

The positives are certainly the large selection of products and ingredients (the butchery counter is 23m long, or some 75 feet) and the huge displays of seasonal treats. The prices also seem to have come down. You could spend a good hour or two touring the store and marvelling at the range of foods and drinks on display. Or maybe just call in for a few veggies. Either is sure to be a good experience. Upstairs, there are a few restaurants.

Zaika 1 Kensington High Street, W8 5NP

020 7795 6533 www.zaika-restaurant.co.uk

In its original site on Fulham Road, this was one of the first top-flight new-style Indian restaurants. Its present site overlooking Hyde Park was once a rather grand bank, and much of the internal architecture has been retained and fused with a rich colour palette. Zaika translates as 'sophisticated flavours', which sums up the ethos behind the menu.

Above **Suzanna Clague, brand manager at Chucs.**

More places to visit in the area

Above **The very chichi Italian Riviera-themed Chucs is both an elegant dining spot and an upmarket menswear label.**

Athenian Grocery
16a Moscow Road, W2 4BT
020 7229 6280 www.atheniangrocery.co.uk
A typical Greek-Cypriot corner shop that's been established for more than 40 years, full of feta cheese, olives, pickled chillies, wines and spirits.

Chucs
226 Westbourne Grove, W11 2RH
020 7243 9136 www.chucs.com
This is an odd combination of an upmarket fashion brand based around the Italian Riviera and food and drink with the same etymology. Worth trying a negroni while you consider some new swimwear.

The Fish Shop at Kensington Place
201–209 Kensington Church Street, W8 7LX
020 7243 6626
A still-impressive fish shop next door to a once-celebrated restaurant.

Four Seasons
84 Queensway, W2 3RL
020 7229 4320 www.fs-restaurants.co.uk
Go for the Cantonese roast duck in this Chinese restaurant (but definitely not for the service or a friendly welcome).

Granger & Co
175 Westbourne Grove, W11 2BS
020 7229 9111 www.grangerandco.com
The first London outpost for Bill Granger and still eternally popular.

Mandarin Kitchen
14–16 Queensway, W2 3RX
020 7727 9012 www.mandarinkitchen.co.uk
Specializes in lobster prepared in six different styles, as well as premium seafood.

Maroush
21 Edgware Road, W2 2JE
020 7723 0773 www.maroush.com
The best place to soak up the Lebanese atmosphere has got to be Edgware Road. The Maroush group operates a few businesses: the original Maroush restaurant at no. 21, Ranoush Juice at no. 43 and the deli selling everything from fresh fish to sweets at 45–9.

Paradise By Way of Kensal Green
19 Kilburn Lane, W10 4AE
020 8969 0098 www.theparadise.co.uk
This former and quite sizeable pub has been converted to something quite fancy. It attracts a bit of a West London celebrity clientele, often for its lively events programme.

R Garcia & Sons
248–250 Portobello Road, W11 1LL
020 7221 6119 www.rgarciaandsons.com
A slice of Spain in the heart of Notting Hill, the deli and food store have been established since 1957, while the tapas bar and café next door opened in recent years. Pedigree España.

Yashin Sushi
1A Argyll Road, W8 7DB
020 7938 1536 www.yashinsushi.com
A high-end modern Japanese restaurant.

Belgravia Knightsbridge Pimlico

Until the 19th century, Knightsbridge wasn't much more than a road linking more interesting parts of London, and providing rich pickings for the highway robbers pouncing on carriages heading out of town. Its change in fortune came in the 1850s, with the arrival of Harvey Nichols and Harrods, hotly pursued by embassies in search of its stately Thomas Cubitt architecture, and ambassadors looking for extravagant lunching opportunities. Today, SW1 may still be the most expensive part of London, but it's not necessarily the chicest. Nowadays, those wanting to see and be seen are more likely to hit Marylebone's Chiltern Firehouse than the fifth floor of Harvey Nichols, or even Shoreditch's Clove Club, in search of the city's culinary glitterati (dinnerati?!). The incredible costs of running a restaurant in this part of London mean that it is only those restaurants with the big chefs required to secure significant backing are able to thrive here. That does mean it's still the place to drop an annual bonus or celebrate an occasion with world-class cooking only serious money can buy. It is also where every five-star hotel (and there are a lot of them in this corner of London) installs a super-chef to run their restaurants – like Dinner by Heston; Theo Randall at The InterContinental; Marcus Wareing at The Berkeley; Eric Fréchon at The Lanesborough; the Arzak family at The Halkin and so on.

With the exception of A Wong in Pimlico, you might not find much in the way of diversity, or surprises in this area, but there is something in the ceremony of the place that is enduringly hard to resist – and not just the flags billowing in embassy porches and the processions of horses trotting out of their barracks. Dining in Knightsbridge means excellent service, a large selection of cutlery and a gratifying amount of pomp and ceremony. As well as a bill weighty enough to sink (or buy) a ship.

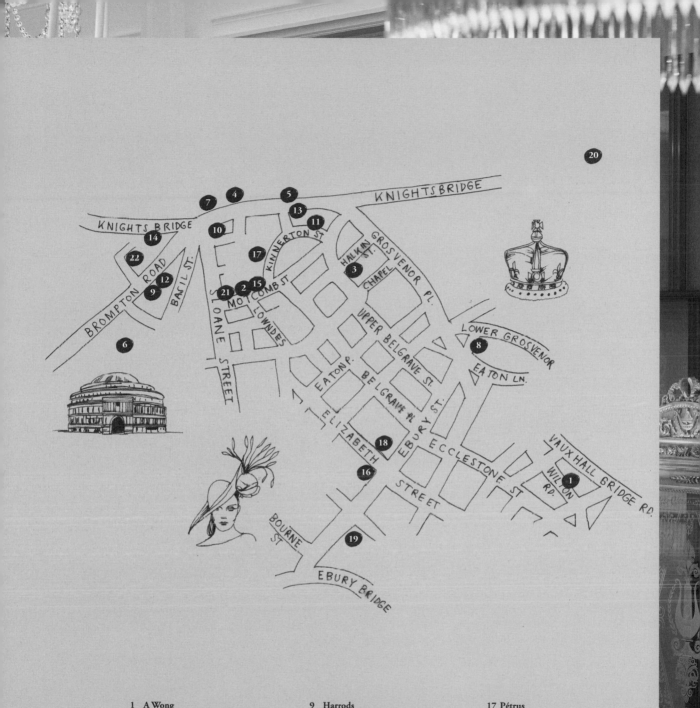

56

A Wong 70 Wilton Road, SW1V 1DE

0207 828 8931 www.awong.co.uk

A few years back Alan Yau helped to bring modern Chinese food to the fore with the introduction of his Hakkasan and Yauatcha concepts, but, other than this, there has been very little in the way of other new and exciting Chinese restaurants in London – until A Wong burst onto the scene. Given the new popularity of other global cuisines, it seems odd that more hasn't been done to bring creativity and innovation to Chinese food, but now it has arrived in an underwhelming street near Victoria Station. Previously his parent's restaurant, called Kym's – after Andrew's grandmother – Andrew (a third generation Chinese restaurateur in London), together with his wife Nathalie, has brought an intelligent and London-savvy approach to a cuisine that has 2,000 years of culinary history. If you give them 48-hours notice, you can enjoy their version of Peking Duck, one of the most iconic dishes dating back to the Northern and Southern Dynasties (420–589). Alternatively, the ten-course tasting menu is a spectacular tour of ten regions. Incidentally, the restaurant is actually named after Andrew's parents, Albert and Annie Wong.

Above **The chic chinoiserie interior at A Wong.** Below **Scallop puffs.**

Right **A wide range of cooking styles being demonstrated at A Wong, from steaming to wok-frying.**

Chinese Chive Pot Sticker Dumplings

Makes 20 dumpling

20 ready-made 8cm round dumpling pastries
40ml (3 tablespoons) cold water
10g (¼oz) plain flour
vegetable oil, for oiling

For the filling

1 tablespoon vegetable oil
6 eggs, beaten and scrambled
200g (7oz) Chinese chives, finely chopped
1 teaspoon sesame oil
salt and white pepper

For the ginger vinegar

100ml (3½fl oz) red wine vinegar
20ml (1 tablespoon) sweetened black vinegar
5g (⅛oz) peeled fresh root ginger, very finely sliced

To make the ginger vinegar, bring all the ingredients to the boil in a non-reactive pan, then leave them to cool and allow the ginger to infuse overnight. Strain out the ginger and store the vinegar in a sterilized airtight container in a cool, dry place for up to a month.

For the filling, heat the vegetable oil in a wok and lightly sauté the scrambled egg and chives. Season to taste with salt and pepper, then set aside to cool. Once the egg mixture is cool, add the sesame oil.

To make the dumplings, divide the filling into 20 portions and place 1 portion in the centre of a dumpling pastry. Lightly brush the edges of the dumpling pastry with water. Bring the edges of the pastry together over the filling to form a neat semicircle, pushing them together with your thumb to ensure an airtight seal above the filling. You will now have a half-moon-shaped dumpling that has a 1cm (½ inch) skirting on the top. Repeat with the remaining dumpling pastries and filling.

Holding the dumplings by their skirting, lift them up and place on a tray with the skirting facing upwards, flattening the base of the dumplings so that they sit upright by themselves.

Steam over a high heat for 4 minutes.

Meanwhile, beat the measured water with the flour to make a light batter.

When the dumplings are cooked, transfer, in 2 batches, to a nonstick frying pan that has been lightly oiled and set over a medium heat. Add half the batter per batch of dumplings, swirling the pan to cover the base with the batter. Watch the heat of the pan create a web around the dumplings in the pan.

When the web of batter is set and crispy, remove the dumplings from the pan and serve immediately with the ginger vinegar.

Recipe from *The A Wong Cookbook* by Andrew Wong, published by Mitchell Beazley

Top and middle
**Andrew Wong on the
pass at his restaurant.**
Right **Intense heat
and steam in the
A Wong kitchen.**

58

Amaya Halkin Arcade, Motcomb Street, SW1X 8JT

020 7823 1166 www.amaya.biz

The focus at Amaya, unlike other modern high-profile Indian restaurants, is on grilled ingredients, rather than curries or spiced dishes with heavy sauces – they say they've got the widest grill selection in England. The theatrical open-grill kitchen focuses on three core methods of Indian cuisine: *tandoor* – cooking food in a really hot clay oven; *sigiri* – cooking over a coal flame; and *tawa* – cooking or griddling food on a hot, thick, iron plate. The food is designed to be eaten with your hands, if you feel comfortable doing so, and shared. The menu includes plenty of fish and shellfish, vegetarian dishes and game in season as well as a small collection of unusual curries and biryanis. They've also got a Michelin star to their name.

Ametsa with Arzak Instruction COMO The Halkin, Halkin Street, SW1X 7DJ

020 7333 1234 www.comohotels.com/thehalkin/dining/ametsa

Ametsa, meaning dreams in the Basque dialect, has been created by the famous Arzak family in partnership with COMO hotels – a formidable team. In San Sebastian, Arzak is a boundary-pushing three-Michelin-star restaurant that is constantly on the list of restaurants that most young aspiring chefs want to visit. The food isn't the top of my list, but you've got to admire their vision and ambition to create a new style of food that has really put this corner of Spain on the global culinary map. And the room in this restaurant is rather good-looking, too, with a wave-like ceiling created from 7,000 glass receptacles filled with spices (PP).

Above **Extravagant flowers to match the food at Ametsa.**

Right **Sergi Sanz Blanco is the head chef at Ametsa.**

Bar Boulud Mandarin Oriental Hyde Park, 66 Knightsbridge, SW1X 7LA
020 7201 3899 www.barboulud.com

While hailing from Lyon, it is in America, and particularly New York City, that Daniel Boulud has made his name as one of the planet's super-chefs. Many say his flagship restaurant is still one of the best in Manhattan. His first venture in the UK, located in the very swanky Mandarin Oriental, is a very welcome addition to the London dining-out scene. The menu is a fun mix of upmarket French bistro, with plenty of very expertly prepared charcuterie, and American de luxe burgers. It is the burgers that have made headlines for this place. We're no great burger experts, but the late restaurant critic AA Gill – acknowledged by many as an authority on the subject – described the three different burgers on the menu as 'supreme' in *The Sunday Times*.

Ruth Rogers

The diversity of food, culture and people – that is what makes London great.
Restaurateur, The River Café

Above **Charcuterie maison, with recipes by Gilles Verot of Paris.** Right **The menu includes a choice of three different burgers: the Yankee, the Piggie and the BB.**

Left **The London outpost of Eric Fréchon's restaurant Céleste, is headed up by protégé Florian Favario.**

Opposite **The gilded and opulent interior at Céleste.**

The Berkeley Wilton Place, SW1X 7RL
020 7235 6000 www.the-berkeley.co.uk

After overlooking their two superstar-chefs, there's still a lot of great food and drink being served at The Berkeley Hotel. First, there is the legendary Blue Bar. Originally opened in 2000, it was designed by the late David Collins and quickly became one of the best bars in London. It has recently had an extension and a makeover by Robert Angell, a protégé of Mr Collins. The drinks and service are exceptional. Secondly, they've just celebrated ten years of their Prêt-à-Portea concept – a light-hearted homage to the fashion world. Do treat all fashionista friends to this fun idea – the cakes are also delicious.

Céleste The Lanesborough, Hyde Park Corner, SW1X 7TA
020 7259 5599 www.lanesborough.com/eng/restaurant-bars/celeste/

The opening of Céleste appears to have been completely missed or perhaps avoided by the London critics, and there is hardly a word spoken about the place. Yes, The Lanesborough Hotel is completely out of step with new modern London, if you exclude the Mayfair bubble that is, but the restaurant is fronted by a major name in Eric Fréchon, from the Le Bristol hotel in Paris where he holds three Michelin stars.

Anxiously, I booked Céleste for a dinner with a few mates – we were looking for something a bit different and we certainly got it. The dining room is richly decorated, with the walls adorned with Wedgwood-like reliefs, chandeliers and posh little details all over the place. I half expected the place to be virtually empty, but in fact it had a lovely atmosphere with a very mixed bag of guests. The only real negative was the pianist – technically the music was good and added a lovely sound to the room, but the playlist was totally naff. The service was exemplary and we all enjoyed our meals. I had a modern take on French onion soup, which was nothing like how it is in your favourite brasserie, followed by a very good hare (not often seen on menus, sadly) with foie gras and pepper sauce.

If you like a cigar after dinner, then this is a good place to head. They've got one of London's very rare hidden areas where you can enjoy a decent Cuban (PP).

Left **Hand-crafted sugar strawberry with gariguette mousse and sorbet.**

Best for... superstar chefs

Céleste – Eric Fréchon's sensational
fine dining at The Lanesborough hotel
Alain Ducasse at The Dorchester –
you can't question three Michelin stars
Dinner by Heston Blumenthal
– arguably far more appealing than
The Fat Duck

Dinner by Heston Blumenthal

Mandarin Oriental Hyde Park, 66 Knightsbridge, SW1X 7LA

020 7201 3833   www.dinnerbyheston.co.uk

Heston is now a household name and this, his first London restaurant, has been a global success, garnering more than a handful of awards, including two Michelin stars. And – shock, horror – this restaurant achieved a higher status than The Fat Duck on the (ridiculous) World's Best Restaurant awards. It could be argued that it's just a must-try experience, and not necessarily a place to visit on a regular basis. But given the demand and the hype, the prices are quite reasonable and the food is extremely good. So maybe it is the best restaurant in London.

Prior to opening, the big talking point was the name of the restaurant. Heston was quick to explain that dinner historically means the main meal of the day, whether it is at midday or in the evening. This is correct, but we're not sure this statement has silenced the doubters.

Don't expect Heston's trademark molecular gastronomy, famous from his Fat Duck restaurant in Bray – this is a new direction in food: new, but looking resolutely to the past. Heston and his head chef Ashley Palmer-Watts have extensively researched British gastronomy and looked to history books for inspiration. Each dish on the menu is given its approximate date of origin, and many are forgotten gems from the past that have been given a modern treatment.

There are some really creative dishes on the menu, yet at the same time the kitchen manages to extract more flavour from the ingredients than you might think possible. This is truly the sign of a great chef. If the main function of the professional cook in today's world of globally available foodstuffs is to maximize the flavour of well-sourced ingredients, then full marks are due to this kitchen.

No expense has been spared when it comes to the kitchen equipment, especially the pulley system that operates the spit roast, a masterpiece that might well be envied by the finest Swiss watchmakers. Dining at the chef 's table, next to the main service counter, has to be one of the most in-demand foodie experiences in London – it is certainly one of the most expensive. The main dining room is not too shabby either; in fact a window table can be one of the best in town. And, naturally, you can be assured of excellent service.

Above left **The now-famous meat fruit – a silky chicken liver and foie gras parfait created to look like a mandarin orange.**

The Goring Dining Room

15 Beeston Place, Grosvenor Gardens, SW1W 0JW

020 7396 9000 www.thegoring.com

Four generations of the Goring family have overseen the most British hotel in the capital. With the Queen as your next-door neighbour, indeed, it would be traitorous for it to be anything other than quintessentially British. The hotel is immaculately managed with every detail addressed with gentlemanly poise. The dining room (designed by David Linley, the Queen's nephew) is light, airy and pleasant, with heavy, comfortable armchairs and large tables with acres of space between them, while Swarovski crystal chandeliers add a more feminine note. This is a restaurant to take one's grandparents or senior grown-up types for important luncheons or dinner, perhaps after an investiture at the Palace. Under the control of Shay Cooper, the kitchen has received its first Michelin star.

Gary Rhodes

"

My favourite corner shop – that would have to be Harrods. This wonderful establishment holds the finest food halls in London, feeding you with great flavours, which always result in a heavier carrier bag!

Chef and restaurateur

Above **A quintessential liveried and white-gloved butler at The Goring.**

Above **Harrods still has some of the finest food counters in London.**

Left **Vying for shoppers, Harvey Nichols also has an impressive food hall although it has become much smaller over recent years.**

Harrods 87–135 Brompton Road, SW1X 7XL

020 7730 1234 www.harrods.com

In the 1980s, when I first arrived in London, I would visit Harrods as often as possible to learn more about food and marvel at the displays. Over recent years the food halls seem to have lost some of their grandeur, but you cannot deny the scale and range of produce available here. The endless counters offer every food possible, from meat, fish and Oriental foods to cheese, coffee and caviar. And, unlike some of the great food halls in London, they still sell foie gras, truffles and many other proper top-end gourmet foods. The seasonal hampers are always going to be ultra special. Also, if you need to buy a very special wine, then the wine department will be sure to cater for your needs, and if you don't have the intention or the budget, do go along and marvel at their selection. Harrods also has a vast array of restaurants and they occasionally run high-profile pop-ups with the likes of Thomas Keller of The French Laundry (PP).

Harvey Nichols Fifth Floor 109–125 Knightsbridge, SW1X 7RJ

020 7235 5250 www.harveynichols.com

Harvey Nicks, as it is affectionately known, is renowned for its street-level window displays and is considered a more fashionable and younger version of Harrods, just a short walk along Brompton Road. When the Fifth Floor first opened, it transformed our conception not only of dining in a store but also of food retail areas within large department stores. Expectations were raised as new, modern interiors were merged with the deli, butcher's, fishmonger's, bakery and cheese counter, and all were wrapped up together in a busy café and excellent restaurant on an entire floor devoted to food and drink. The packaging, especially for own-label products, was also modern, and different from that in most other food halls and department stores. Before the Fifth Floor, restaurants in stores all too often involved appalling hot buffets, soggy foods and tray service.

Today, the format has evolved even further. The food store is a bit smaller, the wine shop is still excellent, the bar remains a hotspot, for various reasons, and now there is more space given over to different restaurant brands.

Ladurée at Harrods 87–135 Brompton Road, SW1X 7XL

020 3155 0111   www.laduree.com

Much hype surrounded the arrival in London of this Parisian institution
that serves an extensive range of French pastries, from éclairs, cakes and
tarts to gâteaux St Honoré and mille-feuilles. But it is the macarons in an
array of attractive colours, made from eggs, sugar and almonds plus a special
Ladurée ingredient, then glued together with ganache-like fillings of various
flavours, that attract most attention. Ideal in the afternoon with a cup of tea
or after dinner as an alternative to a full dessert, they are indeed delicious,
never failing to melt in the mouth. The very chic packaging also makes them
a perfect gift.

Marcus The Berkeley, Wilton Place SW1X 7RL, UK

020 7235 1200   www.marcus-wareing.com

Having operated a restaurant under his full name, Marcus Wareing dropped his
surname in 2014, and we were to understand that everything had changed –
they'd gone informal and relaxed. Well, I'm not sure about that, but we didn't like
the former incarnation, so this modernization is certainly welcome. Whatever our
views, Marcus is an ever-popular restaurant and they've managed the change
without losing their precious two Michelin stars.

Mr Chow 151 Knightsbridge, SW1X 7PA

020 7589 7347   www.mrchow.com

When it opened in 1968, Mr Chow was possibly the first serious designer
restaurant, renowned for its design details and art. The food is authentic
Beijing, but some say it is now eclipsed by more modern Chinese restaurants.
We still think Mr Chow is worth a visit. Its reputation may not be what it once
was, but it is one of those places that you just must experience. It also has
celebrity outposts in New York and Los Angeles.

Ottolenghi 13 Motcomb Street, SW1X 8LB

020 7823 2707   www.ottolenghi.co.uk

Islington and Notting Hill have had the benefit of branches of Ottolenghi
for some time. Now the residents and office workers of Belgravia can enjoy
some of the most attractively presented and best-tasting food of mostly
Mediterranean inspiration in London, with the choice of a daily changing
menu and a wide selection of baked goods and pâtisserie. Yes, it's not cheap,
but in this small but perfectly formed deli and takeaway shop, that is
probably not a major consideration for the locals; in fact it's probably
viewed as more reassuring.

Above **The Ottolenghi
food displays are
as renowned as the
high prices.**

Left and right **If you are planning a lunch or dinner party at home and haven't got time to make everything yourself, then you can only wish for a neighbouring Ottolenghi deli.**

Right **Peggy Porschen's** pretty meringues are the perfect decoration for any cake (see right). Below **A very enviable corner position in a touched away corner of upmarket Belgravia is the perfect spot for Peggy's parlour.**

Peggy Porschen Cakes 116 Ebury Street, SW1W 9QQ

020 7730 1316 www.peggyporschen.com

This boutique bakery is a popular place for groups of girls and mother-and-daughter meetings. A glass of rosé and a cupcake seem like the order of the day. Peggy's edible works of art will make any wedding, christening, baby shower or the like a sweet success.

Chocolate and Raspberry Drip Cake

Serves 18

For the chocolate sponges

120g (4¼oz) unsalted butter, softened, plus extra for the tins
85g (3oz) plain chocolate (minimum 53 per cent cocoa solids), chopped, or in buttons
220ml (8fl oz) milk
290g (10¼oz) soft light brown sugar
80g (2¾oz, or 1–2) eggs
175g (6oz) plain flour
½ tsp baking powder
½ tsp bicarbonate of soda
pinch of salt
20g (¾oz) cocoa powder
chocolate shards, meringues or raspberry macarons, to decorate (optional)

For the raspberry meringue buttercream

160g (5¾oz) raspberry purée (bought online)
270g (9½oz) caster sugar
4½ tablespoons water
135g (4¾oz, or about 4) egg whites
330g (11½oz) unsalted butter
raspberry extract, to taste

For the ganache

4½ tablespoons whipping cream
80g (2¾oz) plain chocolate (minimum 53 per cent cocoa solids), chopped, or in buttons
1 teaspoon liquid glucose

Bake the sponges a day ahead. Assemble and decorate the cake on the day of serving. Prepare the ganache a few hours before use, so it has time to cool.

Preheat the oven to 160°C (325°F), Gas Mark 3. Butter and line 3 x 15cm (6in) sandwich tins with greaseproof paper. (If you haven't got 3 tins, you will have to bake in batches.)

Place the chocolate, 180ml (6fl oz) of the milk and 145g (5¼oz) of the light brown sugar in a saucepan and bring to the boil, stirring.

Place the butter and remaining light brown sugar in the bowl of a stand mixer (or use an electric hand whisk) and cream together until pale and fluffy. Beat the eggs lightly in another bowl and slowly add to the butter mixture, whisking quickly. Sift the flour, baking powder, bicarbonate of soda, salt and cocoa powder together and add to the butter mixture in 2 batches. Mix together slowly until the batter is just combined, then add the remaining milk.

Slowly pour the hot chocolate mix into the batter in a thin stream, mixing at a medium speed. Immediately pour into the prepared tins and bake for 20–30 minutes. The cakes are cooked when the sides are beginning to shrink away from the edges of the tins and the tops spring back to the touch.

Let the cakes rest for about 30 minutes out of the oven. When they are just warm, run a knife all the way round the sides of the tins, remove the cakes from the tins and leave to cool completely on wire cooling racks.

Once cool, wrap the cakes in clingfilm and rest overnight at room temperature. This keeps the moisture in and the sponge will firm up for trimming and layering.

To make the buttercream, put the raspberry purée into a small saucepan, bring to the boil and simmer until reduced by half. Chill until cool.

Place the sugar and measured water into a small saucepan over a medium heat and bring to a rapid boil.

Place the egg whites in the bowl of a stand mixer and whisk at low speed until frothy.

When the sugar syrup reaches 121°C (250°F) on a sugar thermometer, with the electric mixer running, pour it directly over the meringue in a thin, steady stream, taking care not to pour any over the whisk or the sides of the bowl. Whip until cool to the touch; this could take several minutes. With the mixer running, add the butter a couple of tablespoons at a time. Keep beating until completely smooth and spreadable.

Add a little meringue buttercream to the raspberry purée and mix until well combined. Gently fold this into the remaining meringue buttercream and add raspberry extract to taste. If the mixture splits, whip it up until smooth once more.

To assemble the cake, using a cake leveller or serrated knife, trim the top crust off each sponge. Slice each sponge horizontally in half to give 6 even layers.

Place the bottom layer on a cake stand or serving plate, then using a large palette knife and about half the buttercream, sandwich together the 6 sponge layers. Use the remaining buttercream to cover the top and sides. (If you have a turntable, use it, as it may help you to achieve more even layers and a smoother finish.) Chill the cake until set.

To make the ganache, place the cream in a saucepan and bring to a bare simmer. Place the chocolate and glucose in a bowl and pour the hot cream over the top. Whisk together until smooth. Once combined, leave to set at room temperature until the ganache has a thick pouring consistency.

To glaze the cake, place the cold cake on a serving plate or cake stand. Pour the ganache over the top until it starts to spill over the edges.

Decorate with chocolate shards, meringues and raspberry macarons, if you like. The cake tastes best if eaten within 3 days, but can last for up to 1 week.

70

Pétrus 1 Kinnerton Street, SW1X 8EA

020 7592 1609 www.gordonramsayrestaurants.com/petrus

If we weren't so keen on wine, perhaps this place would not be included. The dining room is dominated by the wine display area – it might look better without it, but that would be missing the point of this place. As you would expect, the wine list includes multiple vintages, from 1928 to 1996 Petrus – one of the world's most famous wines, including vintage 1961 at £39,5000 – any takers? Gordon Ramsay has owned the restaurant, and the name, for a long time, and over the years it has reportedly been the subject of various legal disputes – all adding to the allure.

Right **Château Pétrus** – one of the rarest and most expensive wines from Pomerol, Bordeaux.

Poilâne 46 Elizabeth Street, SW1W 9PA

020 7808 4910 www.poilane.com

Pierre Poilâne opened a small bakery in the Saint-Germain-des-Prés quarter of Paris in 1932. Today, Harvard graduate Apollonia Poilâne oversees an international multimillion-pound business. It was always Apollonia's intention to work in the family firm and she underwent a lengthy apprenticeship with her father Lionel at an early age. Following his untimely death, Apollonia was propelled into the role of CEO before her studies were even complete.

Some three per cent of all the bread consumed in Paris today is reputed to be by Poilâne, with daily exports to Milan, Brussels, Berlin, Tokyo and over 3,000 private clients in the US. The bakery in Elizabeth Street has attracted a loyal and distinguished client list for its now legendary sourdough. You can buy a small selection of other breads and *punitions* (literally 'punishments'), or butter shortbread *sablés*, but it is the large 4-lb (1.75kg) sourdough loaves with their trademark 'P' traced in the flour on top that are most certainly the real attraction for the distinguished clientele.

Peggy Porschen

"
One of my favourite breakfast places in London is La Cuisine de Bar by Poilâne near Sloane Square in Chelsea. My guilty pleasure is the truffled egg with Gruyère baked in a thick slice of brioche – it's amazing! The staff are fantastic and the interior is very warm and contemporary. A nice place to relax.

Owner, Peggy Porschen Cakes

Right **The London outpost of the now global Poilâne bakery.**

La Poule au Pot 231 Ebury Street, SW1W 8UT

020 7730 7763 www.pouleaupot.co.uk

This place is old school charm and romance personified, with lots of little corners and niches for intimate candlelit dining. It is a little like a traditional French farmhouse with a few objets trouvés on the shelves and baskets of dried flowers hanging from the ceiling. They've got a quintessential French bistro menu – and it is all generously served. On a summer's day you can enjoy their lovely outside terrace. Bon appétit!

There's something about these places
that makes them more appealing for
a romantic evening out. Of course,
they do all serve French food – *j'adore*.

La Poule au Pot

Le Gavroche

La Petite Maison

Theo Randall at The InterContinental 1 Hamilton Place, W1J 7QY

020 7318 8747 www.theorandall.com

Another top-class chef in a five-star hotel setting. Theo is an ex-River Café
chef where he worked for 17 years before going it alone, and his Italian food is
thankfully more simple and rustic than in some other restaurants in the area.
As tends to be the case with hotel locations, the room and setting are a little
off-putting, but the food is great.

Zafferano 15 Lowndes Street, SW1X 9EY

020 7235 5800 www.zafferanorestaurant.com

Zafferano has been around since 1995 and offers proper Italian food in a rather
grown-up manner. Professional – but never overbearing – service from a mainly
Italian team and the approach of a small and unassuming restaurant combine
to produce an atmosphere of contentment. The room has been extended over
the years and now incorporates a small bar and extra tables, yet it still retains
elements that strike a modest note. This is especially evident in the private
dining room, set in the brick-vaulted wine cellars.

Zuma 5 Raphael Street, SW7 1DL

020 7584 1010 www.zumarestaurant.com

Personally I find the atmosphere and clientele a bit loud (I prefer the sister
restaurant Roka) but the food is quite brilliant. Since Zuma opened in London
in 2002, it has proved hugely popular, which has fuelled a global expansion.
The chef and restaurateur Rainer Becker has created a contemporary version
of a Japanese *izakaya* (an informal bar with simple food). Many of the dishes
are designed to share among friends, and it's a great location for a small party.
The sushi, sashimi and rolls are inventively prepared, and the fish and especially
the pork and beef from the Robata grill are particularly good. The tasting menu
is a full-on gustatory experience, but like most of the menu it carries a heavy
price tag, especially if you go for the black cod or Wagyu beef. The bar is wild
and always busy as the cocktail staff create inspirational drinks, many including
freshly prepared fruit juices with sake and Japanese spirits (PP).

Below **Crab and
asparagus salad
at the enduringly
excellent Zafferano.**

More places to visit in the area

Above right **The Pierre Hermé** *maison* **in Knightsbridge**. Above right **An impressive selection of Pierre Hermé macarons**.

Boisdale
15 Eccleston Street, SW1W 9LX
020 7730 6922 www.boisdale.co.uk
This is a very peculiar place that has a very loyal following for its unique combination of traditional (we're not sure there is any other type) Scottish food, whisky and tartan-heavy décor, plus jazz and cigars on the terrace.

Daylesford
6–8 Blandford Street, W1U 4AU
020 3696 6500 daylesford.com
Knowing a bit about food retail, I can only imagine that this place is coming at a great cost to its owners. It is a marble palace loaded with a wonderful array of fine organic foods, many of which come from the Daylesford-owned farms and estates. It is ultra pricey, but the quality cannot be questioned (PP).

Hunan
51 Pimlico Road, SW1W 8NE
020 7730 5712 hunanlondon.com
One of the key components of a restaurant is the menu. This very special Chinese restaurant, which has been going since 1982, doesn't have one! Instead, you tell the staff what you don't eat, if anything, and how hot and spicy you like your food. They then prepare a special menu for you. Food of this style can be extremely difficult to match wines to, but the Hunan team has carved out a reputation for overcoming these challenges and now have a very special award-winning list.

Pierre Hermé
13 Lowndes Street, SW1W 9EX
020 7245 0317 www.pierreherme.com
This is now a global chain of super-deluxe pâtisseries that specialize in macarons, bonbons and fancy cakes. *Vogue* called Pierre the Picasso of Pastry and certainly it seems that he styles his boutiques more like a fashion *maison* than an earnest cake shop.

Brick Lane
Shoreditch
Spitalfields
Whitechapel

Shoreditch seems to have developed a dual personality. During the daytime it is still home to the cool kids from the creative and digital agencies, but by night certain areas (mostly on the High Street) can be highly undesirable. I'm not talking about crime or it being unsafe, but more in regard to the ugly face of trashy bars, night markets and questionable street food vendors. Possibly no longer the cutting edge of London, it's more like the cutting middle. The area has changed beyond all recognition over the past decade – the fashion students have left Fashion Street in search of cheaper rents and later licences of Dalston and Peckham, and glossy tech start-ups have taken their place. The Shoreditch triangle is lined with all manner of stylish bars and eateries, as well as lifestyle stores, which service the area with filament light bulbs and coffee table tomes. There is still soul left in Shoreditch and at the weekend it adopts a family-friendly vibe. And, unthinkable 15 years ago, it is now chock-full of smart restaurants, hotels and upmarket bars.

While Spitalfields is now turned over largely to chain shops and restaurants, where once there were picnic tables and street food vendors, it has plenty to excite the culinary tourist – Taberna do Mercado is Nuno Mendes's take on the kind of market café you'd find in Lisbon or Barcelona, and makes Spitalfields a real destination again. Go there on a Thursday and the antiques market gives it the tinkerish feel it once had all week. There are still beautiful backstreets with fascinating backstories – slip down Fournier Street and you might notice that all the buildings are a storey higher on one side, with large attic windows. That was so the Huguenot weavers at work on the top floor got as much light as possible in the days before electricity. Now, of course, it's the likes of Tracey Emin and Gilbert & George who take advantage of the airy lofts for their work. Brick Lane stubbornly refuses to be gentrified – it may have a controversial cereal café, but its eastern end is still Bangladeshi to the bone – with supermarkets, curry houses and Asian sweet shops running all the way to Whitechapel. And the queue to legendary Punjabi caterer Tayyabs is almost as long.

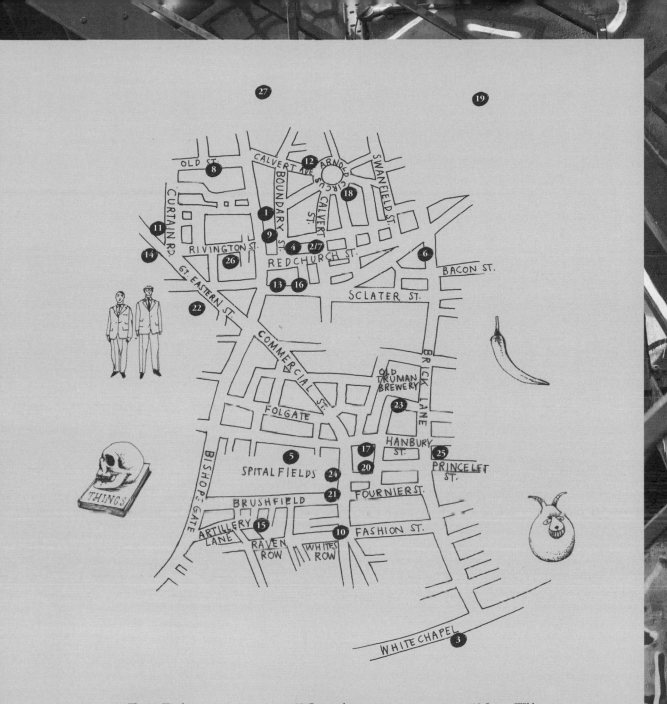

1	The Ace Hotel	
2	Albion	
3	Ambala	
4	Andina	
5	Androuet	
6	Beigel Bake	
7	Boundary Rooftop & Restaurant	
8	The Clove Club	
9	Dishoom	
10	Gunpowder	
11	Joyeux Bordel	
12	Leila's Shop	
13	Lyle's	
14	Oklava	
15	Ottolenghi	
16	Pizza East	
17	Poppies	
18	Rochelle Canteen	
19	Sager + Wilde	
20	Som Saa	
21	St John Bread & Wine	
22	Street Feast	
23	Sunday Upmarket	
24	Taberna do Mercado	
25	Taj Stores	
26	Tramshed	
27	Viet Grill	

Left **A fixed-wheel bike in the lobby window of the Ace Hotel speaks volumes about the area and the hotel itself.**

76

The Ace Hotel – Hoi Polloi, Bulldog Edition and the Lobby

100 Shoreditch High Street, E1 6JQ

020 7613 9800   www.acehotel.com/london

I'm not sure the bedrooms are ace, but the hotel is relatively cheap and the location hard to beat. Instead, it is the ground-floor spaces, all designed by the brilliant design duo Barber & Osgerby, that have helped make this property become a social hub among the cool, young (they seem to get younger everyday) creative set at the heart of Shoreditch.

The main restaurant is run by the Bistrotheque guys (see page 216), so you know everything is going to be stylishly put together – from the staff uniforms to the menu graphics. And, they've brought in some top talent in the kitchens. I particularly like the simplicity and calmness of the wood-panelled dining room.

The lobby is dominated by a 16-seater long communal table made from cast iron, oak and copper. I know this because it was created by Benchmark, a furniture company owned by Terence Conran, and made on his estate in Berkshire. Every day, this table is full with Macbook-toting boys and girls planning the world's next biggest tech start-up. It seems this is the exact point where a new form of socializing meets a new way of working.

If I'm not having my morning kick-starter coffee at Albion around the corner, I'll head to Bulldog Edition. They rightly take their art very seriously and have the World's Barista Champion at their helm. The breakfast cakes, buns and panini are also worth dropping in for (PP).

There's a club downstairs and on the top floor a great event space with a small roof terrace. All in all, a great addition to the area.

Right **Steak skewers from Hoi Polloi.**
Opposite, above **The view from The Ace Hotel top floor over the rooftops of Shoreditch towards the City.**
Opposite, middle **Inside the wood-panelled Hoi Polloi restaurant.**
Opposite, below **The ground-floor bar at The Ace Hotel.**

Albion 2–4 Boundary Street, E2 7DD

020 7729 1051 www.albioncaff.co.uk

We should start by declaring an interest. Albion is our version of a French all-day pavement café done in a British style, with an adjoining bakery and a small shop.

The menu is all about typical British caff foods, nothing challenging or complicated, just straightforward hearty ingredients and recipes. Breakfast is served throughout the day, alongside fish and chips, half pints of prawns, mussels cooked in cider, a minimum of three different pies (often more, including delights such as cottage pie, chicken and crayfish pie and game pie), plus Irish stew, kedgeree, devilled kidneys, doorstop sandwiches, fruit jellies, puddings and crumbles. There's nothing that you won't recognize and everything that you want to eat. The breakfast menu is eternally popular, whether with weekend shoppers or with the local creative community, who love to scoff everything from kippers to duck eggs on toast, or healthy organic yogurt with poached fruits and muesli.

The bakery and pastry ovens are located in the café, so diners can watch the team at work and inhale the reassuring aromas. We now sell 16 different breads, an extensive array of viennoiserie and a full range of English cakes and bakery treats.

Our small shop stocks a range of British foods, from larder essentials and everyday basics, such as Maldon salt and Colman's mustard, to jams and Neal's Yard Dairy cheeses, regional specialities such as Kendal Mint Cake and luxury chocolates, to mention just a fraction of what we cram into it. All of the fresh items, including a range of prepared meals, are made in our kitchen, and we stock a variety of meats and game in season. Gulls' eggs (despite their ridiculous price) and wild smoked salmon are popular. The kitchen garden at Barton Court, Terence's home in Berkshire, provides vegetables and herbs.

Since it opened in January 2009, Albion has far eclipsed our wildest expectations, winning awards and local support. It just goes on growing. We hope you enjoy it.

Ambala 144–6 Whitechapel Road, E1 1JE

0207 247 2042 www.ambalafoods.com

From swirls of *jalebi* to *besan ladoo*, made with gram flour, almonds, pistachios and brazil nuts, and luminous (thanks to food colourings) *kaju* fruits fashioned from cashew nut marzipan, Ambala stocks an impressive selection of traditional sweets from the Indian subcontinent, in addition to baklava in every possible shape and variety. While the sweet counter is impressive, Ambala is even prouder of its *rasmalai*, ideal as an after-dinner dessert on a sweltering hot evening.

Above **The Albion outside terrace below Boundary Hotel.** Right **Inside the Albion café.**

Left **HP Sauce and ketchup are essential condiments at Albion.**

Devilled Kidneys

Serves 1

100g (3½oz) plain flour

10g English mustard powder

5g (¼oz) cayenne pepper

5g (¼oz) paprika

3 lambs' kidneys, cut in half, with fat removed and cleaned

25g (1oz) butter

20ml (¾fl oz) veal jus

1–2 thick slices of bread, toasted

small handful of parsley, finely chopped

salt and freshly ground black pepper

Mix the flour, mustard powder, cayenne pepper and paprika together and season with salt and pepper. Dust the kidneys with the flour mix.

Heat a frying pan over a medium heat and add the butter. When the butter has melted, add the kidneys and cook until golden brown on 1 side, then turn over to seal the other side. Add the veal jus and boil until it is reduced to a sauce consistency. Season with salt and pepper to taste.

To serve, place the kidneys on slices of toast, pour the sauce over and finish with a sprinkling of chopped parsley.

Andina 1 Redchurch Street, E2 7DJ

020 7920 6499 www.andinalondon.com

Located at the corner of Redchurch Street and Shoreditch High Street, Andina is at the gateway to a great night out. You start with a pisco sour, or perhaps multiple piscos. They are so easy to drink, almost like a refreshing juice, but with a kick – so restraint is needed. This is relaxed Latin America mixed with party central on a weekend night. The music is loud and the fellow diners are generally louder, in every sense.

Over the years, I've got to know Martin Morales, the guy behind this Picanteria and Pisco Bar. He's fanatical about his homeland and most sincere about bringing the best of Peru to London, in different guises – whether that's music, art, ingredients or a sense of enjoyment. The menu fuses superfoods native to the Peruvian Andes with seasonal British produce (PP).

You might also try to visit the very attractive private dining room; it's decorated with a nod to Martin's past in the music business, thanks to the display of records adorning the walls.

During the daytime, it's all about healthy recipes and juices, good for a restorative brunch.

Androuet Spitalfields Arts Market, 10 Lamb Street, E1 6EA

020 7247 7437 www.androuet.co.uk

A name with resonance for Parisian cheese-lovers is now to be found on the edge of Spitalfields Market. The House of Androuet was founded in 1909 and now boasts this brilliant London shop and cheese bar. Perhaps not as atmospheric as La Fromagerie or Neal's Yard Dairy, but the service is good and cheese is the star here. Perfectly conditioned French and Italian cheese dominate, but due to a partnership with Paxton & Whitfield, a very upmarket shop in Jermyn Street, they also have boast excellent British cheeses. (If you visit, do ask for Alex and perhaps quote my name and he might give you a few freebies.) As you would expect, their menu is dominated by cheese dishes – think tartiflette, fondue, raclette and so on, even cheese cake. I'm salivating as I write (PP)!

Beigel Bake 159 Brick Lane, E1 6SB

020 7729 0616

Open 24/7, Beigel Bake serves everybody and has been doing so for decades. Go at four in the morning and watch the post-clubbing crowd, or on Saturday afternoons when London cabbies enjoy salt-beef sandwiches. The milky cholla still attracts the Jewish old-timers, and true East Enders come for the pastries. They bake more than 7,000 bagels a day.

Left **A Peruvian twist on pork belly at Andina.**

Above **A green Vayeho juice at Andina – with avocado, pear juice, spinach, lime and Broccocress.**

Best for...
a glamorous
night out

Boundary Rooftop followed by Tratra at Boundary – hard to beat this combination of cocktails followed by a romantic meal in a dining room designed by Terence Conran

Chiltern Firehouse – after the hype has diffused, this is still a special place to visit

Sushisamba – atop one of the City's skyscrapers, the atmosphere is pure dressed-up night out

Avocado Burger with Pineapple Salsa

Serves 4

For the patty

1 red onion, finely chopped

olive oil

1 ripe avocado

240g (8½oz) cooked white quinoa

3–4 garlic cloves, crushed, to taste

2 eggs, lightly beaten

4 tablespoons quinoa flour

2 teaspoons maca powder

2 teaspoons chia seeds

8 tablespoons Greek yogurt

4 seeded buns, split

handful of spinach leaves

4 slices of beef tomato

sea salt flakes

For the salsa

4 slices of ripe pineapple, finely chopped

1 red onion, finely sliced

juice of 2 limes

8 coriander sprigs, finely chopped

For the chilli relish

1 onion, finely chopped

8 red chillies, finely chopped

2 small tomatoes, chopped

8 tablespoons honey

8 tablespoons white wine vinegar

2 teaspoons freshly ground white pepper

Start with the patty. Sauté the onion in a little oil in a small frying pan until soft, but not browned. Cut the avocado into quarters, peel and pit, and mash the flesh in a bowl. Add the cooked onion, two-thirds of the quinoa, the garlic, eggs, quinoa flour, maca and half the chia seeds. Season with salt and mix until creamy and thick. Form into 4 patties and coat with the rest of the quinoa and chia seeds. Leave in the fridge for 1 hour to set.

For the salsa, mix all the ingredients and season. Set aside.

For the relish, sauté the onion until soft in a little oil, then add the rest of the ingredients with a pinch of salt. Bring to the boil and cook for a couple of minutes until it thickens to a chutney consistency.

Splash some oil into a frying pan, place over a medium heat and fry the patties on each side for 7–8 minutes until crispy. Spread half the yogurt on the cut sides of each bun and toast each side in a hot pan for about 10 seconds, to give them some humidity and crunchiness. Spread the rest of the yogurt on the base of each bun, add the spinach, then the salsa. Place the avocado patties on top and add the tomato slices. Finally, spread a generous portion of the relish on the inside bun lids, place them on top and enjoy.

This page **On the pass and in the dining room at Andina.**

Boundary Rooftop & Restaurant 2–4 Boundary Street, E2 7DD
020 7729 1051 www.theboundary.co.uk

Boundary was our first Prescott & Conran project and we are rightly very proud of it. So much so, that we have no qualms about saying that it can be the setting for a perfect night out. Or, with the hotel attached, even more, with a relaxing overnight stay added. Start on the Rooftop with a sexy cocktail and some Provençal tapas while admiring the garden and taking in the east London skyline. Then, when the sun starts to drop, head to Tratra, the main restaurant. *Tratra* is a colloquial French term meaning 'traditional with a hint of modernity'. It also helps explain the jolly *bonhomie* that the team at Tratra try to create. The menu, and many of the ideas behind Tratra, has been created by bestselling author Stephane Reynaud. It was his wonderful books, particularly *Ripaille*, *Pork & Sons* and *Rôtis*, that attracted us to Stephane, and we're now pleased that he's bringing the same spirit to the restaurant at Boundary. As the grandson of a butcher, the menu is unashamedly meat oriented. And, there is an extensive selection of charcuterie. The Tratra menu encourages sharing and a convivial atmosphere, underpinned with great quality ingredients, confident cooking and friendly service.

Wine is very important at Tratra. The all-French multi-award-winning list includes more than 700 bins that range from aristocratic first growths and the finest grands crus from Burgundy to simple table wines from the Languedoc, with a good selection of large-format bottles. These magnums, jeroboams, methuselahs and rehoboams look very impressive and are ideal for large tables. The sommelier team also runs a very successful wine club, Château Boundary, which offers everything from regular tastings to wine holidays.

Alongside the restaurant is a small bar promoting purist versions of the great British and American cocktails. An exceptionally stiff martini is the house speciality. A fine digestif selection, including a range of vintage Armagnacs, many different eaux de vie, and the very rare Louis XIII Cognac, is also available.

Left **Making passion fruit soufflé.**

Above, top and opposite **Tratra before a light refurbishment where tablecloths have now been replaced by beautiful pewter surfaces.** Opposite (top) **The Rooftop, Bar and Grill, complete with a huge fireplace to keep you warm on cold evenings.**

Eat London

82

The Clove Club Shoreditch Town Hall, 380 Old Street, EC1V 9LT
020 7729 6496 www.thecloveclub.com

The Clove Club was recently announced as number 26 on the curious (that's the kindest thing I can say about these awards) World's 50 Best Restaurants list. The other major thing you need to know about this excellent bar and restaurant is that you can't just make a dinner reservation and turn up and choose from the menu. No, that would be too conventional. Here, you need to purchase a ticket in advance from a menu (although no details on the actual food you might eat) giving different tasting menu options for differing table sizes in differing parts of the restaurant, with or without different wine flights and so on.

I visited The Clove Club prior to them introducing the ticket system and it was pretty good. Subsequently, I've been put off by the ticket process, but, fortunately, friends have not, and my wife and I have been the willing recipients of some even better food. Unlike other restaurants in this category, I was pleased to see that the ingredients and presentation hadn't become too overwrought and we enjoyed some relatively simple ingredients in peak condition. The staff here are particularly well informed about the menu and seem keen to tell you about every detail on each plate. While this was informative and interesting, it was the dessert brought to our table by the pastry chef that really caught our attention as something genuine and heartfelt (PP).

Michael Sager

"My all-time favourite restaurant has to be The Clove Club – I always have the buttermilk fried chicken – I simply love that I can be in a space of that calibre without feeling uncomfortable.

Co-owner, Sager + Wilde

Dishoom 7 Boundary Street, E2 7JE
020 7420 9324 www.dishoom.com

Dishoom is wildly successful, with several locations across London. Everything is based on their idea of a modern version of the age-old Irani cafés of Mumbai. The space is massive inside, split over two floors, and they have a small veranda for the summer. It's constantly busy and very often there is a ridiculous queue of people outside. Despite this, it is fun, with music, killer cocktails and an interior that is in tune with expectations.

One of their biggest successes has to be their Indian breakfasts and brunches. The naan rolls with bacon, sausage or egg are a perfect start to the weekend.

Above left **The renowned buttermilk fried chicken with pine salt at The Clove Club.**
Above **The Clove Club has its own little charcuterie room.**

Right **Interior details at Gunpowder.** Right, below **The unprepossessing Gunpowder façade on a back street in Spitalfields.**

Above **Harneet Baweja, co-owner of Gunpowder.** Left **Get there early to secure a table.**

Gunpowder 11 White's Row, E1 7NF

020 7426 0542   www.gunpowderlondon.com

I really wanted to go to Gunpowder all of the time but now that I've been once, it will be a long time before I go back. This mindset isn't because of the quality of the food or the service, which are both excellent. It is the no bookings policy that drives me mad. Before my eventual success in snagging a table, I tried on three prior occasions and on each visit I was told that the wait for a table would be at least 60 minutes. Infuriating! However, unlike other restaurants that don't take bookings, you don't have to queue outside in the cold. They have a really efficient system that sends a text to your mobile phone when the table is ready. I've tried this method and waited in St John Bread & Wine (see page 98), just up the road. When the text didn't materialize, it was rather hard not to resist the B&W menu. Anyway, when you do get a seat, in this intimate single room, you'll find a selection of very modestly priced good Indian home-style dishes with vibrant, confident flavours (PP).

Joyeaux Bordel 147 Curtain Road, EC2A 3QE

www.joyeuxbordel.com

Shoreditch was one of the original late-night bar and club destinations, but the licences are now drying up and the bars are tidying up. Run by the guys from Experimental Cocktail Club, this bar is very chichi and a bit louche. The cocktails are excellent, and you can still enjoy a very late drink (they're open until 3am.)

Leila's Shop 15–17 Calvert Avenue, E2 7JP

020 7729 9789

The quality of produce at this bijou café and neighbouring food store is second to none. The range is sometimes a little sporadic, probably because only the best is permitted, and is therefore ideal for impulse purchases with a particular culinary creation in mind. Whether it is artichokes, blood oranges, chocolate, cheese, pulses, rice or Ortiz products, they are all – always – exemplary. The café is a favourite weekend breakfast spot, serving an interesting range of egg dishes, all brought to the table in the pan.

Best for... new favourites

Honey & Co. – watch out for their new place Honey & Grill

Lyle's – just around the corner from our office – is rapidly becoming one of my favourites, but I do wish it was a slightly more comfortable place to be. Anyway, almost everything else is really good (PP)

Portland and Clipstone – two separate places that both have great wine and drinks lists

Below **The sun shining through the Crittall windows at Lyle's, which is located in a former tea warehouse.**

Lyle's Tea Building, 56 Shoreditch High Street, E1 6JJ
020 3011 5911 www.lyleslondon.com

There's a certain calmness about this place that I really enjoy. I think it's due to a culmination of its many simple interior details – set within the iconic Tea Building, it is all-white walls, big high windows with Crittall frames, a concrete floor, metro tiles, Ercol furniture, light oak table tops, and stainless steel – almost no colour, not dissimilar to a gallery without any art and instead the people and the kitchen are the content. It starts with the website, which is reminiscent of some new cool architecture or lifestyle magazine with serene images of isolated buildings, landscapes or skylines. This calmness puts me in the perfect state of mind to enjoy the food, which also exudes confidence and an intelligence rarely found. Every dish I've had seems to be perfectly judged in terms of the number of ingredients. Keeping it simple works: the balance of the dish, the complementing of tastes, the portion size, the plate or dish that it is served on, and, of course, the maximizing of flavours. I think a lot of chefs forget that they must buy well and then also nurture and coax the ingredients in the right way to make the most of the natural flavours. This happens with aplomb at Lyle's.

The list of ingredients is also right up my street – there's always a fair share of offal, eel, game birds, foraged things – and you can tell that the kitchen is obsessed with seasonality.

James Lowe, the chef behind these fantastic menus, has an impressive pedigree. While he came to cooking quite late at 23, he's been on the fast track ever since, with spells working with Heston at The Fat Duck and Fergus at St John.

I'm also a big fan of their menu formats. At lunch, it is based on à la carte pricing with a list of about a dozen dishes with no separation between first, and main-course-style dishes, although the pricing suggests the more substantial plates. It is all very relaxed and easy: choose how *you* want to eat, not what the restaurant suggests that you should be eating, be it two or three small dishes or just one large. It's your privilege and all at very, very reasonable prices. In the evening, it is a set four-course menu at a fixed price – again, it is always just right for a pleasant evening out.

My only gripe is the wine list, but let's not bother about that (PP).

Left **The leftovers from a delicious blackcurrant leaf ice cream with fresh blackcurrants at Lyle's.**

Above **Light floods into the restaurant space at Lyle's.**
Above left **The admin side to being a chef at a top restaurant such as Lyle's.**

Left **The hugely impressive James Lowe at his restaurant Lyle's in Shoreditch.**
Right **John Ogier, the manager at Lyle's –** he's also an alumni of the great St John.

Left **Biodynamic wine at Lyle's.**
Right **Simple Ercol chairs, wood table tops, a polished concrete floor, white wall tiles, Crittall windows and salvaged factory lights complete the design at Lyle's.**

Lyle's Barbecued Whole Brown Crab

Makes 2 (serves 2 very generously, or 4)

10 heads of wild fennel blossom
150g (5½oz) unsalted butter
2 x 800g (1lb 12oz) live brown crabs
a little fennel pollen
sea salt flakes

Build a barbecue with charcoal and then allow the coals to die down to white-hot.

With scissors, cut the fennel blossoms off the stems, put into a small lidded container and keep in the fridge. Chop the stems finely. Melt the butter and mix in the stems.

To kill the crabs in the most humane way, turn them over so they are lying on their shells. There is a triangular flap on the bellies that can be lifted. Do so, and push a spike into the bodies. You will see the crabs go limp.

The important thing here is to find a height above the coals where the crabs will take 20 minutes to cook. You will know if the coals are at the right level when you can hold your hand at the height of the crabs for about 5 seconds before it gets too hot. Brush the crabs with the flavoured butter and place over the coals. Turn regularly and cook for 20 minutes. This should be enough time for the flavours to make their way through the shells.

Using a digital probe thermometer, check the crabs' internal temperature. Probe in the cracks between the plates around the claws and also into the middle of the bodies. You want them to reach 60°C (140°F). When they do, take off to a cooler part of the grill and allow to rest for 5 minutes.

Joint the crabs when cool enough to handle, then remove the gills and cartilage from the heads. Crack the claws and brush with more of the flavoured butter.

Add fennel pollen to the brown head meat, along with salt, and mix, before returning the meat to the shells.

Brush all the shell again with the flavoured butter and sprinkle fennel blossom all over the crab. Serve with a finger bowl... if you're feeling civilized!

Peas and Ticklemore

Serves 2

6 tablespoons apple juice, ideally tart
2 teaspoons lemon juice
125ml (4fl oz) olive oil
8 chervil sprigs
12 mint leaves
6 lovage leaves
200g (7oz) super-fresh podded peas, chilled
pinch of freshly ground black pepper
80g (2¾oz) Ticklemore cheese, thinly sliced
60g (2oz) pea shoots
40 wild pea flowers or 16 nasturtium flowers
sea salt flakes

In a small pan, reduce the apple juice by half, leave to cool, then chill. Combine the reduced apple juice with the lemon juice and olive oil. Set aside.

Pick the herb leaves into iced water, stir, then remove to dry on a cloth.

Using a mortar and pestle, combine half the chervil with salt and grind until bright green and broken down.

Chop the mint and lovage leaves roughly and mix with the peas. Add some apple dressing, a pinch of pepper and the chervil salt to taste. Plate the peas, spreading them into a thin layer. Cover with the Ticklemore.

Mix the pea shoots in the same bowl you just mixed the peas in; think of using the shoots as a 'sponge' to mop up whatever is left in the bowl; they will end up lightly dressed. Don't overdo it, as they are fragile things and will wilt easily. Put on top of the cheese.

Add the flowers and remaining chervil and serve.

Selin Kiazim

"

My favourite restaurant in London
would have to be Barrafina – it has a
special place in my heart. I always
order a few of the specials; something
like a whole grilled brill and their
baby Gem salad, which is to die for.
What makes Barrafina so special is
the simplicity of their dishes, which
always taste amazing and their
consistently high level of execution.

Chef patron, Oklava

Below **Diners who eat
at the bar at Oklava
can admire the skills
of the chefs in the
open kitchen.**

Left **Bar stool seating
outside Oklava.**
Right **Hellim (Turkish
halloumi) with a fried
duck egg and sherry
vinegar caramel.**

Oklava 74 Luke Street, EC2A 4PY

020 7729 3032 www.oklava.co.uk

The menu here is all about Selin Kiazim's (watch out for this name – it is
going to be big in the future) modern take on the food of her Turkish-
Cypriot background. So, you can expect some strong flavours and delicious
salads such as chilli roast cauliflower or courgette, feta and mint fritters,
as well as *pides* (filled flatbreads), crispy pomegranate glazed lamb or
baharat-spiced pork belly. I keep returning for the (phenomenal) value-
for-money Sunday brunch fixed-price sharing menu. They bring you
wave after wave of lovely things to eat, such as *börek* (baked, filled filo
pastries), grilled Cypriot pastirma sausage, *menemen* (Turkish one-pan eggs,
tomatoes and peppers), salads, seasonal fruits and spoon sweets served
with *çay* (Turkish tea), plus lovely breads and their addictive Medjool
date butter. Incidentally, in Turkish, *oklava* means 'rolling pin'. They've
chosen this name because the breads, pastries and *pides*, made with the
help of a rolling pin, are central to this restaurant's appeal.

Courgette, Feta and Mint Fritters

Serves 4–6

8 courgettes, coarsely grated
1 teaspoon fine salt
2 bunches of spring onions, thinly sliced
bunch of mint, leaves picked and shredded, plus extra to serve
1 large egg, lightly beaten
800g (1lb 12oz) Turkish white cheese or feta cheese, crumbled
200g (7oz) plain flour, or as needed
sunflower oil, for deep-frying
freshly ground black pepper
yogurt, to serve

Mix the courgettes and fine salt together and put them in a colander set over a bowl. Put a plate directly on top of the courgettes and then put several weights on top of the plate. Set aside for up to 1 hour to drain.

Put the courgettes in a clean tea towel and roll them up into a cracker shape, twisting the ends. Squeeze out as much liquid as you possibly can. The secret to lovely fritters is to put just enough flour so that the fritters hold together when frying, so use as little flour as you can get away with – it all depends on how much moisture is in your mixture. Bearing this in mind, put the courgettes into a bowl and add the spring onions, mint, egg, cheese, flour and black pepper. Using your hands, mix together the whole lot, squeezing it through your hands as you go to combine the ingredients really well.

If you are using a deep-fat fryer, heat the oil up to 180°C (350°F). Alternatively, place a deep frying pan over a high heat and add enough oil to cover the fritters. Add a small cube of bread to the oil when you think it is ready and, if it sizzles immediately, the oil is at the right temperature. Working in batches of 6–8, shape the fritter mixture into very tight quenelles using 2 identical spoons, and drop them individually into the oil. Fry for 1–2 minutes, turning halfway, or until golden brown and crisp on each side. Remove and drain on kitchen paper. Repeat with the remaining mixture. Sprinkle with mint and serve with yogurt.

Recipe from *Oklava: Recipes from a Turkish-Cypriot Kitchen* by Selin Kiazim, published by Mitchell Beazley

Ottolenghi 50 Artillery Lane, E1 7LJ

020 7247 1999 www.ottolenghi.co.uk

This book includes a few Ottolenghi references because you can always be assured of great food at them all – without exception. If you find yourself in this corner of town, head to this branch; it is slightly larger than the others, just like the pricing.

Pizza East 56 Shoreditch High Street, E1 6JJ

020 7729 1888 www.pizzaeast.com

Located on the ground floor of the Tea Building, Pizza East is a design triumph and makes a very enjoyable night out for the young, cool crowd. Great credit is due to Nick Jones, founder of the Soho House Group, and the designers involved. The reclaimed floors and furniture, leather banquettes and sharing tables combine with polished tiles, attractive bars and an open kitchen with inferno-like wood ovens. It's no ordinary pizzeria, of course – you need to add the 'gourmet' tag – it offers much more than just pizza. The kitchen also gives serious attention to antipasti, salads, baked items and desserts.

Poppies 6–8 Hanbury Street, E1 6QR

020 7247 0892 www.poppiesfishandchips.co.uk

A retro-looking 'chippy' with a proper 1950s vibe and service values, all underpinned by experience and tradition. Pop, aka Pat Newland, has been serving the East End with fish and chips for decades. There is a full range of fried or grilled fish, with home-made mushy peas and pickled onions, plus saveloys, whitebait and jellied eels. They've also got some tasty rotisserie chicken dishes.

Above and right **You can eat in or take away at Poppies – the latter being wrapped in newspaper.**

Rochelle Canteen Arnold Circus, E2 7ES

020 7729 5677 www.arnoldandhenderson.com

This used to be a little-known canteen principally for occupants of the adjoining former Victorian school, now studio space for various designers and creatives. Established in the late 1990s by James Moores, the project also includes an interesting gallery and event space.

The canteen is now one of the coolest locations for the fashionistas of east London. Entering via the solid metal gate and secret club-like entry buzzer, you cross the grassed-over former school playground and head toward the converted bike shed, where you will find a very simple Shaker-style interior with seating for about 20, alongside a fully open kitchen. When weather permits, dining extends to the outside area, which is also within a watering can's distance of the herb garden and plant pots.

Fans of the St John 'nose to tail' argot will love this simple menu. The business is run by Margot Henderson (wife of Fergus) and Melanie Arnold, who also operate a very successful outside catering business that specializes in feeding London's burgeoning art crowd.

I remember visiting this place when it first opened. The menu was much shorter then, and the bills were presented on scraps of paper. While setting up Boundary nearby, I visited the canteen about once a week and enjoyed every mouthful. The choice and range of drinks have moved on since those early days, but thankfully it has retained all its beguiling mannerisms. The only negatives are no wines (but you can bring your own) and limited opening hours (just breakfast and lunch, Monday to Friday) (PP).

Above **Melanie Arnold (left) and Margot Henderson in Rochelle Canteen.**

94

Sager + Wilde Arch 250 Paradise Row, E2 9LE
020 7613 0478   www.sagerandwilde.com

A tiny wine bar with a big list of wines, and it's also had a big impact on this corner of Hackney Road. It is named after the husband and wife wine expert partners originally fronting the project – although I understand it is now just Michael Sager-Wilde – and you can be sure of a great glass of wine. And you've got to try one of their great toasties – the jalapeño and cheddar one is addictive, possibly more so than the wine.

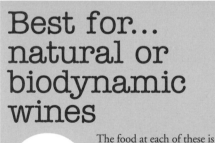

Best for...
natural or
biodynamic
wines

The food at each of these is also excellent.

| Brawn |
| 40 Maltby Street |
| Sager + Wilde |
| Terriors |

Above **The outside terraces along Paradise Row.** Far left **English raspberries and leaf ice cream.** Left **Al fresco dining at Sager + Wilde.**

Crab, Millet and Rice Porridge

Serves 4

50g (1¾oz) millet
2–3 heads of celery (optional)
fine salt
50g (1¾oz) sushi rice
800ml (1½ pints) water (optional)
1 small crab, live, or 160g (5¾oz) picked crab meat
100g (3½oz) Coolea cheese, plus extra to serve
2–3 tablespoons unsalted butter
juice of 1 lemon (omit if you don't want to make the celery juice)

This dish is based on the Chinese comfort food, congee.

The first thing you'll need to do is ferment the millet. Take a sterilized jar, add the millet and cover with water; you want at least 5cm (2 inches) of liquid above the millet. Cover the jar with some muslin and tie off securely. Leave somewhere warmish (around 30°C/85°F) for 2 days or up to 1 week, depending on how far you want to take it; the millet will become increasingly sour the longer you leave it. A strong aroma will start to emit from the millet, very cheesy and powerful. After a few days, put a lid on the jar and allow it to mellow out in the fridge for a day or so.

To make the fermented celery juice, if you want, take the heads of celery and wash well. Juice the celery in a centrifugal juicer and strain through a fine sieve. Weigh the juice and add 2 per cent of the weight in fine salt. Mix well to dissolve, then pour into a sterilized jar or tall plastic container and cover with muslin. Leave in a warm place for at least 1 week and up to 1 month, carefully stirring with a clean spoon every day or so. Taste from time to time and you'll find a nice sour, lactic flavour develops. When ready, store in a sealed jar in the fridge.

To make the porridge, strain and reserve the liquid from the millet, add the rice and millet to a large saucepan, then add a pinch of salt and 800ml (1½ pints) of liquid: for a full-flavoured and rich finish, use the liquid the millet was fermented in and some fermented celery juice; otherwise, just use water. Place over a low heat and start cooking with a lid on, stirring occasionally to make sure it isn't sticking to the bottom. The porridge will take about 1½ hours to cook out fully.

Meanwhile, cook the crab. Boil a large saucepan of water with a good pinch of salt. Drop in the crab and cover, then return to the boil and turn the heat off. Leave, still covered, for 30 minutes. It should now be cooked. If you have a probe thermometer, you can check by inserting a digital probe in between the body and the claw going into the head: the core temperature should be about 70°C (160°F). Once cooked, cool down quickly on a tray in the fridge to catch all the juices that come out. Crack the claws and legs and pick through the meat a few times to ensure all traces of shell are gone. Scoop the brown meat out of the shell and pass through a fine sieve.

Once the crab is prepared, reserve in the fridge until the porridge is ready to be finished.

When the rice and millet are broken down and you have a thick and creamy porridge, grate in the cheese. Add the butter and adjust the consistency with more celery juice, or lemon juice. Taste the porridge: it should be creamy, sour and rich from the butter and cheese. Adjust with lemon or celery juice as you see fit.

Warm 4 bowls and divide the brown crab meat between them. Gently pour the porridge over the top so as not to completely mix it in with the brown crab. Scatter with the white crab, then finish with a bit more grated cheese. Serve immediately.

You can try this with grilled prawns instead of crab, or serve sprinkled with Chinese pickled vegetables, some roasted peanuts and chilli oil for a tasty and warming winter meal.

Som Saa 43A Commercial Street, E1 6BD

020 7324 7790   www.somsaa.com

This was one of the hottest restaurant openings in 2016. Yes, it has been a smash hit with the critics and young cool restaurant-going Londoners, but I am referring to a hotness delivered via chillies and spices. There's no holding back when it comes to the fiery food. I'm far from an expert on Thai food but more than a few people are saying this is the real deal – the best Thai food in London.

When you walk in, you are affronted by both loud music and the smell that is synonymous with Thai food. Immediately, your senses are awakened, before they get full-on accosted. Mark Dobbie and Andy Oliver, the guys behind this fabulous new edition to the east London dining scene, have previously worked with the amazing David Thompson of Nahm restaurant – one of the first Thai restaurants to get a star, and that was back in the day when Michelin were far more selective and certainly not accustomed to giving away their gongs to anything other than fancy French formal restaurants.

The conversion of a former fabric warehouse on the edge of Petticoat Market, not the most appealing corner of east London, is bang near perfect for this type of place – high ceilings, exposed beams, industrial light fittings, scuffed-up floorboards, distressed walls and so on. Again, no design is the best design, certainly as far as young Londoners on a fun night out are concerned.

On their website they say that they are mainly a walk-in restaurant and only really take bookings for larger parties. Well, I tried to walk in, as they say, on four separate occasions only to be met with a massive wait time. The bar is a great hang-out spot while you wait, but do be prepared to do so.

Below **The interior at Som Saa – not as hot as the food, but it seems to be more than appropriate for the young crowd that it attracts.**

Som Saa

Deep-fried Sea Bass with Isaan-style Salad
Nahm dtok pla thort

Serves 2–4 as part of a shared meal

For the fish
vegetable oil, for deep-frying
1 sea bass, 500–600g (1lb 2oz–1lb 5oz), gutted and scaled, fins and tail left on
3 tablespoons light soy sauce
pinch of sugar

For the salad
1 generous tablespoon of roasted rice powder (see method)
2 lemon grass stalks, finely sliced
4–5 small red shallots, finely sliced
2 spring onions, finely sliced
small handful of sawtooth coriander (Thai parsley), finely sliced (optional)
3–4 kaffir lime leaves, cut into very fine strips
small handful of mint and coriander leaves
2–3 dried chillies, fried in a little oil until crisp

For the dressing
5 tablespoons lime juice, or to taste
1½ teaspoons caster sugar
4 tablespoons fish sauce, or to taste
3 tablespoons water
1 tablespoon roasted chilli powder (see method), or to taste

To make the roasted rice powder, dry-toast raw sticky rice in a heavy-based pan over a low heat until golden brown in colour. Allow to cool, then grind to a coarse powder using a mortar and pestle or clean spice grinder. Set aside.

To make the roasted chilli powder, slowly dry-toast hot dried chillies in a wok or frying pan over a medium-low heat until dark red and a little blackened in places (10–15 minutes), then grind into a coarse powder using a mortar and pestle or clean spice grinder. Set aside.

Heat the oil in a deep-fat fryer, or a deep saucepan, to 180°C (350°F); if using a saucepan, make sure the oil does not come more than halfway up the sides of the pan. Score the sea bass with 3–4 angled cuts on each side, then roll it in the light soy sauce and sugar. Place the fish in a deep-frying basket, or old metal sieve, so it curls slightly (this is just for presentation) and deep-fry for 8–10 minutes, until crispy and deep golden brown.

Meanwhile, place all the salad ingredients, except the roasted rice powder and fried chillies, in a mixing bowl.

Now make the dressing: mix together the lime juice and sugar until the sugar has dissolved, then add the fish sauce, measured water and roasted chilli powder. Taste and adjust: it should be hot, sour and slightly salty. Set aside.

Once the fish is cooked, carefully remove it from the fryer and allow to drain and cool slightly on kitchen paper. Put the fish on a large plate or wide bowl and pour one-third of the dressing over it. Add the remainder of the dressing to the salad and serve the salad over the top of the crispy fish. Sprinkle with the roasted rice powder and fried chillies.

Stir-fried Duck with Holy Basil
Pad grapow bet kai dao

Serves 2

For the stir-fry
300g (10½oz) boneless duck meat, plus
1–2 tablespoons fatty duck skin (optional)
5 garlic cloves
6–10 bird's eye chillies, depending how hot you like it
small pinch of sea salt
3 tablespoons vegetable oil
2–3 tablespoons fish sauce, plus extra to taste
½ teaspoon caster sugar
150–200ml (5–7fl oz) chicken stock
2 generous handfuls of Thai holy basil leaves (from larger supermarkets)
freshly cooked jasmine rice, to serve

For the sauce
5 tablespoons fish sauce
5 bird's eye chillies, sliced
2 garlic cloves, finely sliced
¼ lime, roughly chopped

For the crispy eggs 'kai dao' (optional)
4–5 tablespoons vegetable oil
2 eggs

First make the sauce: combine the fish sauce, chillies and garlic in a bowl, squeeze in the lime pieces, then add the squeezed-out pieces to the sauce, too. Set aside.

With a knife or cleaver, chop the duck meat and fat, if using, to a coarse but fairly even mince. Using a mortar and pestle, pound the garlic with the chillies and salt into a coarse paste.

To make the crispy eggs, if you like, place a wok over a medium heat and add the vegetable oil. When the oil is starting to shimmer, break in 1 egg and fry until crispy around the edges and still runny in the middle. Carefully lift out with a slotted spoon and place on kitchen paper to absorb excess oil. Fry the other egg in the same way. Discard the oil and keep the eggs warm.

Clean and dry the wok, place over a high heat and add the 3 tablespoons of oil. Once it is hot, add the garlic and chilli paste, stir-fry for a few seconds, then quickly add the meat. Stir-fry for another minute, then add the fish sauce and sugar, followed by about three-quarters of the stock. Cook for 30 seconds more, then throw in all the basil and the rest of the stock if your pan is looking a little dry. Cook just until the basil wilts (about 20 seconds) and turn off the heat. Taste: it should be rich, hot, salty and fragrant. If it needs a touch more fish sauce, feel free to add and toss through now, but remember there is a salty sauce to come.

To serve, place warm jasmine rice on each plate, top with most of the stir-fry, then add the crispy egg (if liked), followed by a final spoon of stir-fry and any juices. Serve with the sauce on the side.

Above **Nahm dtok pla thort.**
Below **Pad grapow bet kai dao.**

Right **St John have several of their own-label wines as well as a small winery in the Minervois in the south of France.**

Left **The now mandatory St John Eccles cakes.**

St John Bread & Wine 94–6 Commercial Street, E1 6LZ

020 3301 8069 www.stjohnbreadandwine.com

A sibling of the seminal St John, Bread & Wine opened in 2003 in a former bank building. Although they've recently added a small bar area, the St John aesthetic prevails, with white walls, a reclaimed parquet floor, a few pendant lights, Shaker-style coat hooks, counters clad in stainless steel and an open kitchen.

Fergus Henderson continues the 'nose to tail' cooking, and the menu always proffers something slightly unusual and delicious. Just when you think you've sampled all of their dishes, something new pops up – you give it a try and instantly it is yum. There are so many great things to choose, but it is important to keep a little space for the puddings and ices. Bread & Wine seem to have a mystical way of making the ordinary very brilliant – brown bread ice cream comes to mind. And, you cannot leave without ordering some madeleines – eat in or takeaway.

Some people prefer Bread & Wine over its older sibling for its edgier and artier crowd. It is closer to my office so I tend to visit more often – on average once a month, and it never lets me down. Expect queues for lunch at the weekend, when it can get very busy, but it's certainly worth any wait. The staff, in their signature uniform of chef-style white jackets, also deserve an appreciative mention (PP).

Right **The legendary
St John doughnuts.**

Right **A late lunch
table at Bread
& Wine, with
Spitalfields Market
in the background.**

This page **Crowds of young people** flock to Street Feast. Alongside the buzzing atmosphere there are a multitude of street-food style dining options.

Street Feast 19 Great Eastern Street, EC2A 3EJ

020 7033 3903 www.streetfeast.com

This book is all about the diversity of the food and drink offerings in London and it also aims to show how the idea of dining out has been stretched to new lengths. Street Feast/Dinerama is a key part of that point. Essentially, it is a great big drinking and partying destination for those in their 20s and early 30s. I went with my wife on a Friday at about 9pm and it was totally rammed with people this age all having fun. And, now, alongside the booze, which is also quite good here – think artisan beers and ciders, decent wine on tap and funky cocktails – there is now great food. The project is based on lots of individual food vendors each doing their own thing under one big roof. This means that you get specialists that are focused and passionate about their own things, and whether that's a burger, tacos, sliders, a Thai curry, a pizza or doughnuts – they're all fantastic (PP).

Anthony Martin

I grew up in Bermondsey in London, and having family that worked in Billingsgate fish market, Spitalfields and New Covent Garden veg market, I was able to see first-hand the wonderful array of bustling artisanal food sellers and the produce that flooded the London food scene. London itself is one of the food capitals of the world and such a diverse place to grow up and live in, with great wine and places to eat… what's not to love?

Head Chef, Tate Modern

Above **While it's called Street Feast, for many a visit to Dinerama is all about booze.**

Sunday Upmarket Ely's Yard, Old Truman Brewery, E16 QL
Sundays 10am–5pm www.sundayupmarket.co.uk

On Sundays, all around Brick Lane, you'll find various markets and street food vendors. It gets very, very busy with lots of people from all over London (not many locals) and a large portion of tourists. The Sunday Upmarket is the best, with a vast array of foods from all around the world, from sushi, paella and empanadas to falafel and Sri Lankan curry. Alongside the food stalls you can also find some aspiring fashion and lifestyle stalls.

Taberna do Mercado Old Spitalfields Market, 107B Commercial Street, E1 6BG
020 7375 0649 www.tabernamercado.co.uk

As the name suggests, this is a Portuguese tavern inside the bustling Spitalfields Market. However, it is certainly a modern interpretation. Yes, there are authentic aspects and then there are interpretations for a London market. The latter aspect is no bad thing in my view. I've never really thought of Portugal as producing great food; yes, great wine and port, but not really hitting the high notes with their recipes and ingredients. This is a project by culinary superstar Nuno Mendes and chef Antonio Galapito, so perhaps they've selected the good from the less good and given us the best.

As an example of what social media can do for a restaurant, I was drawn to this place thanks to innumerable images on Instagram of their signature dessert – a steamed egg yolk with pork fat and port caramel. It was such an unusual and brightly coloured dish that I soon became desperate to try it. Before getting to the treasured dish, I enjoyed plenty of savoury treats and a few glasses of wine – white and reds, from the all Portuguese list. I could happily work my way through all of the wines and not have any food, but that would be missing out. You should try their house tinned fish. Anyway, I eventually got to the egg yolk dish and thought it was delicious, though my wife was less keen!

On the two occasions that I have visited all of the staff were Portuguese and enormously proud of their restaurant, offering much information and knowledge on each and every dish and the same for the wines (PP).

Taj Stores 112 Brick Lane, E1 6RL
020 7377 0061 www.tajstores.co.uk

If you thought your knowledge of rare and unusual fruit and vegetables could match that of most chefs, try naming the ingredients as you enter this cornucopia of foods from India, Bangladesh, Malaysia, Thailand, Greece, Jamaica, Lebanon and Japan, to mention just a few of the sources. Chow chow, turia, ravaya, gourds, muki and eddoe are just a few of the unusual products displayed in large crates alongside a profusion of peppers and chillies.

At the rear of the store you will find large chest freezers filled with a multitude of different ingredients, from prawns set in blocks of ice to 4cm (1½in) long, deliciously oily, translucent keshi fish and 1m (39in) long, very ugly, rita fish.

The halal meat counter includes pheasant, duck, pigeon and goat, alongside lambs' brains and chicken hearts. This is a specialist food supplier at its best. If you're thinking about cooking an Indian supper for friends, your starting point has to be a visit to Taj Stores. Even if you only buy a tarva pan for your chapati, it will certainly impress your guests.

Tramshed 32 Rivington Street, EC2A 3LX

020 7749 0478 www.hixrestaurants.co.uk

This is one of the best spaces in east London, and Mark Hix is the perfect person to fill it, with his fantastically simple, and very popular, chicken and steak restaurant. At the centre of the Tramshed is a specially commissioned, massive Damien Hurst installation that overlooks everything, called 'Cock and Bull'. There are lots of different things to do and see here, from the gallery in the basement to Mark Hix's kitchen library. And, as with all Hix joints, you can be assured of more than decent drinks.

The name is slightly misleading; it is not a place to store trams, but in fact a place where the electricity was generated to run them.

Whenever I walk past the Tramshed, I always have a tinge of regret. At one point, before Mark took on the project, we were going to do something with it. It's probably a good thing that Mark did it before us, but it does make me think of what could have been (PP).

Viet Grill 58 Kingsland Road, E2 8DP

020 7739 6686 www.vietnamesekitchen.co.uk

On a stretch of Kingsland Road known for its Vietnamese restaurants, Viet Grill is renowned as a favourite among those who appreciate great food. The prices are very reasonable, the food authentic and the service sweet – unlike some of the other restaurants on the 'strip' – and they are also serious about matching wine with food to ensure you have a truly enjoyable experience.

Dan Keeling

"

The Regency Club at the northern end of the Jubilee line is London's best-kept secret. Once you gain entry (by ringing a doorbell and signing a members' book), you can enjoy an atmosphere akin to a bustling Mumbai restaurant and the finest tandoori chicken wings in the world.

Co-owner, Noble Rot

Above and opposite
Street scenes from around Shoreditch.
Left **George, the dog, and his owner live and work on the streets of Shoreditch, with one of the local galleries recently putting on a show of their/his work.**

More places to visit in the area

Allpress
58 Redchurch Street, E2 7DP
020 7749 1780   www.uk.allpressespresso.com
A brilliant espresso bar on one of the best streets in London.

Fifteen
15 Westland Place, N1 7LP
020 3375 1515   www.fifteen.net
Jamie Oliver's first restaurant, where he launched his innovative not-for-profit charitable foundation that helps unemployed and disadvantaged young people to join a proper apprentice scheme leading to a positive future.

The Grocery
54–6 Kingsland Road, E2 8DP
020 7729 6855   www.thegroceryshop.co.uk
A favourite resource for local hipsters, with everything from organic vegetables and meats to kitchen cupboard essentials. They've recently added a decent wine shop – a signal how this well-stocked food store has evolved over the years as the area has grown up.

Merchants Tavern
36 Charlotte Road, EC2A 3PG
020 7060 5335   www.merchantstavern.co.uk
Backed by the lovely Angela Hartnett MBE, this place is really quite good, but there are so many other great things in Shoreditch it tends to get overlooked. They've got a great bar and the food is more than reliable.

Smokestak
35 Sclater Street, E1 6LB
020 3873 1733   www.smokestak.co.uk
Smoked and barbecued meat in a cool east London setting, with fantastic cocktails.

Tayyabs
83–9 Fieldgate Street, E1 1JU
020 7247 9543   www.tayyabs.co.uk
Opened in 1972, it still has queues around the block – few restaurants have achieved such success. This family-run Punjabi restaurant, specializing in tikka – you've got to have the lamb chops – is great value for money and the whole experience is lots of fun.

Camden
Hampstead
Holborn
Islington
King's Cross
Primrose Hill

Before the decision was taken to move the Eurostar terminal to St Pancras, King's Cross was a place you travelled through, not to. And as quickly as you could manage, unless you were specifically looking for trouble. There were one or two cool nightclubs back in the day, but they've all gone now. Perhaps mindful of the culture shock of leaving Haussmann-perfect Paris and arriving in London's vice heartland, developers staged a massive King's Cross takeover. Now 67 acres of industrial wasteland have been turned over to residences, 20 new streets, an open-air swimming pool, a new postcode and a superb canal-side development in the old granary buildings. The area feels alive and buzzing – the developers have done a great job. They have given us wide-open spaces, a lovely mix of architecture and a carefully curated list of tenants. It is no longer at the axis of trade by road, water and rail, as it was in the 1800s – and the canal (yet another project of the prolific John Nash, architect of all of Regency London's best bits) has long since been turned over to day trippers and boat dwellers – but business is booming. Google is building a vast European HQ here, complete with running track, and the presence of Central Saint Martins ensures a youthful and cosmopolitan feel about the place. The university shares the granary buildings with Caravan, Dishoom and Grain Store, and lunchers can dine al fresco with a view of fountains, canal boats and not a few cranes. From here, the canal will take you north to Camden – for an enduringly punky and unappealingly touristy taste of the city – or east to the eatery-packed Islington. This has changed from the seat of New Labour (the famous Blair/Brown pact was struck in a restaurant on Upper Street) to the seat of New Old Labour – Jeremy Corbyn is the local MP. For further political colour, it's also on the bike route of one Boris Johnson – do look both ways when you cross the road.

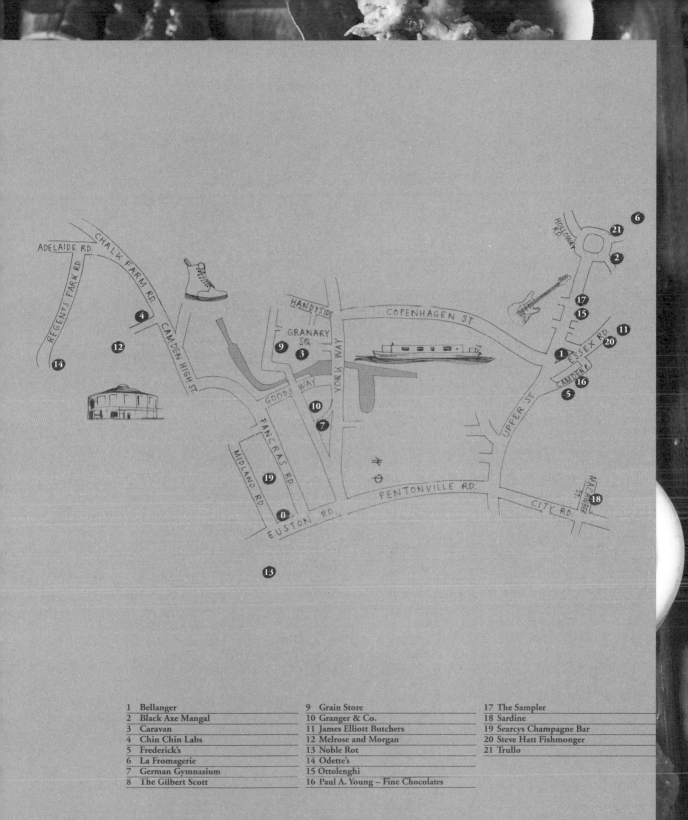

106

Bellanger 9 Islington Green, N1 2XH

020 7226 2555   www.bellanger.co.uk

Whenever I go to a restaurant I try to have their signature dish and that is exactly what I recommend is done when visiting Bellanger. It is based on the idea of a large Alsatian brasserie in Paris, but this iteration is planted on the edge of Islington Green. Not as chic as the Left Bank, but this one is particularly well appointed inside! You start with a wafer-thin tarte flambée and then progress to choucroute with salted and smoked pork belly, ham hock, a frankfurter and various French sausages, all served on pickled cabbage. And you finish with some ice cream. They've even got the old green and brown stem glassware, which might be taking the idea a bit too far. Bellanger is brought to us by Corbin & King, the restaurant impresarios behind many of London top eateries, all of which are in this book, which tells you exactly how admired they are for their success (PP).

Black Axe Mangal 156 Canonbury Road, N1 2UP

www.blackaxemangal.com

This is what you might call something a bit different – a Turkish kebab shop fused with heavy metal rock music. It's all a bit crazy and loud and the flavours and tastes are louder, but it works. Seating only about 20, with plastic wipe–down table coverings and graffiti design details, you start to wonder how this was dreamed up. It is full of things to love and hate, but all to remember. Apparently, 2016 was the year of the kebab, and it was certainly celebrated here. Sadly, this is another joint where you are expected to queue.

Miles Kirby

"

As always, trends will come and go in the food scene. What stays and stands the test of time is the provision of quality in food, drinks and service. Bold flavours will always please me and I often look to Asia to provide me with these. Regional Chinese and Malaysian are two cuisines that I have always felt were under-represented on the food scene in London, so watch this space.

Co-owner and Executive chef, Caravan

Above **The capacious former warehouse Caravan dining room.**

Caravan 1 Granary Square, N1C 4AA

020 7101 7661 www.caravanrestaurants.co.uk

The trick with this place is working out when to arrive to avoid the queues. Get it wrong and you could be facing a very long wait. With friends, around 11.30am at the weekend is a good time to have brunch – just after the up-early lot have cleared off and before the lunch mob arrive. Sitting on the outside terrace overlooking the water fountains, with a special brunch cocktail in hand, you can easily be transported to a more relaxed state of mind.

Inside is huge, with an industrial and stripped-back-to-the-bare-brick look, a massive open kitchen and bar. It is loud, but also fun. The diverse menu is one of the best in London if you want to graze and have a good time with friends without being stressed about the food. Order lots of different things and share.

This was the first restaurant to open at the new King's Cross development and more than any other it has been a universal success. This doesn't happen by accident; the owners and management are brilliantly in tune with modern London and we are all happy beneficiaries.

Left and right **Caravan have their own coffee roastery alongside the kitchen.** Below **This kitchen churns out hundreds of brilliant brunches every weekend.**

Fried Cornbread with Chipotle Butter and Lime

Serves 5

For the flavoured butter

100g (3½oz) unsalted butter, softened

1 dried chipotle chilli, rehydrated and chopped, or 1 tablespoon chipotle in adobo

For the fried cornbread

½ loaf Cornbread (see below)

2 tablespoons olive oil

25g (1oz) coriander leaves

2 spring onions, finely chopped

2 limes, cut into wedges

Mix the butter with the chilli, then form into a log shape, wrap in clingfilm or baking parchment, twist the ends to seal, and store in the fridge.

Trim the ends of the cornbread and cut it into 5 equal slices.

Heat the oil in a large frying pan set over medium heat, then fry the sliced cornbread on both sides until golden brown.

Serve straight away on warm plates with slices of the chipotle butter, the coriander leaves, spring onions and lime wedges.

Cornbread

Makes 1 loaf / Serves 10

60g (2oz) unsalted butter, melted

3 eggs

400ml (14fl oz) milk

170g (5¾oz) instant polenta

80g (2¾oz) strong white bread flour

1 tablespoon caster sugar

½ teaspoon fine sea salt

1 tablespoon baking powder

3 spring onions, finely chopped

150g (5½oz) sweetcorn kernels (fresh or canned)

Preheat the oven to 220°C (425°F), Gas Mark 7. Line a 23 x 13 x 7cm (9 x 5 x 3in) loaf tin with baking parchment.

Pour the melted butter into a large bowl and add the eggs, whisking to combine. Add the milk and whisk together. Sift the polenta, flour, sugar, salt and baking powder into another bowl. Now combine the wet and dry ingredients until there are no dry bits, being careful not to overwork the batter. Mix in the spring onions and sweetcorn.

Pour into the prepared loaf tin and allow to rest for 10 minutes, then bake for 10 minutes. Reduce the oven temperature to 200°C (400°F), Gas Mark 6 and bake for another 20–25 minutes until a skewer comes out clean. Remove from the oven and allow to cool for 5 minutes, then turn the loaf out of the tin on to a wire rack.

This is delicious served warm with butter, or can be fried as above. Keep, well wrapped, in the fridge for up to 3 days.

This page: **Ice cream made in seconds at Chin Chin, thanks to the chilling effect of nitrogen.**

Chin Chin Labs 49–50 Camden Lock Place, NW1 8AF

www.chinchinlabs.com

Europe's first nitro ice cream parlour is great fun for the kids, and interesting and indulgent for adults. Essentially, it offers fast-track and ultra-fresh ice cream made to order in front of you. In fact, it is all rather simple: they pour the custard mix into a table-top blender, add liquid nitrogen and, hey presto, there's your ice cream. The flavours are seriously tempting and highly prized ingredients are used. Beware: on Saturdays expect to queue – all the more anticipation for little ones.

Frederick's Camden Passage, N1 8EG

020 7359 2888   www.fredericks.co.uk

Established in 1969, Frederick's has seen Islington boom while at the same time retaining its excellent reputation as a location for business entertaining, social gatherings and special occasions. The restaurant is family-run and you can tell. The main dining room lies in a glass-vaulted conservatory and there is a small space for al fresco dining. The wine list is seriously attractive. This is the ideal restaurant for a sedate supper after seeing a performance at nearby Sadler's Wells.

La Fromagerie 30 Highbury Park, N5 2AA

020 7359 7440   www.lafromagerie.co.uk

Patricia Michelson is definitely one of my food heroes, and I just adore everything in this shop, from the cheese maps and the pork pies to the tinned cassoulet and *confit de canard*, not forgetting the all-important cheese room. Absolute heaven (PP).

German Gymnasium 1 King's Boulevard, N1C 4BU

020 7287 8000 www.germangymnasium.com

The original German Gymnasium was England's first purpose-built gym in 1865 and helped to host London's first Olympic Games. Thanks to a Herculean task by super-chic architect Tina Norden at Conran and Partners, it is now one of London's most impressively designed restaurants – opposite King's Cross Station, it's on a massive scale, split across two floors, and serves Mittel-European food from sausages, schnitzels and *knödel* to sachertorte and Black Forest gâteau.

The Gilbert Scott St Pancras Renaissance Hotel, Euston Road, NW1 2AR
020 7278 3888 www.thegilbertscott.co.uk

The building has an illustrious history and pedigree, and the internal
and external architecture are both hugely impressive and the potential is
tremendous. Marcus Wareing, the restaurateur chosen for this grand stage,
has devised a familiar menu with some excellent British ingredients. The
Sunday lunch menu is recommended for traditional family get-togethers.

The interior design is a great success, especially the bar with its magnificent
bell chandeliers. But when all the excitement of the opening has died down,
we do wonder who, apart from hotel residents, will dine here.

Grain Store Granary Square, 1–3 Stable Street, N1C 4AB
020 7324 4466 www.grainstore.com

We've all been told that eating less meat, especially red meat, and more vegetables
and fruit, is going to make us live longer and have a healthier outlook. Yes, this
might be true, but would a longer life without a great steak be worth having?
(Joke!) Bruno Loubet is the mega-chef behind this restaurant with sustainability
and social responsibility at its heart. Followers on Instagram will see that he is
passionate about his beloved *potager* – or veg patch. His menus are all about
giving vegetables equal billing to meat and fish, and they sometimes steal the
show. Bruno also has a thing for fermenting, sprouting, pickling and smoking –
all the current trends – and fresh and seasonal ingredients. You can expect recipes
inspired by Bruno's travels and be assured of a great cocktail, thanks to the
involvement of Tony Conigliaro, the best drinks maestro in town.

Left **Bruno Loubet in buoyant form.**

Right, above and below
Mise en place is the
key to success at the
very busy Grain Store.

Best for... wine bars

Les 110 de Taillevent – very much up-market with no natural wines in sight. It's not cheap – these are *grand vins*, but they are available in small measures and the mark-ups are quite modest given the calibre of the wines

Noble Rot – if you're an oenophile, you're going to absolutely love this place

Terroirs – one of the original new-wave wine bars

Granger & Co. 7 Pancras Square, Unit 1 Stanley Building, N1C 4AG

020 3058 2567 www.grangerandco.com

I certainly prefer the Clerkenwell outpost (see page 165), but this location is not to be missed. It's the same brilliant menu but the dining room has a different look and feel that are perfectly in tune with the surroundings and spot-on for the new modern King's Cross.

James Elliott Butchers 96 Essex Road, N1 8LU

020 7726 3658 www.jameselliottbutchers.co.uk

Rosy-cheeked butchers are always on hand here to offer a friendly greeting and expert advice. They seem to know a large number of their customers personally, which is surely a good sign. James Elliott specialize in free-range, dry-plucked ducks and chicken, Suffolk pork, aged foreribs of beef and Lincolnshire lamb, accompanied by a thoughtful selection of condiments, a few cheeses, butter, quails' eggs and a small collection of black puddings.

Melrose and Morgan 42 Gloucester Avenue, NW1 8JD

020 7722 0011 www.melroseandmorgan.com

M&M produce almost all of their wares in their own kitchens. This may seem obvious, but a large number of delis across London buy in the prepared foods and just sell on. Not at M&M, where the whole range is very carefully selected and considered. They also produce foods for Selfridges and you should watch out for their excellent Christmas puddings. Alongside the prepared foods, you can find a fine range of deli and grocery shop essentials.

Chickpea Crêpes with Fennel Purée, Herbs and Anchovy Salad

Serves 4

For the crêpes
240g (8½oz) chickpea flour
400ml (14fl oz) water
2 tablespoons olive oil, plus extra for cooking
sea salt and freshly ground black pepper

For the purée
1 fennel bulb
2 garlic cloves
finely grated zest of ¼ lemon and juice of ½ lemon
3 tablespoons olive oil
100ml (3½fl oz) water

For the salad
handful of basil leaves
2 tablespoons chopped chives, cut in 1cm (½ inch) lengths
½ handful of young parsley leaves
½ handful of fennel fronds
3 handfuls of wild rocket
2 tablespoons olive oil
16 anchovy fillets in oil, halved lengthways

Put the chickpea flour in a bowl. Pour over the measured water in a steady stream, mixing all the time with a whisk. Whisk in the oil and season to taste. Leave to rest for at least 2 hours, then split the batter equally between 4 small bowls.

Cut the fennel into small wedges and place in a saucepan with the garlic. Add the lemon zest and juice, the olive oil and measured water. Season with salt and pepper. Bring to the boil, then cover, reduce the heat to medium and leave to simmer for about 20 minutes. After that time, tip the contents of the pan into a blender and process to a smooth purée.

Heat up a frying pan over a high heat and lightly oil it with kitchen paper dipped in oil. Pour in the batter from 1 of the bowls, swirling the pan to spread the mix all over the pan. Colour 1 side, then flip to colour the other, then slide on to a plate. Repeat 3 times with the remaining batter to make 4 crêpes in total.

Divide the fennel purée evenly over the crêpes, spreading it out with the back of a spoon.

Meanwhile, make the salad. In a bowl, toss the herbs and leaves with the olive oil and season. (If you like you can also add some of the oil from the anchovies, but it will be stronger.)

Arrange the salad over the crêpes, place 8 halves of anchovy fillet over each plate and serve immediately.

Quinoa and Aubergine Stuffed Nasturtium Leaves

Serves 4 as a starter

For the stuffed leaves

12 large nasturtium leaves
320ml (11fl oz) water
120g (4¼oz) white quinoa
1 aubergine
1 onion
3 tablespoons olive oil
2 garlic cloves, finely chopped
3 tablespoons chopped mint leaves
1 teaspoon chopped oregano leaves
100g (3½oz) feta cheese, crumbled
1 lemon, cut into wedges
sea salt flakes and freshly ground black pepper

For the tomato dressing

3 tablespoons olive oil
30 cherry tomatoes, halved
1 tablespoon sherry vinegar
⅓ teaspoon smoked paprika
3 tablespoons water

For the black olive oil

100g (3½oz) black olives, pitted
100ml (3½fl oz) olive oil

Bring a saucepan of water to the boil, add a bit of salt and plunge the nasturtium leaves in for 30 seconds, then remove them with a slotted spoon and place them in iced water.

Now bring the measured water to the boil in the saucepan, then add the quinoa. Cover, reduce the heat to low and leave to cook for 20 minutes.

Meanwhile, cut the aubergine and onion into 5mm (¼in) dice. Heat the oil in a frying pan, then add the aubergine and onion. Stir from time to time until the vegetables get a light golden brown colour, then add the garlic. Cook for another minute.

Place the quinoa in a bowl, add the aubergine mixture, herbs and feta, mix well and taste for seasoning, adjusting if necessary.

Take the nasturtium leaves out of the iced water, pat dry on a clean tea towel and lay them out completely flat and open. Share the quinoa mix between them in widthways lines, leaving a 1.5cm (¾ inch) border on each side, then fold the right and left sides over the ends of the line of filling and roll the leaves up tightly.

Now make the dressing: heat the oil in a wide sauté pan, then add the cherry tomatoes, stir and leave to cook for 2 minutes. Now add the vinegar, paprika, measured water and salt and pepper, cover and leave over a low heat for 2 minutes, then turn off the heat. Place the stuffed leaves on top and cover once more.

Place the black olives in hot water to wash, then drain and pat dry. Place the olives in a blender with the oil, blend until smooth, then pour into a small dish.

Place 3 stuffed nasturtium leaves on each warm plate with the tomato sauce scattered around. Dot with black olive oil and serve.

Left **The bountiful
cellar at Noble
Rot and a case of
very desirable Vina
Tondonia Rioja.**
Above **Every meal at
Noble Rot starts with
a plate of their own
excellent bread.**

Noble Rot 51 Lamb's Conduit Street, WC1N 3NB

020 7242 8963 www.noblerot.co.uk

Noble Rot started out as a magazine all about wine, with some interesting
interviews with great food personalities. However, it was not in the typical
crusty-wine writing style; instead, it had attitude and new ideas, plus a much-
welcomed informality. Founded by Dan Keeling, a former A&R music guy
and Mark Andrew, a vastly experienced wine buyer, they've now progressed to
historic premises on the rather attractive Lamb's Conduit Street.

As a wine-lover, you won't be surprised to read that this is one of my
favourite places to open in London for a long while. However, it is more than
just a great wine bar; it is also a great restaurant with fantastic food. Overseen
by Stephen Harris from The Sportsman in Whitstable, the menu is described as
Franglaise – a mix of old-school French ideas with fantastic British ingredients,
all prepared simply and deliciously. You start with some of the finest bread to be
offered at a London restaurant and then progress to a lovely menu of seasonal
treats, often topped with a few oysters, as you might expect from a link to
Whitstable (PP).

Odette's 130 Regent's Park Road, NW18XL

020 7586 8569 www.odettesprimrosehill.com

Odette's has been around since 1978, and in 2006 was acquired by the concert
promoter and legendary Irishman Vince Power, who installed Bryn Williams
as the chef. Bryn now owns the joint, and has introduced a sprinkling of
ingredients from his native Wales to the menu.

Right **Chocolate
soufflé at Odette's.**

Slip Sole and Homemade Smoked Butter

Serves 4

1kg (2lb 4oz) very good-quality crème fraîche, chilled, or 400g (14oz) very good-quality cultured butter

1 tablespoon smoked sea salt

2½ teaspoons smoked sweet paprika

1 tablespoon ground Espelette chilli powder

a little olive oil

4 x 200g (7oz) slip soles, skinned

sea salt flakes

Put the bowl of a food mixer into the fridge in advance, to allow it to chill.

Place the crème fraîche in the mixer bowl and, using the beater attachment, beat for about 5 minutes at high speed. The cream will start to thicken and you will eventually hear a splashing sound as the buttermilk separates from the butter fat. At this stage, turn the mixer speed down. The buttermilk and fat will separate completely. Turn off the mixer and strain the buttermilk into a separate bowl. (This can be used in other recipes, as a marinade ingredient for tenderizing chicken, or in dressings, or baking.)

Leave the butter in the mixing bowl and turn the machine to its lowest setting. Add the smoked salt, paprika and Espelette pepper until fully incorporated. Form the mixture into a log shape, wrap in clingfilm or baking parchment, twist the ends to seal, and store in the fridge. (This will make more than you need, but will keep in the fridge for up to a week. It also freezes very well.)

Rub a little oil on a large grill tray (or use 2 small trays) and sprinkle with sea salt (this will season the bottom side of the fish). Lay the 4 soles on the tray (or trays) and lay a couple of slices of smoked butter on each fish. Grill for about 1½ minutes, then baste the fish with the melted butter. Grill for a further 1½ minutes, then remove from the grill and allow the fish to finish cooking on the hot tray for a further 2 minutes.

Ottolenghi 287 Upper Street, N1 2TZ

020 7288 1454   www.ottolenghi.co.uk

Following the success of the Notting Hill branch, Ottolenghi opened in Islington.
This not-inexpensive delicatessen and restaurant serves Mediterranean foods with
an occasional North African influence, all made with the very best ingredients.
All the food is made on site in the kitchen below the shop.

The all-white room is dominated by a long, central, all-white dining table,
surrounded by iconic white 1968 Verner Panton chairs. The beautiful displays
of salads, prepared *traiteur* foods and bakery items, all looking as though they
are straight out of the pages of *Vogue Entertaining + Travel*. The epic display of
meringues in the window ensures the patronage of elegant ladies who lunch.

Paul A. Young – Chocolatier 33 Camden Passage, N1 8EA

020 7424 5750   www.paulayoung.co.uk

Yorkshireman Paul Young – a former head pastry chef for Marco Pierre White,
and winner of a gold medal at the World Chocolate Awards – also boasts shops
in the City and Soho. This is where the semi-professional pâtissier comes to
buy the best-quality pure Amedei or Valrhona chocolate. The chocolate truffles,
all handmade in the shop, are gracefully crafted and delicious, especially the
sea-salted caramel. The small bars of chocolate, featuring complementary
combinations such as Szechuan chilli paired with 70 per cent cocoa, or pink
peppercorn and white chocolate, make an ideal mid-afternoon snack. In the
summer months the shop offers home-made ice cream with hot chocolate sauce.

The Sampler 266 Upper Street, N1 2UQ

020 7226 9500   www.thesampler.co.uk

No meal is complete without a bottle of wine, so it seems to us only right to
include this multi-award-winning destination, one of the top independent wine
shops in London. One of the reasons why The Sampler is so important is that it
was the first to introduce the Enomatic wine preservation system to Londoners.
Thanks to this system, which involves injecting nitrogen gas into the bottle when
wine is drawn off, we can try before we buy. Or maybe just try and not buy. Some
80 wines are available to sample, from iconic vintages to everyday table wines.

Sardine 15 Micawber Street, London N1 7TB

020 7490 0144   www.sardine.london

When I was told that the inspiration for this dining room was the book *Lulu's
Provençal Table* by Richard Olney, I knew I was going to like it. The book I refer
to is a beautiful story all about the châtelaine of Domaine Tempier and her recipes,
life at the winery and the traditions of the Bandol region in southern France.

The Sardine signature dish is *lamb à la ficelle* with white beans and green
sauce – a mess on the plate but it tastes delicious. You start with some radishes,
crème fraîche and bottarga and perhaps some saucisson seiche or pissaladière
– as though you were on the terrace of some charming house under an azure
blue sky with a glass of rosé at hand. There is a choice of about five or six main
courses. As the name suggests, this is a very small place with rather cramped seating,
but it does seem to work quite well. The volume can creep up, but it is a lovely
and informal setting with subtle use of some well-selected decorative colours.

Searcys Champagne Bar Upper Concourse,
St Pancras International Station, Euston Road, N1C 4QL

020 7870 9900 www.searcysstpancras.co.uk

The perfect place to meet for a glass or two of fizz before a trip on Eurostar. The owners claim that this Champagne bar, located in the monumental vastness that is the Barlow Shed, is the longest in Europe. Allowing for poetic licence, it certainly makes an interesting meeting spot. The architectural setting is jaw dropping. At 213m (698ft) long, 73m (240ft) wide and 30.5m (100ft) high at its apex, this was the world's largest enclosed space when it was built. For a period of four years before its completion in 1864, this part of the station employed no fewer than 6,000 men, 1,000 horses and 100 steam cranes. The refurbishment at the turn of millennium took seven years and over £800 million. Is this progress or regression? One feature of the Barlow Shed that would not have been given much consideration when it first came into use would have been the lighting. Today, the lighting is one of its greatest successes, really bringing the structure to life both by day and by night.

Steve Hatt Fishmonger 88–90 Essex Road, N1 8LU

020 7226 3963 (closed Sunday and Monday)

The queues early on a Saturday morning speak volumes about the freshness of the fish available here. This no-frills shop is small, but the stock displayed on mounds of crushed ice is exhaustive. Hatt offers everything from tuna for sushi suppers to monkfish, turbot and sea bass for elegant Islington dinner parties. This is a place to buy proper palourde clams for your *spaghetti alle vongole* or oysters and prawns to make your loved one swoon. They also smoke a fine range of fish on site. We can't think of a better fishmonger in all of London. This is one of the finest food retailers in the capital: if you are planning a special meal, you should seriously consider making the journey to Steve Hatt. It will be worth it. Incongruously, during the game season, they also sell a fine selection of birds from the moors and excellent wild duck, such as mallard.

Trullo 300–2 St Paul's Road, N1 2LH

020 7226 2733 www.trullorestaurant.com

The more informed in the London food world would argue that the most enjoyable restaurant food is to be had at St John, The River Café and Moro. Trullo is influenced by all of them, plus the virtuous Jamie Oliver. Head chef Tim Siadatan was one of the stars of the *Jamie's Kitchen* television programme in 2002, and went on to work at St John and Moro, while co-owner Jordan Frieda (son of celebrity hairdresser John and singer Lulu) worked front of house at The River Café. This excellent pedigree permeates the menu, service and ambience at Trullo.

If it weren't so hard to get a table, this would be the model neighbourhood restaurant. Prices are modest, especially the wine, and the service is polite and willing. There are no airs and graces, and the love of simple seasonal Italian produce and cooking is palpable. Like the reassuringly simple dining room, the menu is quite small, focusing on silky home-made pasta or sparklingly fresh fish and meat cooked over hot coals. If you're tired of the loud and overblown restaurants in central London, we urge you to try Trullo. Located just a few hundred yards from Highbury and Islington tube station, it's easier to reach than you might think.

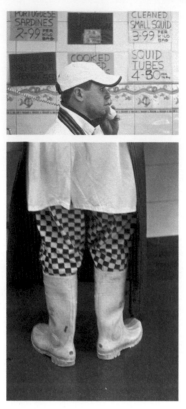

Right **Many Londoners believe that Steve Hatt is the best fishmonger in the capital.**

Robert Reid

Bar Esteban in north London ('where Barcelona meets Brooklyn') has to be my favourite restaurant. It's where I go with my family. The food there is simple and tasty and the atmosphere is homely and friendly – exactly how it should be.

Executive chef, Balthazar

Left **Tomato, bean and tarragon salad from Oldroyd.**
Right **The Dishoom at King's Cross is massive and probably one of the largest restaurants in London, yet they still manage to attract huge queues to get in.**

More places to visit in the area

The Blues Kitchen
111–113 Camden High Street, NW1 7JN
020 7387 5277 www.theblueskitchen.com
All of a sudden, Texan BBQ and Blues-style food, including catfish jambalaya, pulled pork, corn breads, ribs and so on, have become enormously popular, especially when combined with live music and a fun atmosphere.

The Bull & Last
168 Highgate Road, NW5 1QS
020 7267 3641 www.thebullandlast.co.uk
Just a stone's throw from Hampstead Heath, this former 19th-century coaching inn is the perfect combination of a proper London pub with decent ales and some hearty British recipes.

Dishoom
5 Stable Street, N1C 4AB
020 7420 9321 www.dishoom.com
There are now a number of Dishoom's around London but you've got to see the sheer scale of this place, which is part of the King's Cross regeneration story.

Kipferl
20 Camden Passage, N1 8ED
0207 704 1555 www.kipferl.co.uk
An authentic Viennese coffee house and kitchen. From spicy Hungarian goulash soup to Wiener schnitzel and sachertortes.

Oldroyd
344 Upper Street, N1 0PD
020 8617 9010 www.oldroydlondon.com
Tom Oldroyd, the chef and owner, is the small plates king – he set up nine Polpo restaurants and has now branched out on his own.

The Wells
30 Well Walk, NW3 1BX
020 7794 3785 www.thewellshampstead.co.uk
A good pub with food. The classic Georgian building perched about halfway between the sedate, semi-rural charms of Hampstead Heath and the village high street makes a good place to stop for a light lunch and a beer (cold or warm, according to taste).

Yasar Halim
2a/2b Hedge Lane, Palmers Green, N13 5SH
020 8882 3100 www.yasarhalim.com
An urban souk and a local institution since it was opened in 1981 by Mr Halim. This is the perfect Turkish Cypriot food emporium – everything from olives and the most impressive fruit and veg displays to a proper butcher's counter. They've also got their own bakery producing flatbreads, baklava and other sweet treats.

Canary Wharf
The City

These two areas are not adjacent to each other and they are, on many terms, arch enemies. They are both competing to host global financial institutions and head offices for the world's leading companies. But this is the only point of comparison – their characteristics are quite different. Canary Wharf represents the new financial district of London, built on the old London docklands, while the 'City' is the location of the traditional financial district and bordered by the old city walls, dating from medieval times. In the past, you only dined in these areas if you were working there or meeting a client, but now there is far more to offer.

At a time when many traditional London businesses struggle to generate more revenue than the land they occupy could yield as a property development, it's surprising that Billingsgate Fish Market still exists in its current lucrative location. But perhaps there are parallels to be found in the frenzied trading that takes place on the fish market floor before 7am, and over the dock in the offices that house the bankers and brokers of Canary Wharf.

Despite a recent marketing push by Canary Wharf designed to attract weekend visitors, it's still probably not an area you'd visit if you weren't about to clock in at work. Unless, that is, you wanted to chew with a view – for with most towering office blocks comes a restaurant with a panorama of the city. In Canary Wharf, Plateau serves up fish pie (stuffed with the morning's catch) from the top of Canada Place – one of the best views in London. Up the river in the city, there are many more high-altitude options, designed to expedite bonus-blowing and feed those leaving the office in the small hours – Duck & Waffle is open 24 hours. The Shard, The Walkie Talkie and Tower 42 all now have glossy restaurants that carry a sense of occasion, thanks to their lofty positions. At weekends, city slickers are replaced by date nighters and birthday celebrators. And now that Shoreditch, just a short walk away, offers world-class dining options, the City has to fight a little harder to keep hold of its moneyed clientele. And the result? Dramatic dining rooms, exciting food, slick service – a bonus for everyone.

As we go to press, The City is getting ready for a mammoth new project soon to open called The Ned which is sure to be another game changing dining destination.

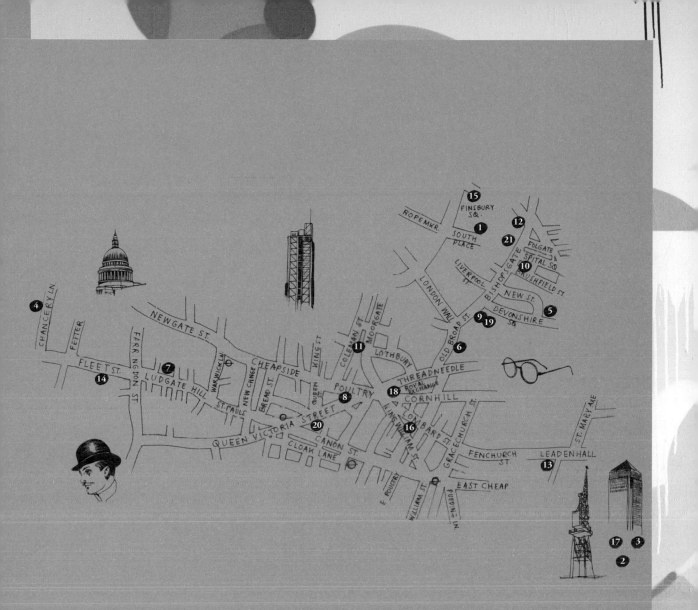

1   Angler
2   Billingsgate Fish Market
3   Boisdale
4   Cigalon
5   Cinnamon Kitchen
6   City Social
7   Cojean
8   Coq d'Argent

9   Duck & Waffle
10 Galvin La Chapelle
11 Hawksmoor Guildhall
12 HKK
13 Leadenhall Market
14 Lutyens
15 The Modern Pantry
16 One Lombard Street

17 Plateau
18 Royal Exchange Grand Café
19 Sushisamba
20 Sweetings
21 Yauatcha

124 **Angler** South Place Hotel, 3 South Place, EC2M 2AF

020 3215 1260 www.anglerrestaurant.com

This restaurant has a lot going for it, which is probably why they've managed to secure a Michelin star for a menu that focuses on British fish and shellfish. Positioned on the top floor of an ambitious hotel, the restaurant sits under a mansard-style roof and looks a little like a show home, but it is quite pleasant once it fills up. And the outside terrace is perfect for an early evening glass of fizz. Given all these positives, it is such a shame that a better name couldn't have been selected.

Billingsgate Fish Market Trafalgar Way, E14 5ST

020 7987 1118 www.billingsgatefishmarket.org

Tuesday–Saturday 4–8am

The largest inland fish market in the UK covers a 13-acre site that is open to the public from Tuesday to Saturday (though you have to get up early, as trading is from 5 to 8.30am). This pungent, fascinating place is an essential experience for any aspiring young chef, and given the fact that fish stocks in our oceans and seas are declining at a rapid rate, it is something that should interest us all. Children under 12 are not permitted.

José Pizarro

I love Duck & Waffle, at the Heron Tower, for breakfast or brunch; the variety of flavours, sweet and salty, different kind of eggs and the views of London are all just wonderful.

Restaurateur and chef, José

Boisdale Cabot Place, Canary Wharf E14 4QT

020 7715 5818 www.boisdale.co.uk

What exactly is a Scottish restaurant, traditional or modern? Scotland certainly has some amazing ingredients – best in classic, in many cases – but the concept of a specific restaurant based around these ingredients seems to be missing. The Boisdale team say that they are a traditional Scottish restaurant, but when you look at what they offer, it is so much more. Of course, haggis is on the menu, something that a strange number of people want to taste, plus very good Scottish beef and game, plus wonderful shellfish and oysters. All of that would be enough, but at Boisdale you also get caviar, a massive cigar terrace, live jazz, an extensive selection of whiskies and a good wine list. It is all very decadent – just like Ranald Macdonald, the man behind the brand. Having known Ranald for a while, I can say with confidence that everyhing on offer are also his personal passions (PP).

Cigalon 115 Chancery Lane, WC2A 1PP

020 7242 8373 www.cigalon.co.uk

Named after Marcel Pagnol's 1935 film about a renowned chef who opens a restaurant in a small Provençal village, Cigalon is an *hommage* to the life and food of Provence – think lavender, pine trees, cicadas, pastis on the terrace, azure skies, terracotta walls and captivating food markets... The menu includes all the treats you'd expect from the south of France, with well-executed regional specialities including salade niçoise, soupe au pistou, anchoïade, ratatouille, panisses, aïoli, Camargue rice and beef. The exclusively French wine list specializes in wines from Provence and Corsica.

Cinnamon Kitchen 9 Devonshire Square, EC2M 4YL

020 7626 5000 www.cinnamon-kitchen.com

The City now has a modern Indian restaurant to be proud of: Vivek Singh's innovative and creative cooking is highly impressive. Anyone with concerns about the suitability of spices and curries for lunch is probably a bit dated in their opinions, though it may be a better fit for a fun and relaxed supper. The interior spaces are very glitzy, with dining and drinking options ranging from the tandoor bar and grill to the sexy Anise bar.

125

Left **At Cigalon with
the open kitchen
and Robata grill in
the background.**

City Social 25 Old Broad Street, EC2N 1HQ

020 7877 7703 www.citysociallondon.com

Designed by legendary architect Richard Seifert, the NatWest Bank building (one of the first skyscrapers in the City) took almost nine years to build before it was officially opened by HM Queen Elizabeth in 1981. At the time, it was the tallest building in the UK and it remained the tallest building in the Square Mile until 2009, when the nearby Heron Tower was completed. Quite astonishingly, when viewed from above, the building mirrors the NatWest logo – three chevrons in a hexagonal arrangement. NatWest have long departed the building but their identity lives on. That's what you call brand legacy! The building has since formally changed its name but many, like me, still call it the NatWest Tower.

At level 24, in what is now called Tower 42, is a rather swanky restaurant by Jason Atherton in partnership with a firm of industrial-scale caterers. The interiors are all moody and dark, but you do look out toward some spectacular views across London. The view is equally good during the day as it is when darkness falls.

To distract you from the views is some pretty decent food from Paul Walsh, a chef with a quite distinguished CV, having worked at The Savoy among others. At City Social, his menus are quite pricey, but they do mostly include premium ingredients, and there are more than a few flourishes on the plate.

I've visited twice over the past year and was astonished to see on both visits so many suited people drinking at lunch, both fancy cocktails and bottles of wine. This seems to be where the younger corner of the City goes to play, especially in the adjoining bar, which is massive. If you ascend to the top of the building at level 42, you will discover an amazing viewing gallery and bar (PP).

Cojean 50–2 Ludgate Hill, EC4M 7EX

020 3841 9771 www.cojean.co.uk

Cojean is a Parisian version of Pret a Manger or Leon, which aren't exactly very French. In Paris it is a successful chain of clean-living, healthy and modern takeaway/café joints. This is their first London outpost – an odd location to start at, but the food is very good, with lots of on-trend values. Most important, the food is well thought through, fresh and seasonal. The packaging is very attractive and so is the space – all light and bright, thanks to huge windows allowing you to dine inside and watch the City go by.

Coq d'Argent 1 Poultry, EC2R 8EJ

020 7395 5000 www.coqdargent.co.uk

If you work in the Square Mile, then you must have been to Coq d'Argent. If you haven't, you're certainly missing out. Set atop James Stirling's bold and spectacular post-modern building at the heart of the City, near Bank, it has spacious gardens designed by Arabella Lennox-Boyd and a Conran-designed restaurant. This is the place you'll find your bankers celebrating deals and bonuses. The interior is modern, with black-and-white photographs of French artisans on the wood-panelled walls, and is a rampant coq–piece sculpture by Anthony Caro at the reception desk. Go in the summer when the gardens are at their best. It's a massive space, including a 150-cover formal dining room with an outside terrace, a large grill restaurant and barbecue terraces, a busy bar and a buoyant events business. Le Coq, as it is known, is a stunning destination for a celebration.

Best for... late night/ 24-hour restaurants

Bagel Bake

Duck & Waffle

Ranoush Juice

Vingt-Quatre

Dan Doherty

"

For breakfast or brunch it has to be Bellanger in Angel, Islington. The food is always on point, the hospitality never ceases to amaze me and it's dog-friendly too! Go for the Full English – you won't be disappointed.

Chef director, Duck & Waffle

Left and right **The exterior and interior at Duck & Waffle on the 40th floor of the Heron Tower.**

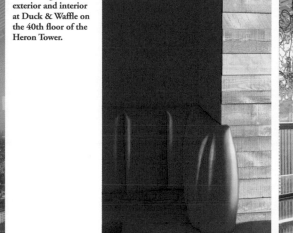

Duck & Waffle Heron Tower, 110 Bishopsgate, EC2N 4AY

When I first heard the name of this restaurant, I was a little bemused and became more so when I heard that they actually have a duck and waffle dish on the menu. Initially sceptical, I was quickly corrected: the combination, also including a fried duck egg and mustard maple syrup, was in fact really very good.

Located on the 40th floor of über-developer Gerald Ronson's Heron Tower, now called 110 Bishopsgate, it started out as the understudy and second option if you weren't able to grab a table at Sushisamba. Now, many prefer the more playful and informal setting at Duck & Waffle, which has a rather incongruous rustic element, especially when compared with the shiny and ultra-smart building.

One of my team has previously worked at this restaurant and he tells me that Dan Doherty, the chef director, is hugely impressive and at the same time mercurial. Certainly, he seems to have created very individual menus that seem to respond to what young City folk want to eat.

This is one of the very few restaurants in London that is open 24 hours a day. I've not visited in the middle of the night, but having looked at the menu and considered the possible views at dawn, I can't help think it would be a wonderful thing to watch the sun come up while munching on a delicious breakfast (PP).

As we go to press, Duck & Waffle have opened a second, more informal restaurant, Duck & Waffle Local, in Piccadilly's St James's Market.

Left **Dan Doherty** burst on to the London scene with the launch of Duck & Waffle and is now a major food personality and cookbook author.

Duck and Waffle with Mustard Maple Syrup

Serves 4

4 duck legs
500g (1lb 2oz) duck fat
butter, for frying
4 duck eggs

For the duck cure
90g (3¼oz) salt
90g (3¼oz) caster sugar
zest of 1 orange
pinch of ground cinnamon
1 each clove and star anise
3 pink peppercorns
10ml (2 teaspoons) brandy

For the waffle mix
175g (6oz) plain flour
10g (¼oz) caster sugar
1 teaspoon baking powder
½ teaspoon bicarbonate of soda
pinch of salt
175ml (6fl oz) buttermilk
35g (1¼oz) butter, melted
1 small egg

For the mustard maple syrup
200ml (7fl oz) maple syrup
25g (1oz) yellow mustard seeds
1 teaspoon mustard powder
2.5cm (1 inch) piece of cinnamon stick
thyme sprig

You will also need a waffle iron

The day before serving, mix the ingredients for the duck cure and sprinkle all over the duck legs. Leave in the fridge, covered, overnight.

The next day, preheat your oven to 140°C (275°F), Gas Mark 1. Take the duck legs and brush off all the cure. Place in a casserole dish and cover with the duck fat. Cook for approximately 3 hours, or until the meat just falls off the bone. Allow to cool in the fat.

To make the waffle mix, put the flour, sugar, baking powder, bicarbonate of soda and salt into a bowl and whisk together. In another bowl, whisk together the buttermilk, melted butter and egg, then whisk this into the flour mixture until just combined. The mixture will be quite thick, which is normal. Set aside in the fridge.

Combine all the ingredients for the maple syrup in a pan and bring to the boil. Take off the heat and leave to cool. Remove the cinnamon and thyme, but leave the mustard seeds.

When ready to serve, heat your oven to 180°C (350°F), Gas mark 4 and turn on your waffle iron. Heat an ovenproof frying pan and add the duck legs, skin-side-down. Once the skin starts to crisp, turn the legs over and put into the oven for about 8–10 minutes, or until crisp.

Meanwhile, make your 4 waffles. Gently fry the duck eggs in butter, spooning the hot butter over the yolk right at the end. Serve a duck leg on top of each waffle, with an egg on top and maple syrup on the side.

Recipe from *Duck & Waffle: Recipes & Stories* by Dan Doherty, published by Mitchell Beazley.

Baked Alaska

Serves 6

6 balls of vanilla ice cream, frozen hard

For the dulce de leche sponge

70g (2½oz) unsalted butter, at room temperature, plus extra for greasing

30g (1oz) golden syrup

1 (397ml) can of dulce de leche (milk caramel)

2 eggs

100g (3½oz) self raising flour

For the Italian meringue

225g (8oz) caster sugar

150ml (¼ pint) water

90g (3¼oz) egg whites

You will also need a sugar thermometer and a piping bag with a plain 10mm nozzle

Preheat the oven to 180°C (350°F) Gas Mark 4. Lightly grease a 30cm (12 inch) lipped baking tray and cover with baking paper.

To make the sponge, put the softened butter, golden syrup and dulce de leche (milk caramel) into a mixing bowl and, using an electric mixer, or a wooden spoon if mixing by hand, cream together until lighter in colour – this should take about 5 minutes. Crack the eggs into a bowl and whisk together. Still creaming the butter mix, add the eggs, then mix together for another 2 minutes, or until completely smooth. Sift in the flour and mix for 1 more minute. Spoon your sponge mix on to the prepared baking tray and spread out until it is 1cm (½ inch) thick. Bake for 8–10 minutes, then remove and cool on a wire rack. Using a 10cm (4 inch) diameter cookie cutter, cut out 6 discs of sponge and set aside.

To make the meringue, put the sugar into a small saucepan over a low heat and gently pour over the water. Make sure no sugar has come up the sides of the pan, as this will make the syrup crystallize. Put the egg whites into a mixing bowl and, using an electric hand mixer, whisk on slow speed. Once the sugar has reached 116°C (240°F), increase the speed of whisking to create soft peaks. When the sugar has reached 121°C (250°F), pour it slowly on to the egg whites while still whisking on a high speed. Once the sugar syrup has been added, continue to whisk until the meringue has cooled to room temperature, then put into a piping bag with a plain 10mm (½ inch) nozzle.

To finish, put the sponge discs on individual pieces of baking paper on a baking sheet and place a ball of ice cream on each sponge disc. Pipe the meringue all the way around, to completely cover. At this stage place in the freezer until you are ready to cook and serve.

When ready to cook, preheat your oven to 200°C (400°F) Gas Mark 6. Place the baking sheet on the bottom shelf for 3 minutes, or until the meringue is nice and browned. Carefully transfer to serving bowls and decorate with edible flowers, mint springs or anything you fancy.

Recipe from *Duck & Waffle: Recipes & Stories* by Dan Doherty, published by Mitchell Beazley.

Left and right, below
The former St Botolph's Hall now houses Galvin La Chapelle.
Right **Staff in suits and bow ties welcome you at Galvin.**

Galvin La Chapelle 35 Spital Square, E1 6DY

020 7299 0400 www.galvinrestaurants.com

Chris and Jeff Galvin's City restaurant is named after the celebrated Hermitage La Chapelle wine, itself named after the chapel that overlooks the vineyards in the Rhône valley. As you would expect, the wine list includes many different vintages of this prized wine, including the 1961, one of the most mythical wines of the 20th century, at an eye-watering £19,500. Set in the stunning 19th-century St Botolph's Hall, the restaurant has been described by reviewers as the kind of place you see in movies. Dining in the Gallery on the mezzanine level gives you sweeping views of the room below and brings you closer to the impressively vaulted ceiling. Many of their dishes are quite elaborate and decorative, with a mixed bag of distinct flavours. You need to clear your diary and set aside the afternoon so that you can truly enjoy the experience at this restaurant: try the eight-course menu gourmand, with a different wine to accompany each course. The head sommelier has prepared a highly informative wine list that should perhaps be read online in advance.

Best for... cocktail bars

Think about visiting one of these places before dinner at a nearby restaurant or you could simply stay all evening and also enjoy great bar food.

The Blue Bar at The Berkeley
The Connaught
Zetter Townhouse

Above **The best time to visit Leadenhall Market is Friday morning, when a few extra stalls sell charcuterie, olives, antipasti and other snacks.**

Right **The wrought-iron and glass Leadenhall Market was designed by Sir Horace Jones, also the architect of Old Billingsgate and Smithfield. Here it is complete with bunting and flags.**

Hawksmoor Guildhall 10 Basinghall Street, EC2V 5BQ
020 7397 8120   www.thehawksmoor.com

Hawksmoor is renowned for its excellent steaks and cocktails and an appropriately good wine list, but for this location it is the breakfast menu that deserves special attention. It was voted Best Power Breakfast in London by *GQ* magazine and it is much deserved. The menu is topped with a list of breakfast cocktails that they call anti-fogmatics. It includes drinks like Shaky Pete's Ginger Brew, which is made with gin, ginger syrup and lemon juice and is topped with London Pride beer – quite a drink, especially for breakfast. The food menu is equally full-on, with an epic breakfast for two, and, of course, you can have a breakfast steak.

HKK 88 Worship Street, EC2A 2BE
020 3535 1888   www.hkklondon.com

Don't be put off by the location or the nondescript and underwhelming office-like entrance, because once inside you are in for some very high-end Chinese fine dining cuisine. You should go to this restaurant for one of the extensive tasting menus and you must have the signature cherry wood Peking duck. It is served in two waves, the first with black truffle and caviar (very sinful) and the second with sesame pancakes in a rather more traditional manner. So, either go on a day off or in the evening, not for a quick business lunch.

Leadenhall Market 4–5 Leadenhall Market, EC3V 1LR
020 7929 1697   www.cheeseatleadenhall.co.uk

If you work in the City of London, this place must be a blessing. The spectacular market building by Sir Horace Jones (Victorian architect du jour) dates back to 1881. The site's long connection with British cheese, meanwhile, goes back as far as 1397, when cheesemongers from across the land were bound by law to bring all their cheeses to Leadenhall Market. Cheese at Leadenhall stocks more than 100 different cheeses, plus chutneys, biscuits, ports and a few carefully selected wines. You could buy your chilled cheese at lunchtime and store it in your briefcase until after the train home, by which time it should be perfectly ripe for supper.

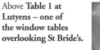

Lutyens 85 Fleet Street, EC4Y 1AE

020 7583 8385   www.lutyens-restaurant.com

In the summer of 2009, we opened Lutyens at 85 Fleet Street – the same address where Samuel Pepys was born on 23 February 1633. It was designed by Sir Edwin Lutyens in 1939, and for half a century to come the area was renowned as the home of journalism and newspapers in London. Over the last 20 years all this has changed, and the denizens of Fleet Street are now high-flying bankers and lawyers.

Lutyens offers a range of dining and drinking options; it's open from breakfast to late night and has four private meeting and dining rooms, a wine bar and bistro, a small outside dining terrace in the shadow of St Bride's church garden and the main dining room, which seats 120. Of course, we are also very proud of the restaurant design and of its many different details, from the mosaic floor that references Reuters ticker tape to the black lacquer furniture that evokes the period of the building's heyday. The club area houses a collection of Lutyens books, we have acquired a few original Lutyens chairs, and the walls of the private dining rooms feature the great architect's drawings. Daniel Mertl, our head chef, has an excellent CV, having worked at some of the best restaurants in London, and before joining us, he worked at The Glasshouse in Kew, where he won and retained a Michelin star for three years. Our other star at Lutyens is Yves Desmaris. He's a master sommelier, one of only a few hundred with this qualification across the world. His brief is to provide the best wine list in the Square Mile, and many say that he has achieved this objective. It is our aim to provide a grown-up and sophisticated City restaurant that is ideal both for clinching that global deal and for simple suppers with friends.

Above **Table 1 at Lutyens** – one of the window tables overlooking St Bride's.

Opposite **The charcuterie counter in the Wine Bar at Lutyens.**

Dover Sole with Beurre Mâitre d'Hôtel

Serves 10–12

1 Dover sole per person, approximately
600–700g (1lb 3oz–1lb 5oz), head, fins
and back skin removed, and trimmed
(ask your fishmonger to do this)

olive oil

1 lemon, sliced

For the beurre mâitre d'hôtel

250 g (8 oz) unsalted butter, at room
temperature

25 g (1 oz) chopped parsley

juice of 1 lemon

pinch of salt and finely ground black pepper

Make the butter in advance so it can be chilled:
place the butter in a medium bowl and cream
with a spatula or wooden spoon. Add the
remaining ingredients and mix well. Place the
mix on a sheet of greaseproof paper and roll
into a sausage shape about 5 cm (2 inches) in
diameter. Store in the refrigerator until you are
ready to use for up to a week, or in the freezer
for longer.

Brush the sole with a small amount of
olive oil. We bar-mark the top fillet to create
the criss-cross pattern by heating metal skewers
over a gas flame and pressing to the flesh. Cook
on a baking tray under a hot preheated grill
on just one side (white skin on the underside)
for 8–10 minutes. Alternatively, you can cook
the sole in a ridged griddle pan to achieve the
bar marks, although you must ensure that the
pan is very hot before adding the fish and do
not touch it for a couple of minutes to avoid it
sticking to the pan.

The cooking time will obviously depend
on the size of the fish and the intensity of your
grill. Try to avoid putting the fillet too close
to the heat. Once the fish flesh is cooked and
flakes easily or cooked to your liking, place a
disk of the butter about 1 cm (½ inch) thick
on the fillet and place under the grill for
another 30–60 seconds until the butter just
begins to melt. If you are cooking for a few
people or your grill isn't that large you could
use the oven for this final stage.

Season with salt and pepper, and serve
with a slice of lemon, steamed new potatoes
and spinach.

The Modern Pantry The Alphabeta Building, 14 Finsbury Square, EC2A 1AH

020 3696 6565   www.themodernpantry.co.uk

Located at the corner of a Grade II listed art deco building, this is the second Modern Pantry and I think it is the better one of the two. The space is good-looking and much larger than the first site. As you enter, you are greeted by a lovely U-shaped dining bar that seats about 15 and offers fantastic tapas. This might not be the first choice location for most people, but it is quite close to the Barbican Centre, where there are no decent restaurants, certainly none that are open for Saturday brunch, which is very good at The Modern Pantry.

One Lombard Street 1 Lombard Street, EC3V 9AA

020 7929 6611   www.1lombardstreet.com

With changes in the banking world over the last 15–20 years, many restaurants and bars have sprung up in former banking halls or local branch buildings. Many such conversions are to be found in the City: one of the grandest of all must be One Lombard Street, located opposite the ultimate bank, the Bank of England. The neoclassical Grade II listed building, which dates back to 1776, features an internal domed ceiling by Pietro Agostini. In 1998 owner Soren Jessen, himself a former banker, created a multi-faceted dining destination, now one of the City's most renowned, that is open from breakfast through to late supper.

Plateau 4ᵗʰ floor, Canada Place, Canary Wharf, E14 5ER

020 7715 7100   www.plateau-restaurant.co.uk

From the outset, Plateau has been the destination of choice for the senior bankers, lawyers and newspaper people of Canary Wharf. It's certainly the top ticket during the working week, and it also has a thriving weekend business. Located on the top floor of an incongruously low building, the restaurant benefits from a half-glass ceiling and an entire glass wall overlooking the lawns and sculpture of Canada Square Park. At night, when you look up toward the surrounding 40- and 50-storey buildings, you can't help being reminded of New York or even Gotham City (in fact, part of *Batman Begins* was filmed at the restaurant).

There are two dining options: a grill and bar area, plus the smarter restaurant. The interior design is iconic 1950s, with Arco lamps, Eero Saarinen Tulip swivel chairs and tables with beautiful marble tops and wavy eau-de-nil upholstered banquettes. The silver cutlery is designed by David Mellor, and the other table accoutrements are also very stylish.

Royal Exchange Grand Café The Courtyard, Bank, EC3V3LR

020 7618 2480   www.theroyalexchange.com

This impressive all-day upmarket café and oyster bar is laid out in the airy courtyard that was once the trading floor of this truly grand Grade I listed building. It was a great trading centre and stock exchange for London in its day, but the original building and a second one on the same site were both destroyed by fire. The current building first opened for trading on 1 January 1845, and has subsequently endured radical change to now house a galaxy of luxury shops and offices, cafés, restaurants and bars. The restaurant's logo features the grasshopper (*sauterelle* in French, also the name of the restaurant on one of the mezzanines) of the Gresham family crest, a motif echoed by the weather vane on the roof.

Above **Eero Saarinen-designed Tulip chairs and tables, and an Arco lamp at Plateau restaurant.**
Right **The glamorous sweeping staircase in Sushisamba.**

Sushisamba Heron Tower, 110 Bishopsgate, EC2N 4AY

020 3640 7330 www.sushisamba.com

I'm told that this is the largest revenue-generating restaurant in the Square Mile. This a restaurant that a large number of people from outside the City and those from within – want to visit; they all want to enjoy the view and the (very loud) party atmosphere feeling of the place. It is all more than a little over the top, from the design, the cocktails and, of course, the views from the 38th and 39th floors, especially from the outside terraces. The food is a blend of Japanese, Brazilian and Peruvian, which seems to tell you everything you need to know.

Left and above left
The cocktail bar at Sushisamba.

Above **The stunning view from Sushisamba of the Gherkin at 30 St Mary Axe, which was designed by Norman Foster and Ken Shuttleworth.**

Sweetings 39 Queen Victoria Street, EC4N 4SF

020 7248 3062 www.sweetingsrestaurant.co.uk

The term 'institution' is applied to restaurants all too often and too easily, but in the case of Sweetings – which has been trading since 1889, with few apparent changes, and is still full most days – the accolade is fully justified. The devastating damage suffered by Queen Victoria Street during the Blitz reputedly destroyed the wet fish counter, which was replaced by a large window. In the 1980s, when the City started to become the global financial centre it is today, word went around that a compensation cheque for £10,000 had been delivered by a recently relocated German bank. Apocryphal, perhaps, but a nice addition to the legend that is Sweetings.

The menu, although they appropriately call it a 'Bill of Fare', is based on a proper traditional oyster bar and fish restaurant with a nursery fare emphasis. So, you can gorge on potted shrimps, cods' roe, skate wings with brown butter, crab, Dover sole, fish pie, lobster bisque, good smoked salmon and so on.

In recent years many chefs have taken to featuring traditional English puddings on their menus, though in a lighter and less liberal manner. Not at Sweetings. Here the steamed syrup pudding and baked jam roll are vast. And they are one of the few restaurant in London still to offer good savouries as an alternative to a pud. Sweetings is open only for lunch, Monday to Friday, you can't make a reservation, and they don't serve coffee, but it's definitely worth a visit. There are lots of quirky and lovely details. Take your godson to show him how things used to be done!

Yauatcha Broadgate Circle, EC2M 2QS

020 3817 9888 www.yautcha.com

Probably the best dim sum in the City, both traditional style and some ultra-modern variations – the venison puffs and the scallop *siu mai* are essential. Yauatcha is part of the Hakkasan group, which generally means that there will be other outposts around the world but, more important, the quality will be good. This is a very big restaurant with two large outside terraces overlooking the recently redeveloped Broadgate Circle – not the best view, but it can be a very lively place with people coming and going to their offices, Liverpool Station and some of the other very good neighbouring restaurants. Go midweek, on a summer's evening, especially if you can't get a table at the Yauatcha in Soho.

Chris
Galvin

"

London is the greatest melting pot of ethnic cuisine in the world today and finally, we are blessed with lots of 'young guns' cooking and serving daring dishes and concepts.

Owner, Galvin La Chapelle

Above **The London Eye**
– food isn't served on
board, but perhaps it
should be?

More places to visit in the area

28°–50°
140 Fetter Lane, EC4A 1BT
020 7242 8877 www.2850.co.uk
The name refers to the degrees of latitude within which virtually all the world's wine is grown. This is a great little wine bar with decent food.

Barbecoa
20 New Change Passage, EC4M 9AG
020 3005 8555 www.barbecoa.com
This striking Tom Dixon-designed restaurant specializes in cooking meat and seafood using different forms of fire – Robata grills, tandoors, wood pits and so on. The stunning view of St Paul's, especially at night, is another asset for this restaurant by Jamie Oliver.

The Don Restaurant and Bistro
The Courtyard, 20 St Swithins Lane, EC4N 8AD
020 7626 2606 www.thedonrestaurant.com
Here, on the site of the old Sandeman port cellars, you can enjoy solid City dining and a far-reaching wine list. The atmospheric rooms and friendly staff make this a preferred destination for City dining.

Goodman
11 Old Jewry, EC2R 8DUA 020 7600 8220
3 South Quay, E14 9RU 020 7531 0300
www.goodmanrestaurants.com
Two outposts of the New York-style steakhouse that serves both USDA corn-fed beef and grass-fed beef from Scotland and Ireland.

Konditor & Cook
30 St Mary Axe, EC3A 8BF
020 7633 3333 www.konditorandcook.com
A fantastic bakery and cake shop in the City, though in an awkward location at the base of the Gherkin.

ROKA
4 Park Pavilion, 40 Canada Square, E14 5FW
020 7636 5228
71 Aldwych, WC2B 4HN 020 7294 7636
www.rokarestaurant.com
There are a number of ROKAs in London and overseas, with the first and best one at Charlotte Street, but these two outposts in the two financial districts of London offer convenient access to their unique version of contemporary *robatayaki* cuisine.

Above **Each new skyscraper in the City doesn't seem complete without a top-floor bar or restaurant.**

Chelsea
Fulham
South
Kensington

This suave and sophisticated corner of London is perhaps where most people would live, if they could live anywhere. Everyone from JK Rowling to Eric Clapton has chosen a white wedding cake of a Chelsea home, within walking distance of some of the best museums in London, especially the stunning Victoria and Albert Museum, and a very easy-on-the-eye stretch of the Thames. We have the Victorians to thank for the cultural mecca of Exhibition Road – or the Albertopolis, as it was known during the period of Queen Victoria's reign when her husband was instrumental in the Great Exhibition, the subsequent purchase of land in South Kensington for museum building, and the foundation of the great institutions that followed. Londoners will be forever in his debt. You can walk around any of these for free, and then in just a few minutes find yourself in the august Hyde Park, perhaps dining on the edge of the Serpentine, watching pedalos circle the pond, and eyeing intrepid Londoners cleaving up and down the outdoor lido. It's now 40 years since the term Sloane Ranger was coined to describe the jet set that took advantage of Chelsea's more exclusive haunts. By and large, they're still there – and after a walk around Sloane Square and along King's Road, ending with a tour of the Shop at Bluebird, and a plate of something nice at the adjoining café, or an afternoon visit to the Victoria and Albert Museum, it's hard to find a reason why they'd leave.

Further west in Fulham it's possible to see what an earlier period of gentrification has done for London. In the 1950s this was a so-so, downmarket residential area. Now it's a distinctly established upper-mid market zone with some buzzy restaurants and other attractions, but still retains some characterful institutions.

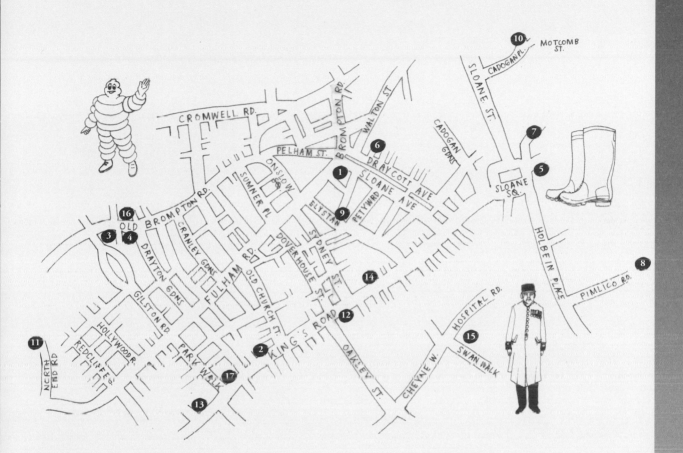

1 Bibendum Restaurant & Oyster Bar	9 Elystan Street
2 Bluebird	10 The Good Life Eatery
3 Cambio de Tercio	11 Harwood Arms
4 Capote Y Toros	12 The Ivy Chelsea Garden
5 Colbert	13 Medlar
6 Daphne's	14 Rabbit
7 David Mellor Sloane Square	15 Restaurant Gordon Ramsay
8 Daylesford	16 Tendido Cero

Left and below right
**The corpulent
form of Monsieur
Bibendum.**

Bibendum Restaurant and Oyster Bar Michelin House,
81 Fulham Road, SW3 6RD 020 7581 5817 www.bibendum.co.uk

With its handsome architecture (the former main headquarters of the
Michelin Tyre Company from 1911) and its excellent location, Bibendum
is one of the most sophisticated places to dine in the capital. In the upstairs
dining room the atmosphere is elegant, but without any pretentiousness.
The armchairs are comfortable and diners are bathed in natural light, and
the space between the white linen-covered tables is conducive to a sociable
ambience. Colourful stained-glass images of Monsieur Bibendum, the iconic
Michelin man, keep an eye on things, and his distinctive corpulent form is
immortalized in the decanters, flower vases, table legs, bar, graphic art, coat
stands and the butter dishes.

Bibendum (not to be confused with the wine company of the same
name, with which it has no connection) has over the years won a multitude
of awards, not least Tatler's 'Most Consistently Excellent Restaurant' award.
Simon Hopkinson, the founding chef who has inspired so many other top
chefs, and Matthew Harris have consistently delivered classic dishes with a
French bias and the occasional contemporary twist. This has been the case for
30 years and it has remained successful throughout. However, times change.
Recently, the founding directors have announced some exciting changes.
Claude Bosi, famous for his two-Michelin-starred Hibiscus restaurant (now
closed), has replaced Simon Hopkinson, and the dining room has received a
little refresh – all very exciting.

Above **The Bibendum** café on the ground floor is open all day. Right and far right **The crustacea counter in the forecourt at Bibendum.**

This page **The Bluebird Café** on King's Road includes a bar, a big restaurant as well as a small food store and wine shop.

Bluebird 350 King's Rd, SW3 5UU

020 7559 1000   www.bluebird-restaurant.co.uk

The King's Road isn't quite what it used to be, especially when compared to the Swinging Sixties when it was the epicentre of style. However, the Food Store at Bluebird, within the same building as the restaurant but otherwise not connected, is certainly worth a visit. Afterwards, repair to the bar or to one of the café tables on the courtyard. The upstairs dining room has recently had a (another) makeover and now attracts reality-show celebrities.

Left **The modern and innovative Cambio de Tercio.**
Right **Abel Lusa at Capote Y Toros.**

Below **Mousse Oloroso at Capote Y Toros.**

Cambio de Tercio 163 Old Brompton Road, SW5 0LJ

020 7244 8970 www.cambiodetercio.co.uk

The Spanish government awarded the founders of Cambio de Tercio, Abel Lusa and David Rivero, the 'Premios Alimentos de Espana 2003' for being the best Spanish restaurant anywhere outside Spain. This is the flagship of Abel Lusa's mini-group of four restaurants, and it certainly deserves recognition as one of the finest exponents of modern Spanish food and culture in London. As with all Lusa's restaurants, the interior is awash with colour, with vivid yellow and pink walls and bullfighter art and references.

You could immerse yourself in Spanish food and drink by trying all three of Lusa's restaurants on the Old Brompton Road in one evening, as they are just a short step away from each other. Start with a glass of fino and cured ham at Capote Y Toros (see below), then cross the road to Tendido Cero (see page 155) for some hot tapas or maybe a gourmet paella, before crossing back to Cambio to enjoy one of the chef's specialities of oxtail or suckling pig, finishing with a caramelized torrija (Spanish bread pudding) with crema catalana ice cream or maybe some manchego. What a night that would be.

The fourth tapas bar and grill in the stable, Tendido Cuatro, is on the New King's Road.

Capote Y Toros 157 Old Brompton Road, SW5 0LJ

020 7373 0567   www.cambiodetercio.co.uk

The latest offering from Abel Lusa is simply fantastic. With just eight tables and some bar stools with dining shelves, it is small but perfectly formed. The offer is principally based on Iberico hams, Andalucian tapas and more than 40 different sherries, though there is also a decent wine list. The shelves are lined with bottles of sherry, from the salty dry Finos and Manzanillas to sweet Pedro Ximenez, while hams hang from the ceiling and collages of bullfighting scenes and posters cover the walls.

144 **Colbert** 50–2 Sloane Square, SW1W 8AX

020 7730 2804 www.colbertchelsea.com

This has got to be one of the most perfect locations for an up-market pavement café, especially a French one: located on the distinguished Sloane Square and at an axis leading to Chelsea, Belgravia, Pimlico and Knightsbridge, the Royal Court Theatre just happens to be next door. It also has the most appropriate façade, with large windows, huge awnings and a row of rattan chairs and marble-top tables, perfect for watching the world go by. Added to the location is the fact that it is operated by London's classiest operators in the form of Chris Corbin and Jeremy King – business partners in the restaurant world for 35 years.

Inside you'll find all the essential grand café essentials: a black-and-white tiled floor, mirrors, poster art, red leather banquettes and so on. The menu is quintessentially *vrai*. For me, the best experience has got to be a croque monsieur and a café crème or a tray of oysters with a jolly glass of fragrant and easy-going picpoul. You can, of course, get much much more.

Daphne's 112 Draycott Avenue, SW3 3AE

020 7589 4257 www.daphnes-restaurant.co.uk

Daphne's has been around for a long time and is now part of the Caprice Holdings group, which generally means that it is a lavishly decorated space and little expense has been spared on the details. In this case, designer du jour Martin Brudnizki has given it a sprinkle of his magic, making it a very welcoming space on a pleasantly modest scale. The food is all about well-known and reliable Italian classics, including plenty of white truffles when they are in season.

Miles Kirby

"

I love Bar Shu on Frith Street in Soho – I love the intensity of flavour you get from Sichuan food. I always order the dry-fried green beans and the gong bao chicken. I always take serious food lovers there to test the metal.

Co-owner and Executive Chef, Caravan

Above **Getting a table on the pavement outside Colbert on Sloane Square is a real treat.**

David Mellor Sloane Square 4 Sloane Square, SW1W 8EE

020 7730 4259   www.davidmellordesign.com

This book is principally about dining out in London but it does also include a few specialist food stores. We also wanted to include this very special shop selling some of the best-designed and best quality tableware and kitchenware. Originally opened in 1969 by David Mellor himself, and part of the Chelsea Swinging Sixties design thing so synonymous with the area, this is a fantastic location to get everything from a humble kitchen whisk to the ultimate cast-iron or copper pans. They've got the most beautiful bone china and, of course, the best cutlery you can buy. I particularly enjoy all of the David Mellor cutlery, some of which dates back to the 1950s and is still in production; it continues to look modern and sharp (PP).

Keeping things in the family, David's son, Corin, has also designed some very elegant cutlery and other dining table accoutrements. You'll also find very good table and kitchenware at The Conran Shop on the Fulham Road nearby.

Daylesford 44b Pimlico Road, SW1W 8LP

020 7881 8060   www.daylesfordorganic.com

This farmshop and café close to Sloane Square is an offshoot of the very impressive farmshop in the village of Daylesford in Gloucestershire. Both are definitely worthy of a visit.

The Daylesford brand was set up by Lady Bamford many years ago – well before organic produce was popular in the UK. Now the Daylesford operation comprises its own organic cattle farms, a creamery making its own cheeses, a bakery producing bread, cakes and pastries, a market garden and kitchens that create an extensive range of own-brand soups and prepared meals. All of these products, plus much more, are available at this shop.

The produce comes directly from the farm, although the elegant shop – very easy on the eye with masses of beautiful marble – scarcely brings to mind the concept of farm to fork. All of the produce is not only of an exceptionally high standard but also very stylishly presented and packaged.

This page **No expense is spared on anything at Daylesford – only the best of everything will suffice, and that applies to all ingredients.**

Elystan Street 43 Elystan Street, SW3 3NT

020 7628 5005 www.elystanstreet.com

This place is all about Philip Howard and his change of step. After a couple of decades cooking two-star cuisine at The Square in Mayfair, he sold up and could have easily retired, but no. The call of the kitchen was too much, apparently, and he set up this more informal restaurant with Rebecca Mascarenhas – they already own other restaurants together elsewhere in London. They say it is more accessible and everyday, but don't forget this is Chelsea and the area has a different type of understanding of the words informal and affordable. Personally, I find the room and the bare tables all a bit inappropriate, trying too hard to be relaxed when in fact not much else about the restaurant is simple or understated. The service is slick, technical and informed, but not very personable. And the food is of an exceptionally high standard. Mr Howard's years of experience and his intelligence result in some inspired dishes and excellent flavour combinations. The clean and elegant presentation is also to be admired (PP).

The Good Life Eatery 20 Motcomb Street, SW1X 8LB UK

020 7838 9172 www.goodlifeeatery.com

If clean eating is your thing, then The Good Life Eatery is the place to go. This is the sort of restaurant that feels the need to tell their patrons all about their beliefs and ideology. Thankfully, they recognize taste, local suppliers and sustainability more than organic credentials. As you might expect, they actively welcome and attract those with special diets and intolerances, be it gluten or dairy. The drinks menu is all about cold-pressed juices with the likes of Dr Green Love, including kale, spinach, apple and coconut, plus Drink Your Salad, containing everything you might expect from the name. While the lunchtime soups, salads and wraps have a particular appeal, it is the breakfast menu that I find the most rewarding. At the weekend, we might revel in a full English or some devilled kidneys, whereas in the middle of the week, a bowl of something healthy and fulfilling provides more of a wellness and confidence boost.

Another admirable thing is the 'no-Wi-Fi policy', which is designed to encourage people to speak to each other and not be obsessed by their smartphones.

José Pizarro

"

I love a good pub. Somewhere informal and off the beaten track.

Restaurateur and Chef patron, José

Left **More and more health food restaurants are appearing in London serving more juices and smoothies and less wine and fewer cocktails.**

Best for... secret assignations

76 Dean Street or other private members' clubs – blag your way into one of them

Park Chinois – this place is jaw-dropping in its opulence and over the top in everything it does. Even the hardest cheese will melt

Quaglino's – it is so big and generally packed out that you're never going to get noticed

Harwood Arms Walham Grove, SW6 1QP

020 7386 1847   www.harwoodarms.com

The Harwood Arms was the first pub to secure a Michelin star for its seasonal and resolutely British food. As we're not great fans of either gastropubs or the Michelin star system, it follows that we shouldn't be too keen on the Harwood Arms. But in fact the opposite is true.

One of the reasons why we enjoy this particular offering is the amount of game peppered across the menus. The triumvirate who manage the pub include chef Mike Robinson, who is equally well known for his shooting and hunting activities in rural Berkshire, and who apparently personally shoots much of the game in season. Mike is also the proprietor of The Pot Kiln, a country pub specializing in game located in Frilsham near Newbury. The other partners are Brett Graham from The Ledbury in Notting Hill (see page 44) and Edwin Vaux of Vaux Brewery, who looks after the pub side. While it cannot be said that the Harwood Arms is a true boozer, it hasn't lost all of its pub charm, with Edwin contributing his fair share of character in the form of some great beers.

Some of the table details are a little over the top, arguably, and the plates are a bit fancy, but the service is very professional without being too starchy, which makes the overall experience very enjoyable.

If you are planning a visit to the Harwood Arms, we suggest you also call in at the nearby Vagabond Wines, one of the new wave of wine retailers that are popping up all over London. They have more than 100 wines available to taste in small measures and at very reasonable prices.

Right **The Ivy Chelsea Garden is located on Chelsea's iconic King's Road.**

Right **The very pleasant dining room at The Ivy Chelsea Garden.** Below **The Ivy's chocolate bombe with milk foam, vanilla ice cream, a honeycomb centre and hot salted caramel sauce.**

The Ivy Chelsea Garden 195–7 King's Road, SW3 5EQ

020 3301 0300   www.theivychelseagarden.com

Having interviewed some chefs who have worked in the kitchens of this offshoot of the original Ivy restaurant (see page 195), I'm reluctant to dine here, but I do think the garden, the atmosphere (although quite loud) and the cocktails are all worth visiting for. It is a fantastic-looking space with an extraordinary-pleasant garden dining area. My comments about the food menu are probably unfair: the menu is massive and I've been told that much of it is prepared elsewhere and shipped in. This does help with consistency and can make the value for money better, but perhaps I've got an outdated view that the produce should arrive raw and be cooked from scratch on the premises by a skilled team of kitchen staff – perhaps not (PP)!

Above **Chelsea Garden hamburgers.** Right **It is worth visiting The Ivy Chelsea Garden for the cocktails alone.** Opposite **The lavishly decorated interiors at The Ivy Chelsea Garden are by über-designer Martin Brudnizki.**

Tuna Carpaccio with Avocado, Radish and Lime and Crème Fraîche Dressing

Serves 1

For the avocado purée

1 avocado
juice of ¼ lime
1 tablespoon rapeseed oil
couple of pinches of sea salt

For the lime and crème fraîche dressing

100g (3½oz) crème fraîche
½ tablespoon lime juice

For the carpaccio

85g (3oz) sushi-grade tuna, cut in an 8cm (3 inch) diameter log
1 radish, cut into 5 wedges
1 lime
pinch of sea salt
coriander micro-cress, to serve

To make the avocado purée, peel and pit the avocado and place in a food processor with all the other ingredients. Blitz until smooth, then spoon into a piping bag and store in the fridge.

To make the dressing, place the crème fraîche into a bowl, add the lime juice and a pinch of salt and whisk well. Again, spoon into a piping bag and store in the fridge.

Using a sharp knife, slice the tuna into 2mm (¹/₁₆ inch) slices. Carefully arrange the tuna on a plate, slightly overlapping the slices.

Pipe the dressing in a zig-zag across the tuna, then pipe 5 equal-sized dots of avocado purée on top of the tuna.

Place a piece of radish on each dot of avocado purée. Using a fine grater, grate some lime zest on the tuna.

Season with sea salt and finish with coriander micro-cress.

Field Mixed Salad

Serves 1

For the avocado hummus

½ avocado
125g (4½oz) hummus
1 teaspoon tahini
1 teaspoon lemon juice
1 heaped tablespoon finely chopped red onion
1 tablespoon finely chopped coriander leaves

For the wholegrain mustard and manuka honey dressing

100g (3½oz) wholegrain mustard
2 tablespoons manuka honey
4 tablespoons blossom honey
2 tablespoons water
160ml (5½fl oz) rapeseed oil
sea salt flakes and freshly ground black pepper

For the salad

1 golden beetroot
1 cauliflower floret
small piece of mooli (daikon)
1 courgette
1 carrot
1 radish
20g (¾oz) red and white chicory (endive) leaves
1 rainbow chard leaf
1 teaspoon toasted sunflower seeds, pumpkin seeds and/or linseeds
a few coriander leaves
a few edible petals

To make the avocado hummus, peel and pit the avocado, place it in a food processor and blend until smooth. Scrape into a clean bowl. Add the hummus and tahini and mix well, then add all the other ingredients and mix well to evenly distribute them. Store in a container in the fridge until needed.

To make the dressing, place the wholegrain mustard, honey, measured water, salt and pepper in a bowl and whisk vigorously. Slowly pour in the oil, still whisking, until it emulsifies and thickens. Store in the fridge in a glass jar until needed. (This makes more than you need for this recipe, so store the dressing in the fridge for up to 1 week.)

Using a mandoline, slice all the hard vegetables – lengthways where possible – and place them in a bowl. Finely shred the chicory and chard and add those to the bowl. Dress with some of the honey dressing and mix well to coat.

To serve, place the avocado hummus in the centre of a plate and, using the back of a spoon, spread it out into a circle. Place the dressed vegetables on top, trying to stack them so they have height on the plate.

To finish, scatter over the toasted seeds, coriander and petals and, finally, drizzle a little more of the dressing around the plate.

Richard Gladwin

"

As a chef I am so lucky to have access to a family farm for a lot of our ingredients, but in addition London is fantastically located to take advantage of produce created in and around the city, within a radius that really can be called local and, of course, British.

Co-owner, Rabbit

Medlar 438 King's Road, SW10 0LJ

020 7349 1900   www.medlarrestaurant.co.uk

The food at Medlar is very good and it is all at an attractive price given that they (only) operate a simple *prix fixe* menu with a choice of about eight first courses, eight mains and eight desserts plus cheese. However, it is the wine list that reaches the highest levels. We can say with confidence it is one of the best in the capital, and the restaurant rightfully attracts those in the wine trade due to the breadth and quality of the selection and the modest mark-ups. It is no surprise that the wine list is so good here because they employ Christopher Delalonde MS, probably the most experienced sommelier working in London today. The MS after his name signifies that he is a master sommelier. Like the legendary Master of Wine qualification, MS status is notably difficult to achieve and there are fewer than 200 people across the world who have passed the exam. For those interested, there is a rather melodramatic film called *Somm* that charts the nerves and anxieties linked to securing the MS accreditation.

Opposite and above
**Duck egg tart with
red wine sauce, turnip
purée, lardons and
sautéed duck heart
at Medlar.**

Right **A selection
of cheese served on
a board at Medlar.**

Left **A little bit of the country in Chelsea at Rabbit.**

Left **One of many amusing little details at Rabbit.** Below **A mushroom marmite èclair, confit egg yolk 'mouthful' at Rabbit.**

Rabbit 172 King's Road, SW3 4UP

020 3750 0172   www.rabbit-restaurant.com

After successfully launching The Shed in Notting Hill, the Gladwin brothers progressed to another dining room that inspires wistful dreams of the country life. Brought up on a farm in West Sussex, this seems to come naturally to the brothers. Gregory is a farmer providing the produce, Oliver is the chef and Richard, like his father, is the restaurateur. Together, they make the perfect circle and it shows. Nutbourne Cures indicates a section on the menu that includes produce sourced from their land. Then you can either choose Slow Cooking, which is all about braising and marinating, or Fast Cooking, including raw and grilled items. There is lots of imagination and creativity added to the menus without it becoming too gimmicky, and you can be assured that everything is seasonal and fresh. This is a new form of modern British food, and it is to be enjoyed.

Restaurant Gordon Ramsay 68 Royal Hospital Road, SW3 4HP

020 7352 4441 www.gordonramsay.com

The Gordon Ramsay brand has had its ups and downs over the years, but the one constant is the three coveted Michelin stars it has held since 2000 at its flagship location. Key lieutenants have moved on from Gordon's empire, some acrimoniously, attracting much attention, but throughout all of this, Gordon has managed to achieve the ultimate accolade for a chef of his intentions. I recently read a comment about the potential for this restaurant to lose a star and what Gordon might do in response. Apparently, he said he'd jump back in the kitchen and start to do it all himself until the full complement of stars is achieved. Wouldn't this be interesting to see (PP)!

The restaurant is next door to the Chelsea Physic Garden, which is also well worth a visit.

Tendido Cero 1/4 Old Brompton Road, SW5 0BA

020 7370 3685 www.cambiodetercio.co.uk

If we had to choose one of Abel Lusa's three restaurants in this corner of South Kensington, it would be Tendido Cero. Everything, from the passionate, gesticulating staff to the atmosphere and lighting, is pitched at just the right level. The menu is simply presented in two categories, cold and hot tapas, with all the usual suspects: jamón, quesos, toasted tomato breads, boquerones, calamares, piquillo peppers, croquetas, tortillas, chorizo, gambas and much more. And, of course, every meal must end with either chocolate churros or crema catalana.

Hen in a Bowl

Serves 5

For the mushroom béchamel

15g (½oz) unsalted butter
15g (½oz) tapioca flour, or other flour
105ml (3½fl oz) milk
1 tablespoon sherry vinegar
30g (1oz) dried mushrooms, crushed to a powder, plus 30g (1oz) extra to make mushroom salt
1 teaspoon caster sugar
½ tablespoon truffle oil
sea salt

For the eggs

5 eggs
a little white wine vinegar
handful of oak chippings
150g (5½oz) plain flour
150ml (¼ pint) milk
150g (5½oz) potato starch (flour)
vegetable oil, to deep-fry

To serve

500ml (18fl oz) very good chicken broth, ideally homemade and flavoured with tarragon
small bunch of picked tarragon leaves
1½ tablespoons tarragon oil

For the mushroom béchamel, cook the butter until it starts to brown and then add the flour. Cook, stirring continuously over a medium heat for 1 minute to make a roux. Add the milk bit by bit until you have a velvety paste, then add the sherry vinegar, mushroom powder, sugar and salt and finish with truffle oil. Put in a piping bag and leave to cool.

Blitz the remaining dried mushrooms to a powder in a blender, then stir in double their weight in sea salt. Set this mushroom salt aside.

Gently place the eggs in a pot of boiling water with salt and a splash of white wine vinegar. Cook for 8 minutes at a simmer, then plunge into iced water. When cool, shell the eggs, then cut out a wedge of egg white about a quarter of the size of the egg, so you can easily remove the yolk but still keep the shape of a whole egg white intact. Pull the egg yolk out. (Reserve all the pieces of egg white.)

Set up a hot-smoker. Line a wok and lid with a double layer of foil, put the oak chippings inside, and place on the lid. Set over a medium heat until you can smell or see smoke. Put the 10 egg yolks on a trivet lined with baking parchment, then lower this into the wok, cover and hot smoke for 10 minutes. Remove from the smoker, leave to cool, then crumble to make a smoked egg yolk powder.

Fill the hulled egg white with the mushroom béchamel, then put the egg white wedges back into their cavities to re-form the sealed eggs. Freeze for 20 minutes. Put the flour, milk and potato starch into 3 shallow dishes. Roll each egg first in flour, then the milk, and then the potato flour. Leave on a tray.

Heat the oil in a deep-fat fryer, or large saucepan, making sure the oil does not come more than one-third up the sides of the saucepan. The oil is hot enough when a bread cube thrown in sizzles at once and begins to brown. It will measure 190°C (375°F) on a cook's thermometer, if you have one.

Meanwhile, heat the chicken broth.

Deep-fry the eggs, in 2–3 batches, for 90 seconds each, turning once, or until crisp, then drain on kitchen paper. Now deep-fry half the tarragon leaves until they, too, are crisp, draining them on kitchen paper.

Make a nest in each of 5 warm bowls with half fresh and half fried tarragon leaves. Dot droplets of tarragon oil around and put a fried egg in the middle of each nest. Crumble over the smoked egg yolk powder, then season the egg with mushroom salt.

Serve with small jugs of the hot, tarragon-infused chicken broth, telling your guests to pour it into the bowl around the egg. The egg should eventually fall off its perch by rolling to the side.

More places to visit in the area

Above **Battered fish and chips – Tom's Kitchen style.**

Le Colombier

145 Dovehouse Street, SW3 6LB
020 7351 1155 www.le-colombier-restaurant.co.uk
The embodiment of French charm, with brasserie dishes that have stood the test of time.

Eight Over Eight

392 King's Road, SW3 5UZ
020 7349 9934
www.rickerrestaurants.com/eightovereight
Will Ricker seems to own a pan-Asian eatery in every cool neighbourhood in London. Eight Over Eight, a sister of the celebrity-lined E&O (see page 40), serves good dim sum, sushi and tempura as well as pad Thai and steamed sea bass specials. Its success is down to the quality of the food, stylish interior design and killer cocktails.

The Five Fields

8–9 Blacklands Terrace, SW3 2SP
020 7838 1082 www.fivefieldsrestaurant.com
Old-school fine dining values but more of a modern outlook, especially when it comes to sourcing vegetables and herbs from their own kitchen garden in East Sussex. They've earned their Michelin star through quality on the plate.

Restaurant Ours

264 Brompton Road, SW3 2AS
020 7100 2200 www.restaurant-ours.com
Another place with an odd name. With so many restaurants in London, inevitably there are going to be a few duds. The introduction on the website 'What's Ours, is yours', is equally strange, in my view. However, I'm going to give much credit to Tom Sellers, the young culinary director, for his confidence and drive (PP).

Tartufo

1 Cadogan Gardens, SW3 2RJ
020 7730 6383
Situated on the lower-ground floor of a red-brick Victorian mansion block below a very discreet and high-quality hotel. The modern European food here is refined and elegant. Alexis Gauthier oversees the menus and brings brilliance to bear on the plate.

Tom's Kitchen

27 Cale Street, SW3 3QP
0207 349 0202 www.tomskitchen.co.uk
Open for breakfast, lunch and dinner, Tom Aikens' restaurant is a multi layered operation, with a ground-floor dining room, a first-floor bar, and private dining rooms on the upper floors. The pleasing menu ranges from the signature seven-hour confit of lamb for two to simple delights such as fish and chips and (very fine) sausages and mash with onion gravy.

Toto's Restaurant

Walton House, Lennox Gardens Mews,
Walton Street, SW3 2JH
020 7589 2062 www.totosrestaurant.com
This is very high-end and also very authentic Italian cuisine. Go in the summer and request a table in the very chichi and intimate garden.

The Troubadour

263–7 Old Brompton Road, SW5 9JA
020 7370 1434 www.troubadour.co.uk
The highly atmospheric Troubadour houses a café, delicatessen, art gallery and cellar-club, where it continues its strong links with emerging musical talents.

Clerkenwell
Farringdon
Smithfield

There's a reason that Clerkenwell is the district of choice for many architects and furniture retailers. First, it's a handsome part of town, with buildings old and new juxtaposed a little more naturally than in some parts of London. It's only a few bus stops, or a quick walk, into town from here, but it doesn't feel like it on the beautiful back streets, where the history of the area is rich and dark, with an abundance of proper English pubs that come with macabre back stories. Like its neighbour, the City, this is an area with a colourful history. In the 19th century it became one of the most impoverished and crime-ridden districts of the metropolis. Dickens made Clerkenwell the stomping ground of the Artful Dodger, and set many more of his stories here, perhaps because the names of the streets are so deliciously grizzly – Bleeding Heart Inn is so named because Lord Hatton's daughter was murdered here in the 1500s, her heart said to be found isolated and still pumping blood long after her death. Of course, this is also the bloodiest part of London in a literal sense – the historic Smithfield meat market still stubbornly occupies a glorious old building right in a lucrative patch of land that could be made into 1,000 luxury flats, although the Museum of London will get a wing of it in 2021. It has been a meat market since the Middle Ages and the streets here also ran with the blood of traitors, as Smithfield was a site of execution in the 1300s – William Wallace was executed here. Of course, nowadays it is merely cattle that meet their maker here, and the market is open to any members of the public that can stomach the early rise needed to get the best bits. If not, the Smithfield area has many notable eateries that trade off the reputation and proximity of the meat market. Across London, I often see some cringe-worthy walking tours on guided history lessons, but I can't help thinking that it might be worth joining the tourists to learn more about this area's rich past.

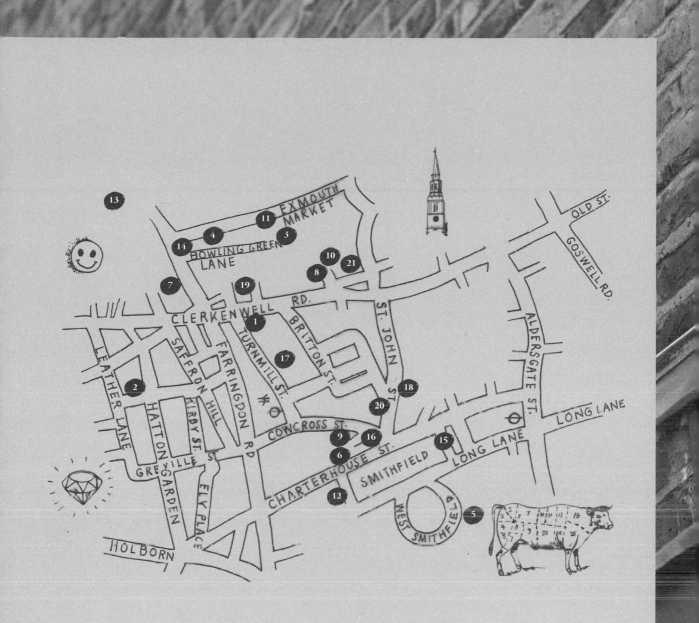

Albion Unit 1, The Turnmill, 63 Clerkenwell Road, EC1M 5NP

020 3862 0750   www.albion-uk.london

This is our third and by far our largest Albion. It is a great lofty corner site at
the axis of Clerkenwell, home to the world's highest concentration of architects'
offices – just one of the reasons why we chose this location. The premises have
had a rather chequered history; before our occupation it was the site of a legendary
all-night club. Unfortunately, there were problems, and it became a rather dodgy
venue, which rarely got going before 3am or later. It is funny now talking with
people that remembered lost nights at this club – I was particularly shocked
when our very straight bank manager said he previously frequented it.

   We appointed the brilliant architect Isabelle Chatel de Brancion to help us
convert the space and I think she's done an amazing job in creating a modern
industrial feel without it being too oppressive or unwelcoming. Spread across
two floors and 650sq m (7,000sq ft), it includes several dining, drinking,
meeting, snacking and shopping opportunities with one clear aim: to provide
informal, unfussy, modestly priced British café food (PP).

Lauren Webster

"
Albion is open from early morning to
late supper every day; with the adjoining
shop and bakery, we aim to provide
a valuable resource and hub for the
local community.

General manager, Albion

Above **The full
Albion breakfast.**
Above left **Albion
Clerkenwell has its
own on-site bakery.**
Right **Signature coffee
and tea pots in post-
box-red at Albion.**

Left **Almond croissant** made at the Albion Clerkenwell bakery.
Above right **Albion's own-recipe gin made** exclusively at the City of London Distillery.

Right **Kedgeree – a** colonial classic that has been on the Albion menu since day one.
Below **British rock** oysters at Albion.

Above **Albion's own-label pale ale.**

Left and right
**Creative and stylish
interiors at Bourne
& Hollingsworth
Buildings.**

Anglo 31 St Cross Street, EC1N 8UH

020 7430 1503   www.anglorestaurant.com

This is a really interesting new arrival that is cooking up a storm with its
own take on (very) modern British cooking. Like so many new places,
it only offers a seven-course tasting menu in the evening, but it seems to
work. At lunch, there is a small à la carte menu or a five-course tasting
menu. The food presentation is rather fussy but it has actually been very
intelligently planned and we think we are going to see more from the
young owners in the future – the current location (just off Leather Lane)
doesn't really do them any justice.

Bourne & Hollingsworth Buildings 42 Northampton Road, EC1R 0HU

020 7724 1617   www.bourneandhollingsworth.com

They call it a club house, and with a bar, café, restaurant, greenhouse and
event spaces, this is a fab location for parties, raucous gatherings, special
occasions and celebrations. They even have their own cookery school.
The weekend brunch is also worth a trip, and the Below & Hidden bar
concealed beneath the main building is a great late-night hangout on a Friday
and Saturday night. However, the key ingredient here is brilliant cocktails in
a beautifully creative space – a blend of old and new, shabby chic with great
charisma. The owners have a track record in creating great parties, such as
their Cocktails in the City and Prohibition Party events, and they also play
host to a wonderful atmosphere at their other London locations in Rathbone
Place and Goodge Street.

Hervé Durochat

"

London's best kept foodie secret?
Anglo in Clerkenwell. Just fantastic!

Co-owner, Casse-Croûte

This page **Great cocktails and an easy-going menu at Bourne & Hollingsworth Buildings make** for a wonderful brunch destination.

Caravan 11–13 Exmouth Market, EC1R 4QD

020 7833 8115 www.caravanonexmouth.co.uk

Pitch perfect, in every sense. The corner location of this Kiwi-managed café-cum-restaurant on the edge of desirable Exmouth Market is hugely appealing: the tables both inside and on the pavement are a pure delight, especially when you catch the aroma of coffee roasting in the basement. The relaxed nature of the setting is matched by the exacting commitment and skill displayed in the presentation of the food, wine and coffee. It is hardly surprising, therefore, that, since its opening in early 2010, Caravan has been a runaway success. Miles Kirby, co-owner, head chef and head roaster (and not many people can claim that title) is an alumnus of The Providores, so you can expect a global roll call of ingredients. Could fusion food be making a comeback, dare we ask? In the right hands it can work, and Miles is certainly one of the few people who can make it enjoyable. The small coffee roastery in the basement has also captured the attention of many other restaurateurs, and now has its emulators around town.

Club Gascon 57 West Smithfield, EC1A 9DS

020 7600 6144 www.clubgascon.com

Pascal Aussignac has created a multiple award-winning and Michelin-starred eatery devoted to the food of south-west France. The dining room seats about 60 people and has a City-boy atmosphere, with dark woods, marble and linen napery. Cellar Gascon next door is a busy wine bar with a peerless list of wines from Gascony. Serious bar snacks follow the same robust duck, foie gras and porcine direction.

Comptoir Gascon 63 Charterhouse Street, EC1M 6HJ

020 7680 0851 www.comptoirgascon.com

The Club Gascon team offers more duck, goose, pork and other meats in this small, rustic 30-seat bistro, with a few bakery and deli items also available. While most people prefer the original Club Gascon site, this more humble offering is more to my taste. The French fries cooked in duck fat are (as the late Michael Winner might have said) historic (PP).

The Eagle 159 Farringdon Road, EC1R 3AL

020 7837 1353 www.theeaglefarringdon.co.uk

Having opened in 1991, The Eagle is reputedly the very first gastropub in London. During years of both metamorphosis and proliferation in the world of gastropubs, The Eagle has thankfully remained unchanged and true to its original idea. This is probably the best format for a business of this type: let pubs remain pubs, with good and inexpensive grub, and let restaurants be restaurants.

The ground-floor open kitchen sets the tone, and everything is stripped back. The Eagle puts on no airs and graces, and it is perhaps a little too scruffy for some tastes, yet the place is packed with integrity and is robust in every sense, with a generally faultless kitchen.

The original chef, David Eyre, has now set up a new Spanish and Portuguese restaurant, Eyre Brothers, with his brother in the City.

Above **Flat whites at Caravan. If you look closely, you'll see that they even have their own unique spoons.**

Right **The Caravan brunch menu and cocktail list is one of the best in London.**

Best for...
brunch

Caravan – the King's Cross location is the best, but expect to queue. It is worth waiting for, not least because of the atmosphere and brunch cocktails

Granger & Co. – the ultimate brunch menu

Oklava – brilliant modern Turkish food and fantastic value for money on Sunday

Above and right **The no-frills dining room at HIX Oyster & Chop House.**

Granger & Co. Clerkenwell Green, 50 Sekforde Street, EC1R 0HA
020 7251 9032   www.grangerandco.com

After dining rooms in Sydney, Japan, Honolulu and Seoul, there are three Granger & Co.'s in London, and I am convinced that this is the best one. I love the slightly elevated situation overlooking the trees and neighbouring churchyard. I'm not exactly sure how they achieve it but the dining room feels antipodean – and it's particularly good on a sunny morning or summer's evening.

Bill Granger is the world's best-known Aussie chef and he's really the face of relaxed brunches. Bill also put communal sharing tables on the restaurant map, thanks to his cafés in Sydney. His recipe books share the same sunny and infectious attitude. Having met Bill, I can also say that he's a great guy, the kind of person everybody wants to be friends with, and his personality seems to pervade the menus and the whole ethos of his restaurants.

His menus are always modestly priced, diverse, modern in their outlook and full of interesting ingredients that deliver some really strong flavours. We can't recommend him enough (PP).

HIX Oyster & Chop House

36–7 Greenhill Rents, Cowcross Street, EC1M 6BN
020 7017 1930   www.hixoysterandchophouse.co.uk

This no-fuss eating house is Mark Hix's first solo project. In his illustrious career he has worked with Anton Edelmann and Anton Mosimann at the grand hotels along Park Lane, and even more impressively chalked up a commendable 17 years with Caprice Holdings. Mark was the head chef at Le Caprice, The Ivy and J Sheekey, before becoming chef director for a much larger group of restaurants encompassing everything from Vietnamese to Italian menus. Mark was also the key figure responsible for devising and establishing the magnificent Scott's in Mayfair. Having been responsible for the food at London's most fashionable restaurants, he certainly knows how to run such places.

The kitchen here serves up hearty and gutsy British food without any frills. Just how we like it. Everything is well sourced and proudly British. From wild herbs, sea vegetables and English garden vegetables to a Barnsley chop or rib steak and excellent flank and oyster pies, there is much to relish here. The fruit puddings and fools are excellent, and the British cheeses live up to their well-deserved international reputation.

Try the De Beauvoir smoked salmon 'Hix Cure', smoked over oak and apple chips using salt and molasses at Mark's home in east London.

The style and layout of the restaurant, formerly a sausage factory, complement the stripped-down food perfectly, while evidence of Mark's design awareness and knowledge of art is all around.

Before 2008, when Anna Hansen opened The Modern Pantry, fusion food (sometimes known disparagingly as 'confusion food') seemed, like *nouvelle cuisine*, to be dead and buried in London. With the exception of The Providores, Peter Gordon's excellent restaurant in Marylebone (see page 254), Londoners had abandoned this sometimes misunderstood style of food just as quickly as they had embraced it in the 1990s. While we might not rush to visit The Modern Pantry, there can be no doubt that the city benefits from diversity and creativity. This is an interesting project that brings together global recipes and ingredients in a pleasingly simple setting. From east-meets-west to wacky flavour combinations, the menus can be challenging and seemingly characterized chiefly by a riot of textures, flavours and aromas. On the whole, the combinations seem to work, and occasionally you will find nuggets of brilliance. Given the different components in each dish, the kitchen certainly deserves credit for championing this style of food. We can't imagine anything further removed from Escoffier's great dictum, '*Faites simple*', or Elizabeth David's advocacy of 'the avoidance of all unnecessary complication and elaboration'.

Set in a handsome Georgian townhouse overlooking St John's Square are three dining spaces. The ground-floor cafe, with its communal table and large windows, is a delight, even if it feels a little like a goldfish bowl as pedestrians pass by. Upstairs is more suitable for intimate suppers, and on a sunny day the outside terrace seating is best. The breakfast and weekend brunch menu also needs a separate mention.

Above right **The downstairs dining room at The Modern Pantry.** Right **Chef Anna Hansen.**

Above and left **In the kitchens at Moro.** Right **Chef patron Samuel Clark.**

167

Moro 34–6 Exmouth Market, EC1R 4QE

020 7833 8336   www.moro.co.uk

According to the first *Moro Cookbook*, the menu was born of a desire to cook within the wonderful traditions of the Mediterranean, while still exploring new and exciting flavours. From its inception in 1997, Moro has been cooking excellent Spanish food with more than a hint of North African flavours and ingredients. The kitchen team manage to capture the influence of the Moorish occupation of Spain from the 8th to the 15th centuries and at the same time present everything in a modern and modest manner. As an exponent of this culinary direction, Moro stands alone: nothing similar or close to this standard of cooking exists in London today. Some chefs might introduce an occasional dish linking saffron and cinnamon, paprika and cumin, but at Moro the link between these two great culinary traditions imbues the entire menu, and it's a delight.

Before opening the restaurant on Exmouth Market, the recently married proprietors Sam and Sam Clark set off in a camper van to explore the food and culture of Spain and Morocco as far as the Sahara. Clearly the journey was worthwhile. The food the Clarks serve shows their previous experience at the seminal River Café (see page 30), and they adopt the same relaxed idiom, yet have created a lively dining room and an impressive open kitchen. Charcoal-grilled meat, poultry and fish, together with dishes such as wood-oven roasted pork with green mojo sauce and wrinkled potatoes, form the heart of the menu.

Along with The River Café, Moro is one of the few restaurants that really understands excellent wood-oven cooking. The long zinc bar is a lively spot from which to enjoy various tapas, cured hams and a glass of sherry. As well as its excellent food and ambience, Moro also offers great value for money. Given its popularity, the temptation to increase the prices on the menu must have been strong; fortunately for us, the passion and belief in running a sustainable, popular restaurant appear to be even stronger.

Over recent years, the team have taken on the lease for next door and opened Morito, a cute and brightly coloured tapas bar.

Best for...
hidden locations

Le Café du Marché – an old French classic accessed via a narrow walkway

Hakkasan – the original hidden-door restaurant and still excellent for dim sum during the day or a decadent, expensive dinner

Rochelle Canteen – just brilliant in every way and best enjoyed in the summer months

Oriole East Poultry Avenue, Smithfield Markets, EC1A 9LH

020 3457 8099   www.oriolebar.com

This is one of the most creative cocktail bars in London. They seem to serve cocktails in anything but a glass and the garniture is certainly edging towards OTT, but it all seems to work. You can't deny that it is a great space and the techniques and skills behind the bar are impressive.

Otto's 182 Gray's Inn Road, WC1X 8EW

020 7713 0107   www.ottos-restaurant.com

Without exception, all UK food critics love this place – and so should you. A large reason for the admiration is the anachronistic menu. If you're not familiar with the work of the world's first celebrity chef Auguste Escoffier or the restaurant La Tour D'Argent in Paris, do your research before you go. And, definitely go with an appetite so that you can enjoy the *canard* or *homard à la presse* – the antique silver press dates back to 1927. If you don't want the duck or lobster, there is a whole roast *poulet de Bresse*, plus many other true classics from the annals of grand French cuisine.

Best for... breakfast

Start the day with great food, a stylish setting and perhaps a little people watching.

Albion

Cecconi's

The Wolseley

Above **The bar at Oriole, under Smithfield Meat Market.**

Below **Next door to Quality Chop House you'll find a very good butcher's, a small, assiduously stocked deli and a liquor store.**
Below, right **The historic Quality Chop House dining room.**

Quality Chop House and Shop 90–4 Farringdon Road, EC1R 3EA

020 3490 6228 www.thequalitychophouse.com

I'm really very fond of this place for several reasons, but I do find the seating to be the most uncomfortable in any restaurant. They are very narrow benches, which are now part of the Grade II listing that covers the premises. Originally opened in 1869, it has been called the Quality Chop House ever since, and there are other little details on the front window and the mosaic floor that allude to its historic past. Now, the food is a lovely blend of traditional British and new ideas. In the evening, it is another one of London's now many fixed, no-choice menus – not in a tasting-menu format, but more akin to supper at a friend's house. All rather charming, with mixed plates and reclaimed cutlery, it has been very carefully considered but planned to look quite natural. You can also drink very well here. The wine list is relatively short, with about 75 brilliant wines from around the world and they are all affordable – the mark-ups are low and the buyer's eye is also highly knowledgeable. It is broad church with strong personalities.

Clerkenwell, Farringdon, Smithfield

169

Smithfield Meat and Poultry Market Charterhouse Street, EC1A 9PS

www.smithfieldmarket.com

One of the oldest markets in London, Smithfield has been supplying meat and poultry to the populace for over 800 years. The building, designed by Sir Horace Jones, suffered a fire in 1958 and was replaced in 1962, though much of its original Victorian splendour survives, and it is Grade II listed.

The market still influences the cost of meat and poultry in the UK today, with hundreds of butchers and suppliers visiting it on a weekly basis. Anyone can visit the market and shop there, but access to certain areas is restricted to those wearing clean protective clothing, in accordance with hygiene standards. Just before Christmas, the market and some of the adjoining butcher's shops all open to a wider audience and great bargains can be enjoyed – expect queues.

Smiths of Smithfield 67–77 Charterhouse Street, EC1M 6HJ

020 7251 7950   www.smithsofsmithfield.co.uk

John Torode, the original personality behind Smith's, has moved on, but this multi-faceted diner still has a certain appeal – something relaxed and absolutely at one with the jacket-off relaxed City folk at play. This former warehouse opposite the meat market offers a multitude of dining and drinking options for them. The common thread that connects the five floors, each with its own distinctive character, is a passion for unpretentious food that tastes great.

On the ground floor the décor is simple, with bench seats, leather sofas and a long bar. An open kitchen serves up an excellent all-day breakfast, along with club sandwiches, meat pies, sausage and mash, brunch and freshly squeezed juices. Good beer is the order of the day. The first floor houses a craft beer bar and a private dining and events space. Above, on the second floor, is a 130-seat dining room and a semi-open kitchen that offers food prepared according to a range of cooking methods, from the wok to clay ovens and charcoal grills. The menu here crosses several continents and includes a grill section and a 10-oz beef burger with mature cheddar and Old Spot bacon.

On the top floor you reach the summit in culinary terms: the menu is dedicated to the best of British meat, organic foods and seasonal vegetables.

Above left **A corner of the Smithfield Meat Market, with Smiths of Smithfield in the background.** Above **The skill level and professionalism among the chefs and front-of-house team at Sosharu is highly impressive.**

Sosharu 64 Turnmill Street, EC1M 5RR
020 3805 2304 www.sosharulondon.com

They say it is an izakaya-style restaurant but I'm not sure that this description is exactly accurate – not that it matters too much. Sosharu is out in a category on its own. They use British seasonal ingredients alongside mostly Japanese recipes and techniques. There are also a few other broader Asian flavours thrown in for good measure. You get tempura, temaki, rice pots, kibachi and yaki grilled items, but no sushi. They've also got a second inner kitchen where diners can watch the talented chefs in action preparing a tasting menu with Japanese specialities.

Downstairs, there is a small cocktail bar called 7 Tales, which also delivers Tokyo flavours, with some particularly intricate cocktails.

You've got to admire the attention to detail at this place, and I've also found the service to be particularly well drilled – it is a big menu with lots to explain and the staff do it with consummate ease. I was impressed. Everything is done with professionalism and the signature of Jason Atherton, who is becoming a major player on the global food stage. He's emerged from, and probably eclipsed, his one-time mentor Gordon Ramsay, and now seems on a trajectory to superbrand chef status (PP).

Above and above right
The talented chefs in action at Sosharu.

St John Bar & Restaurant 26 St John Street, EC1M 4AY

020 7251 0848   www.stjohnrestaurant.com

It's now over 20 years since Trevor Gulliver tempted Fergus Henderson and Jon Spiteri to set up a new restaurant close to Smithfield Meat Market. Fergus's nose-to-tail menu has gone on to gain a much-deserved worldwide reputation and a Michelin star. Jon was indispensable in the early years and has subsequently moved on – he's now one of London's top maître d's, and if you see him in one of his natty suits, you know you are going to receive some lovely service.

When Trevor found the building, it had been used – among other functions – as a smokehouse. He simply painted the walls white, put in a skylight, installed a kitchen and dropped in some tables and chairs. This no-fuss approach is a major factor in the success of the place. However, a refurb is in the offing and much anticipation is clutching those in the know.

The food is beyond reproach, naturally. Laconic and to the point best describes not only the style of the menu, but also what appears on the plate. Nobody else cooks to this standard and uses the range of ingredients pioneered by Fergus. His parents have a lot to answer for, it should be said. His late father, Brian Henderson, always enjoyed the best food and wine in generous quantities. His mother Elizabeth is a fine cook, in the Henderson tradition. Fergus learned at her stove, though he originally trained as an architect.

We thoroughly recommend calling in as often as possible, whether for a morning fillip, a long lunch or a simple supper. Or why not just collect a few Eccles cakes or a seed cake from the bakery?

As well as going to the restaurant as much as possible, I also celebrate my birthdays here. For my 35th, we had a raucous party for 18 and shared a whole suckling pig; for my 40th, things were slightly more sedate with an unimpeachable grouse. For my 45th, my now wife treated me to a special evening and, guess what, I had another plump grouse. It's just a wonderful place to be (PP).

Nicholas Balfe

"

The St John bacon sandwich is, as far as I am concerned, the finest example of this breakfast staple in the capital. The rare breed Old Spot bacon is perfectly charred on the grill, the bread is a classic white sandwich tin loaf, baked at the St John Bakery in Bermondsey, and their gently spiced ketchup is a deep red delight.

Chef patron, Salon

Above **The St John**
signature first course
of roast bone marrow
and parsley salad.

Right **Another**
signature dish at
St John: Lancashire
cheese with an
Eccles cake.

Left **Freshly baked**
Eccles cakes.

Sushi Tetsu 12 Jerusalem Passage, EC1V 4JP

020 3217 0090   www.sushitetsu.co.uk

I agonized about including, or not, this tiny, and I mean tiny, dining room down a discreet passageway in Clerkenwell. It is near impossible to get a booking and it would be foolish to make things harder. However, it really should be recognized as one of the hidden gems of London. Don't expect any hot food or even miso; it is pure (in every sense of the word) sushi only (PP).

Vinoteca 7 St John Street, EC1M 4AA

020 7253 8786   www.vinoteca.co.uk

This is one of London's modern wine bars inspired (as the name suggests) by the popular Italian and Spanish models. There are about 275 wines on offer, with some 25 available by the glass, each listed with eloquent tasting notes. Without ignoring the popular varietals, the lists also include many less well-known grapes and some real exploration wines. With its décor of heavy oak furniture, blackboards and a little poster art, the place is invariably buzzing. While the emphasis is intended to be on the wine, the food is also jolly good and highly appropriate. If you've enjoyed a particular wine, you can also buy a case to take home: an interesting concept thought up by three independent wine merchants. There are a few other locations in London and each has managed to retain a certain independent spirit.

The Zetter Townhouse Cocktail Lounge 49–50 St John's Square EC1V 4JJ

020 7324 4444   www.thezettertownhouse.com

This 13-bedroom sister to the main Zetter Hotel, just across the square, houses an eccentrically decorated cocktail lounge, which they describe as 'more like the private residence of a most beloved and eccentric Great Aunt'. The main attraction is clearly the cocktails, but don't overlook the food by Bruno Loubet.

Tony Conigliaro, widely acknowledged as one of the country's top drink creators, has devised a drinks list simultaneously respectful of the past and ultra-contemporary. The service is pitch perfect, and the attention to details, especially the range of glassware, makes this place a must for any barfly.

Right **Some of the finest cocktails in London can be enjoyed at The Zetter Townhouse.**

Left and above **The eccentrically designed drawing room at The Zetter Townhouse – worth a visit for this alone, let alone Tony Conigliaro's cocktails.**

More places to visit in the area

Bird of Smithfield
26 Smithfield, EC1A 9LB
020 7559 5100 www.birdofsmithfield.com
Named after the former Ivy head chef Alan
Bird, who now runs this five-floor Georgian
townhouse. It starts with club (the Birdcage)
in the basement and ascends to the rooftop
bar via some competent food in between.

The Bleeding Heart
Bleeding Heart Yard, EC1N 8SJ
020 7242 2056 www.bleedingheart.co.uk
What a great name! It is linked to the
murder of Lady Elizabeth Hatton in the 17th
century. Now, this cluster of a wood-panelled
restaurant, bistro, tavern and private dining
rooms, all based around a hidden yard,
serves decent French food in an historic
and atmospheric setting.

Le Café du Marché
22 Charterhouse Square,
Charterhouse Mews, EC1M 6DX
020 7608 1609 www.cafedumarche.co.uk
Hidden away at the end of a cobbled mews,
this charming French eating house is very
atmospheric and ideal for discreet assignations.

Dans Le Noir
30–1 Clerkenwell Green, EC1R 0DU
020 7253 1100 www.london.danslenoir.com
Taking the concept of a blind tasting to the
extreme. Dining in absolute darkness is a
sensory journey. This London outpost is now
part of an international group with social
responsibility at its heart – 50 per cent of the
staff have disabilities.

Look Mum No Hands!
49 Old Street, EC1V 9HX
020 7253 1025 www.lookmumnohands.com
Combining a café with a bicycle workshop.

Sedap
102 Old Street, EC1V 9AY
020 7490 0200 www.sedap.co.uk
I was originally taken here by a rather flash
Malaysian restaurateur friend, and when I
walked in the door I was convinced it was the
wrong place – the décor is very weird, but
the food is not. This is true old-style Malaysian
food (PP).

Shawarma Bar
46 Exmouth Market, EC1R 4QE
020 7837 1726 www.shawarmabar.co.uk
Sister to the brilliant Berber & Q in Shoreditch,
this is a new-style kebab shop with a difference
– the difference being the food is fantastic.
Choose from sizzling lamb, rotisserie chicken
or slow-braised beef short-rib. The desserts
include ice cream pita sandwiches with tahini
soft-serve and caramelized banana. They even
have frozen slushie cocktails.

Workshop Coffee
27 Clerkenwell Road, EC1M 5RN
020 7253 5754 www.workshopcoffee.com
Australians are serious about coffee, and
this London outpost of a highly praised
Melbourne-based coffee roastery and café is
studious about its subject.

Chinatown
Covent Garden
Soho
The Strand

This is the beating heart of London recreation – the home of its best theatres, most famous restaurants, its film industry and its shops. And, in Covent Garden in particular, most of its tourists. Those of a highbrow disposition have the Royal Opera House – one of the world's best opera and ballet venues. Elsewhere, where once there was a thriving produce market in the piazza, there are now performance artists painted silver and chain-store retailers. That said, the area has smartened up considerably since a takeover by a visionary developer/landlord, who has brought in the likes of Apple and Burberry on King Street to replace more touristy establishments, and Chanel and other high-fashion brands to replace the tourist tat pedalled in the piazza. Of course, they are also turning to top-end restaurateurs and bar supremos to bring some gravitas.

Cambridge Circus is the axis that funnels pedestrians between Chinatown, Covent Garden and Trafalgar Square. It's also the 'Circus' of John le Carré's Smiley spy thrillers – the writer imagined the MI6 HQ inhabiting the building that currently houses Macari's Musical Instruments, and its spies padding around Soho at lunchtime. Nowadays, Soho is occupied by film post-production houses and media agencies, and some of the city's best restaurants – you could really dine on any cuisine of your choosing, from modern Israeli at Palomar to Peruvian at Ceviche. By day, it's a buzzy place, with a gratifying number of thriving independent restaurants, shops and bars giving the place real personality. By night, it's lost a lot of its bridge-and-tunnel revellers to other parts of London. In some ways, that's no bad thing, but many of Soho's denizens are running various campaigns to keep its seedy character alive and stop the displacement of the true characters of the area – they don't seem to be succeeding!

10 Greek Street 10 Greek Street, W1D 4DH

020 7734 4677 www.10greekstreet.com

If I worked in an office in Soho, this would be my regular lunch spot,
thanks to its solid food, modest prices for food and wine, and its lovely style.
However, I do find the tables rather close together and it is important to
note that they only take bookings for lunch and it is just walk-ins only in
the evening, which, for me, means that I rule it out for supper, as I'm not
prepared to pitch up and expect to wait for a table, not even in Soho (PP).

26 Grains 1 Neal's Yard, WC2H 9DP

www.26grains.com

Inspired by Scandinavian cooking traditions and spices, 26 Grains is
something quite different. As the name suggests, they are all about
wholesome grain-based dishes and, to a large extent, a healthy positive diet.
There are some out there, especially in the world of 'clean' eating, that have
banned grains from their diet (don't mention Hemsley & Hemsley) and
there are those that see them as essential life-fulfilling foods. Of course,
the best response is a balanced and mixed diet, but hey, what do we know?
Anyway, at 26 Grains they celebrate *hygge* – yes, that annoyingly popular
Nordic concept that seems to suggest something along the lines of a cozy
night around a fireplace with a cashmere throw and somebody you love, or
in food terms, a warming bowl of hearty soup or porridge.

They've got all manner of grains: oats, quinoa, buckwheat, barley,
millet, amaranth, spelt, flaxseed and rye cooked through a variety of
milks – nut milk, coconut milk – or water or juices. Then you add spices
cardamom, ginger, cinnamon, nutmeg and star anise, all followed with
complementary toppings like honey, fresh fruit, maple syrup, yogurt,
compote and coconut. You can also enjoy some decent soups, salads,
savouries, sandwiches – on rye, obviously – and sweet snacks such as
buckwheat banana bread or spelt, honey and dukkah loaf. Plus, the drinks
menu is interesting if you believe in the importance of a healthy gut, with
the likes of hot turmeric drinks.

Robert
Reid

The London restaurant scene reminds
me of a funfair: it's packed full of
different experiences. With time
I believe that there will be more and
more vegetarian restaurants as I feel
that they remain relatively unexplored
and yet are essential to our diet.

Executive chef, Balthazar

Above left
**The distinctive
awning outside the
massive Balthazar
in the former
Theatre Museum.**

Balthazar 4–6 Russell St, WC2B 5HZ

020 3301 1155 www.balthazarlondon.com

I loved the original Balthazar in New York but its arrival in London has possibly been slightly less successful. Saying that, having dined there more than a few times since it opened, I've noticed that the food and service have actually got a lot better. The subtle Americanizaton of the traditional French brasserie menu does have a lot of appeal, not least on the brunch menu, and they are one of the few places remaining in London to offer really fresh *plateaux de fruits de mer*. So, if you are visiting the Royal Opera House, immediately across the road, you can't really go wrong here. And the boulangerie next door is particularly good (PP).

Above and left **The fabulous Balthazar pâtisserie and boulangerie next door to the brasserie.**

Rhubarb and Custard Doughnuts

Makes 12

For the rhubarb jam (makes 4 x 450g/1lb) jars)

1kg (2lb 4oz) pink rhubarb, trimmed

1kg (2lb 4oz) jam sugar (which contains added pectin)

finely grated zest and juice of 1 lemon

50g (1¾oz) stem or crystallized ginger, finely chopped

4cm (1½in) piece of fresh root ginger, peeled

For the custard (makes 500g/1lb 2oz)

1 vanilla pod

500ml (18fl oz) milk

4 large egg yolks

100g (3½oz) caster sugar

60g (2oz) cornflour

2 teaspoons plain flour

For the starter

450ml (16fl oz) milk

90g (3oz) fast-action dried yeast

245g (8½oz) strong white bread flour

For the dough

200g (7oz) caster sugar, plus extra for dusting

4 large egg yolks

495g (1lb 2oz) strong white bread flour

fine sea salt

150g (5½oz) unsalted butter, softened, plus extra for the bowl

sunflower oil, for deep-frying

First make the rhubarb jam: wash the rhubarb and slice into 2cm (¾ inch) pieces. Tip into a large ceramic or plastic bowl and add the jam sugar, lemon zest and juice and the stem ginger. Finely grate the fresh root ginger directly into the bowl. Stir thoroughly, cover loosely with clingfilm and leave to rest for about 2 hours; the sugar will dissolve into the rhubarb juices, though you may need to stir the mixture occasionally.

Scoop the fruit and all the sugary juices into a saucepan and set it over a medium heat. Stir until the sugar has completely dissolved, then bring to the boil. Continue to cook at a swift pace until the rhubarb is tender and the conserve has reached setting point; this should take about 10–15 minutes. (To test for a set, drop ½ teaspoon of the jam mix on to a cold saucer, leave it for 30 seconds, then gently push it with the tip of your finger. If the jam wrinkles, the setting point has been reached. If not, continue to cook for a further couple of minutes and test again.) Remove the saucepan from the heat and set aside for 2–3 minutes before pouring into sterilized jars. Seal immediately and label with the date. This has a shelf life of 3 months (store it in a cool, dry place).

Next make the custard: slice the vanilla pod in half lengthways and scrape out the seeds. Put the remaining pod, seeds and milk into a saucepan and bring to the boil.

In another bowl, whisk together the egg yolks and caster sugar until smooth and light. Add the cornflour and the flour and whisk again until all is combined.

Once the milk is boiling, strain gradually through a sieve into the egg yolk mixture, whisking constantly, until incorporated.

Pour back into the pan and whisk over the heat until the mixture becomes thick enough to coat the back of a spoon. Pour the custard into a cool bowl and cover the surface directly with clingfilm, to prevent a skin from forming. Leave to cool.

For the starter, put the milk and yeast into a mixing bowl and whisk together. Then sift in the flour gradually, still mixing, until a smooth paste has formed. Cover the bowl with clingfilm and leave in a warm place for 30 minutes to ferment.

Put the sugar and egg yolks into another mixing bowl; this time ensure it's heatproof. Place over a saucepan of boiling water; the bowl should not touch the water. Whisk until light and fluffy (this should take around 5 minutes). Remove from the heat.

To make the dough, place the flour, salt and the starter mixture in the bowl of a stand mixer. Begin to mix on a low speed, then add the egg yolk and sugar mixture. Increase the speed and mix until the dough is smooth, elastic and coming away from the sides of the bowl. Add the butter and beat until incorporated.

Place the dough mixture into a clean buttered bowl and cover with clingfilm. Put into the fridge and leave for at least 1 hour (more if possible), before dividing into 80g (2¾oz) pieces and rolling each into a ball about the size of a tennis ball. Put each ball, well spaced out, on a clean tray and leave in a warm place to prove for around 2 hours, or until they have almost doubled in size.

You don't have to use a deep-fat fryer to cook the doughnuts, but if you don't, please be extra careful with the hot oil. Pour about 6cm (2½ inches) depth of oil into a large, heavy-based saucepan or deep-fat fryer. Heat until it measures 160°C (325°F) on a cooking thermometer. Fry the doughnuts, in batches, for about 20 minutes or until golden brown, turning regularly with tongs to keep an even colour. Remove and place on kitchen paper to soak up any excess oil.

To assemble the doughnuts, poke a hole in the side of each doughnut with a small, sharp knife, going through to the middle. Put the rhubarb jam and custard into separate piping bags. Pipe the rhubarb jam into the centre of the doughnut, followed by the custard. Roll the doughnuts in caster sugar. Serve immediately and enjoy!

Left **Outside Bao...
the legendary queue
starts across the road
(see below).**
Below right
**Counter dining
overlooking the
kitchen is compulsory
at Barrafina.**

Bao 53 Lexington Street, W1F 9AS

www.baolondon.com no telephone, no reservations

London has gone mad for the Bao. I happen to think these Taiwanese steamed buns will run out of steam, so to speak, but they're certainly hot at the moment. Sadly, you are expected to queue to get a foot in the door, but, like many of these much-in-demand places, it is actually worth the inconvenience. The food is unusual, delicious and extremely good value for money. I also enjoy the graphics and the very plain timber-clad counter and clutter-free setting (PP).

Barrafina 10 Adelaide Street, WC2N 4HZ, 43 Drury Lane, WC2B 5AJ
and 26–7 Dean Street, W1D 3LL

www.barrafina.co.uk

Modelled on Cal Pep in the El Born district of Barcelona, this proper tapas bar by Sam and Eddie Hart was originally launched in Frith Street. The original site is no longer but thankfully there are now three new locations all within easy walking distance of each other: the Dean Street branch is part of the Quo Vadis building (see page 209). Each looks and feels the same, with marble-top bars where you dine overlooking the open kitchens, but each seems to have a slightly different menu. I personally prefer the Adelaide Street branch, where they have a large chargrill section on the menu to enjoy lovely things like Iberian pork ribs and lamb's kidneys. *Para picar* – meaning 'for picking at' or 'snacks' – heads the menus and you then have a range of lovely fried things that are ideal for eating with your hands, such as *croquetas*, *chipirones* and *pimientos de padrón*. Then comes a selection of cold meats, tortillas, seafood and meat, and you can finish with either a crema catalana or a Santiago tart.

While staunchly British, Sam and Eddie have a mother who is half Spanish and they regularly holidayed on Mallorca when they were young, as well as spending some formative time in Spain – Eddie in Madrid and Sam in Barcelona. They are supported in this venture by Basque-born head chef Nieves Barragán Mohacho. The menu has a strong but not exclusively Basque influence. They do not take reservations at any of the locations, with the exception of larger groups for the private dining space. You might need to queue to get a seat, but it will be worth the wait (PP).

Worst for...
queuing

Bao – steamed Taiwanese buns

Hoppers – inspired by Sri Lanka
and Tamil Nadu

Padella – phenomenal value-for-
money pasta

Barshu 28 Frith Street, W1D 5LF

020 7287 6688 www.barshurestaurant.co.uk

We urge you to call seven or eight friends and arrange to meet for dinner at Barshu as soon as possible. We suggest a large table so that you can taste and enjoy many of the varied dishes. The wide-ranging menu includes traditional Chengdu street snacks with descriptions such as 'numbing and hot eel strips' and 'pock-marked Old Woman's bean curd'.

Barshu specialize in food from the Chinese province of Sichuan, with Fuchsia Dunlop, the highly rated author of *Sichuan Cookery*, as their consultant. The Barshu team have also opened Bashan, just across the road, which is equally good and probably better suited to smaller groups.

Blacklock 24 Great Windmill Street, W1D 7LG

020 3441 6996 www.theblacklock.com

Vegetarians stay away! Especially at lunch on Sundays when they say that the roasts are 'almost as good as Mum's'. They offer individual beef, lamb and pork options, all roasted over an English oak fire, or you can go for their spectacular mixed roast that includes all three. It is all served with Yorkshire puddings, potatoes roasted in duck fat and bone marrow gravy. And if this wasn't enough, they've also got a small list of cocktails for £5 each! The music is loud and, on the day that I visited, the crowd was young and certainly up for a fun lunch – all this in a basement in Soho. Midweek, it is all chops – skinny chops and big chips – at a very reasonable price. If you like Hawksmoor, but think it a bit pricey and that it perhaps takes itself a little too seriously, then you'll love Blacklock (PP).

Above right
The dining room at the rear of Bocca di Lupo with Haidee Becker art.
Right **Shaved radish and celeriac salad with pomegranate, Pecorino and truffle oil at Bocca di Lupo.**
Left **Formerly a seedy corner of Soho, Archer Street is now full of restaurants and bars.**

Left and right **Inside Bocca di Lupo.** You'll need to arrive early to snag one of the stools at the dining counter. Below **Gelupo, opposite Bocca di Lupo, has some of the best ice cream in London.**

Bocca di Lupo 12 Archer Street, W1D /BB
020 7734 2223 www.boccadilupo.com
&
Gelupo 7 Archer Street, W1D 7AU
020 7287 5555 www.gelupo.com

Bocca di Lupo ('mouth of the wolf') is all about authentic regional Italian food, not from one specific part of Italy, but from each of its 20 regions. Most people who are familiar with Italy will know that before they were unified some 150 years ago, each of the country's 20 independent states had its own food culture. The menu lists the source of each recipe and its inspiration, whether it be *buristo* (blood salami) from Toscana, octopus and celery salad from Sicilia, broad bean tortelloni with ricotta from Puglia, or dishes from Lazio, Calabria, Veneto, Campania, and so on. It's all a big geography lesson, with delicious food to boot. The wine list is also pure Italian and offers a Grand Tour of the key wine-producing regions.

Chef patron Jacob Kenedy gleaned his knowledge of Italian regional food from a sabbatical spent touring the country. With partner Victor Hugo he has created one of the most interesting Italian restaurants in London, demonstrating a full appreciation of the credo 'less is more', and of the essential truth that good Italian food is inherently simple. Dining at the bar counter is a great treat for anyone who enjoys watching skilled chefs at work.

During the course of our 'research' for this book, we visited several ice cream parlours, as they used to be known. We can confirm that Gelupo, the gelato offshoot of Bocca located opposite, is by far the best and the ice cream is supreme.

Brasserie Zedel 20 Sherwood Street, W1F 7ED

020 7734 4888 www.brasseriezedel.com

This is possibly one of the largest and most jaw-dropping beaux-arts/art-deco dining rooms in London. It is all based on the idea of a 1930s Parisian grand brasserie, in particular Bouillon Chartier, where the prices are always remarkably attractive. The food is unashamedly classic French, with absolutely no attempt to modernize. On the three occasions that I have visited, I've had their wonderful *choucroute* – the current menu offers three different types but I always opt for the Alsacienne version. Zedel also includes an American bar, where you can have a pre-dinner martini and a live music venue called Crazy Coqs (PP).

Dean Street Townhouse 69–71 Dean Street, W1D 3SE

020 7434 1775 www.deanstreettownhouse.com

Many of the clubs, bars and restaurants in the Soho House group – of which Dean Street Townhouse is one – tend to under-deliver on the food and service, while over-supplying in terms of the clientele and the sexiness of the atmosphere. This seems to be the first establishment to deliver on all fronts, while the restaurant floor and kitchen also seem to be managed in a professional manner. A blissful fusion.

The look of the hotel is very interesting, in that it promotes a style that has otherwise generally been banished to the annals of design history. The look has been lent a few cool credentials in the form of 60 unique pieces of modern art by respected names.

The hotel bedrooms are quite small (the smallest are modestly described as 'tiny'), but if it's location that counts, you can't be more central than the middle of Soho. The slender outside terrace is one of the hottest locations in town – good for everything from breakfast to late-night drinks.

Smoked Haddock Soufflé with Chive Butter Sauce

Serves 4

For the soufflé

150g (5oz) skinless smoked haddock
175ml (6fl oz) milk
25g (1oz) butter, plus extra to coat the moulds
25g (1oz) flour
35g (1½oz) Keen's Cheddar, grated
35g (1½oz) Parmesan cheese, grated
¼ teaspoon salt
nutmeg, to taste
5g (¼oz) anchovy sauce
¼ teaspoon Tabasco
1 teaspoon Worcestershire sauce
8g (generous ¼oz) English mustard
2 egg yolks
4 egg whites

For the chive butter sauce

600ml (1 pint) white wine
75g (3oz) shallots, finely sliced
75g (3oz) leeks, chopped
½ garlic clove
¼ bay leaf
small pinch thyme leaves, picked
small pinch white peppercorns
250ml (8fl oz) double cream
400g (13oz) butter, diced
English mustard, to taste
finely chopped chives, to taste
salt and pepper

To make the soufflé, place the smoked haddock in a baking dish, pour over the milk and and simmer over a gentle heat for 30 minutes. Strain, keep the haddock to one side and chill the milk.

In a saucepan, melt the butter over a medium heat, add the flour and cook, stirring, for 2–3 minutes. Gradually add the milk to the flour mixture to form a smooth, thick sauce. Pour the sauce into a large bowl and add the salt and nutmeg to taste. Flake the haddock into large pieces and add to the mixture. Add the Cheddar and mix, then add the condiments and egg yolks, mixing well again.

In a clean bowl, whisk the egg whites until they form medium peaks, then gently fold them into the fish mixture.

Brush 4 individual 150 ml (¼-pint) plastic pudding moulds with soft butter, then line with the grated Parmesan and tap out any excess. Fill the moulds three-quarters full with the soufflé mixture (to the line of the mould), place in a deep tray and fill it with water to come three-quarters of the way up the sides of the moulds. Bake in a preheated oven, 180°C (350°F), Gas Mark 4, for 13 minutes.

Serve straight away, or chill and store in the moulds in the refrigerator. If chilled, serve by turning out the moulds on to a baking tray lined with a sheet of greaseproof paper and reheat in the oven at 180°C (350°F), Gas Mark 4, for 13 minutes. Check the soufflés are hot in the middle before serving.

To make the chive butter sauce, reduce the white wine with the shallots, leek, garlic, bay leaf, thyme and peppercorns. Add the cream and reduce for 10 minutes. Remove from the heat and slowly whisk in the butter. The sauce should be of a light coating consistency. Leave off the heat to infuse for 20 minutes, then pass through a fine sieve. Keep warm, and when ready to serve add the English mustard to taste and chopped chives.

To serve the soufflés, turn each on to a warm plate and spoon over generous amounts of the chive butter sauce.

The Delaunay 55 Aldwych, WC2B 4BB

020 7499 8558   www.thedelaunay.com

Most Londoners recognize Chris Corbin and Jeremy King as possibly the best restaurateurs in our great city. I think this is their best restaurant. It is modelled on a grand European café that is open all day, from breakfast all the way to a late post-theatre supper. The location on the edge of the City and the fringe of the West End's Theatreland attracts two distinctively different types of clientele throughout the day. You can be assured of excellent service and a wonderful atmosphere. It is always good to make a reservation in advance, but often this is difficult due to the restaurant's popularity. On three separate occasions over the last year, I've tried to make a booking and no tables were available but nevertheless I just turned up and they very courteously found a table for us (PP).

Left and above **Bookings aren't always necessary for bar tables at The Delaunay.**

Right **The cake table sitting on a beautifully polished marble floor at The Delaunay.**

Left **The ground floor café at Les Deux Salons.**
Right **Paris Breast at the Left-Bank styled Les Deux Salons.**

From left **Asparagus and artichoke salad, game pithivier and dover sole at Les Deux Salons.**

Left **Tarte Tatin à deux is always on the menu at Les Deux Salons.**

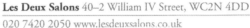

Les Deux Salons 40–2 William IV Street, WC2N 4DD
020 7420 2050 www.lesdeuxsalons.co.uk

At the risk of being accused of a self-serving bias, promoting another one of our own restaurants, we won't say too much about Les Deux Salons. Located in the heart of Theatreland, it is a large space, with two main rooms, each with its own distinctively different setting and atmosphere. Each room shares the same large menu that focuses on the long-established Parisian bistro and brasserie classics. For me, it is the perfect place to enjoy a tray of oysters followed by a choucroute garnie or perhaps entrecôte frites followed by a tarte tatin (PP).

We're not aiming to do anything new or inventive, but we do want to deliver a generous plate of food and decent glass or carafe of wine, all at modest prices, in a setting that we think is redolent of a subtly updated version of the Left Bank eating houses of the 1920s and 1930s.

Praised by *Evening Standard* restaurant critic Faye Maschler as 'an authentic Parisian brasserie' and 'a triumph', that I had at last achieved after a lifetime of effort. I agree with her (TC).

Eneko at One Aldwych One Aldwych, 1 Aldwych, London WC2B 4BZ
020 7300 0300 www.eneko.london

Having visited Eneko Atxa's three-star Michelin restaurant just outside Bilbao, I have great respect for his food here in London. It is all rather experimental and inventive, which seems to be the Basque way, but it does also deliver some really good flavours (PP).

I'm not quite sure about the design of the place (TC).

Above **Just some of the quirky table-top items at Eneko.** Left **It seems the conventional is unacceptable at Eneko – everything must be challenged.**

Right **Edurne Martin Delgado, head chef at Eneko.**

Basque Fried Hake with Peppers

Serves 4

2kg (4lb 8oz) red peppers
4 x 120g (4½oz) hake fillets
20g (¾oz) plain flour
30g tempura flour (bought ready-mixed)
3 tablespoons water
a little olive oil
sea salt flakes

Preheat the oven to 180°C (350°F), Gas Mark 4. Place the peppers on a baking tray and bake for 30 minutes. Remove the stems and seeds, then purée the peppers in (ideally) a food mill, or a food processor. (Press them through a sieve for an extra-smooth sauce if you like, but it's not necessary.) Season with salt to taste.

Season the fish fillets with salt and dredge with the plain flour.

Mix the tempura flour and measured water in a small bowl, add the fish fillets, and turn to coat them on all sides.

Heat some oil in a large frying pan over a medium heat and add the fish. Fry for 2 minutes, then turn and fry for 2 minutes on the other side.

Divide the baked pepper sauce between plates and place the hake fillets on top. We like to add a little parsley emulsion for decoration.

Above **The bar and ground-floor dining room at Frenchie attracts a cool young crowd, unlike many other places in Covent Garden.**

Eneko Atxa

London is a city with such a diverse mix of cultures that has seen a huge growth and interest in different cuisine experiences in the last few years. It's a city where people are constantly searching for something new and different, which is why it's so special.

Restaurateur, Eneko

Left, above **Preparing desserts at Frenchie.** Left **You can dine directly adjacent to the open kitchen pass in the basement at Frenchie.**

Above **Gregory Marchand has brought some much-needed modernization to French cuisine.**

Four Seasons 12 Gerrard Street, W1D 5PR

020 7494 0870 www.fs-restaurants.co.uk

In the past we have been dismissive of the innumerable restaurants in Chinatown because of their overuse of MSG. Four Seasons is an exception, however. The staff may not be very welcoming (this is pretty standard in Chinatown) and you should not be deterred by the plastic laminated menus with photographs of the food. The house speciality is roast duck, which is good, but we recommend something that isn't on the menu. As soon as you are seated, simply ask for the three meats (duck, chicken and barbecued pork) on rice, plus the Chinese broccoli with garlic sauce. The attitude of the staff will change, and they will bring you some delicious food. Look around and you will notice that everybody is eating the same.

If you are feeling particularly ambitious after the Four Seasons and up for a late night, we also recommend the Experimental Cocktail Club at 13a Gerrard Street – open until 3am and very plush.

Frenchie 16 Henrietta Street, WC2E 8QH

020 7836 4422 www.frenchiecoventgarden.com

Named after Gregory Marchand's sobriquet while he was working in London at Fifteen with Jamie Oliver (before that he spent long periods at the Savoy and Mandarin Oriental), this modern bistro follows Gregory's success with the original Frenchie in the 2nd arrondissement in Paris. The space is light and airy and the menu includes dishes from Gregory's travels around the world, but obviously has more than a few French roots. It's not a particularly ground-breaking menu but it is capable of being loveable and has some great individual dishes. The lunch menu is extremely good value for money, but we can't say the same for the drinks.

I happen to have visited this place twice in two weeks and on both occasions I spotted notable Michelin-starred chefs dining at other tables – together they amounted to five stars. This surely must give you some indication of the appeal of the place. Personally, I prefer the original Frenchie in rue du Nil, but this London outpost is certainly well received (PP).

Left **Frenchie himself, Gregory Marchand, splits his time between London and Paris.** Right **Wild berries tart being portioned at Frenchie.**

Gauthier Soho 21 Romilly Street, W1D 5AF
020 7494 3111 www.gauthiersoho.co.uk

When Richard Corrigan decamped to upmarket premises in Mayfair, we feared that Alexis Gauthier would struggle to come close to the excellent reputation of his predecessor on this site. We shouldn't have worried as this new offering is even more popular – and deservedly so. Completely different from the gutsy Irish flavours that Richard delivered, it is more refined and delicate. Everything has been lightened up, from the décor to the waiters' white tunic jackets. The food, also much lighter, is now (as they put it) 'vegecentric'. Alexis is very earnest when it comes to making vegetables the centre of attention. The level of technique and skill in this kitchen is very high: Alexis has previously worked with Alain Ducasse, and it shows in his food.

Alexis was ahead of the curve when he started to list the calorie count for each item on the menu, which is quite a departure for a fine dining destination of this calibre, but we can appreciate why he wants to do it. This is clearly a further indication that we are all thinking more about the food we consume and the impact it has on our health and wellbeing.

This style of food is increasingly appealing to me, and I am constantly impressed by the cooking at Gauthier. In fact, I would go so far as to say that it is the restaurant of the star-chasing variety that has most impressed me over recent years. They are usually so infuriating, whereas I really think that Alexis is doing something interesting here, and that he has an admirable respect for classic French techniques and the key ingredients that should be associated with this level of dining. The service was exceptional and the wine list is also very impressive (PP).

Above right **Gauthier occupies an old Soho townhouse.**
Left **One of the small dining rooms on the ground floor at Gauthier.**
Right **Alexis Gauthier has been ahead of the curve when it comes to light and healthy Michelin-standard food.**

Left and right
Head down to the bar at HIX Soho for a fun night and some brilliant cocktails. Below **The ground-floor dining room and bar at HIX.**

Great Queen Street 32 Great Queen Street, WC2B 5AA

020 7242 0622   www.greatqueenstreetrestaurant.co.uk

This place is all about great, no-nonsense cooking and nothing else. For this reason alone it is very loveable. To describe the interior as utilitarian would be flattering. Don't go to Great Queen Street for physical comfort: go for the reassurance that a slow-roasted joint of meat can bring. No gimmicks, no fuss, just great seasonal ingredients prepared by self-confident cooks. They also seem to specialize in great sharing dishes, such as duck cassoulet for two or ox flank with horseradish or even a seven-hour lamb shoulder. You can make a reservation here, unlike at its sister establishment, the Anchor & Hope (see page 284).

HIX Soho 66–70 Brewer Street, W1F 9UP

020 7292 3518   www.hixsoho.co.uk

Compared with Mark Hix's first restaurant near Smithfield, this serves a slightly smarter version of his trademark modern British cooking. The menu boasts several seldom-seen British ingredients and dishes; Mark is very good at resurrecting long-forgotten foods and highlighting specialist regional food producers. You can be assured of excellent provenance across the menu, in particular the great oysters, steaks and game. If you want a proper gutsy Sunday lunch with roast beef and Yorkshire pudding, you can't go wrong here.

This restaurant is also known for its art, and particularly for the mobiles that hang from the ceiling. The roll call of British artists who show their work at Mark's restaurant is testimony to his many friendships with the art community.

Mark's Bar, below the restaurant, is one of the best cocktail bars in town.

193

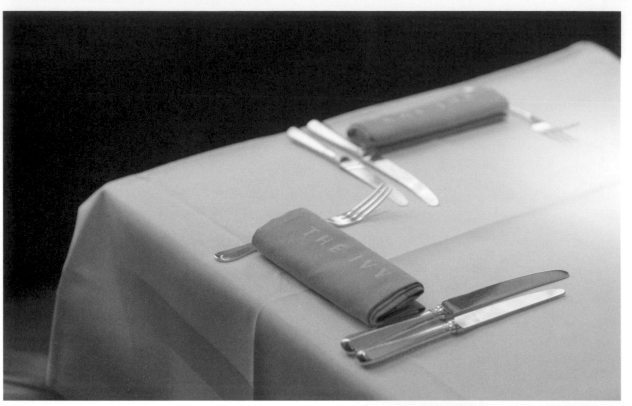

194

Hoppers 49 Frith Street, W1D 4SG

www.hopperslondon.com no telephone, no reservations

Ahead of a holiday to Sri Lanka, I was desperate to visit Hoppers before jumping on the plane. However, this is another one of those infuriating no-reservation joints where you are expected to queue for your supper. No thanks. On my return from Colombo, I made a special effort and visited off-peak. It was worth the inconvenience. As far as I can see, Hoppers is an authentic Sri Lankan experience all based around one of their most iconic foods, the hopper. Unlike Sri Lanka, however, they've got really great cocktails (PP).

So, what's a hopper? It is a little bowl-shaped spongy pancake that is made from fermented rice and coconut batter (gluten and dairy-free, some will like to note) that is cooked in a special wok-like pan called an appachatti. You eat them with curry or perhaps an egg. You also get string hoppers, which are steamed handmade rice flour noodles pressed into string pancakes – all great for soaking up a mild curry. They're associated with street food and breakfast in Sri Lanka and are at the heart of the food culture across this part of the subcontinent.

Robert Reid

Opposite and below
The Ivy management have always been protective of their image and photos of the inside of the restaurant were strictly controlled – it has since had a major facelift.

The Ivy 1–5 West Street, WC2H 9NQ
020 7836 4751   www.the-ivy.co.uk

About ten years ago, Richard Caring bought The Ivy from Chris Corbin and Jeremy King and there were immediately prophecies of doom and the end of an era etc. etc. etc. However, this has certainly not been the case. And, just about a year ago there was a very bold refurbishment that, again, everybody suggested would be the death knell. In fact, this major overhaul has probably given The Ivy another 50 years of life. Now, there is a large central bar, and the space seems to have been increased, with much better dining positions. The old spirit has been retained and also glamorously added to.

Everybody talks about the celebrity clientele and how difficult it is to get a table at this legendary restaurant, but underneath all the glitz lies an extremely well-managed business serving good and reassuring food. The menu is massive and almost more than comprehensive. In fact, there is too much for us to comment on here.

The main front-of-house players are still at The Ivy, and this surely contributes to the success of the service. The calibre of the managers and waiting staff eclipses that of most other restaurants: they seem to communicate with each other at some telepathic level, and their skill at the table is undeniable. I often choose The Ivy when I know that the staff have to be particularly discreet and you can also rely on them providing quick service at breakfast and lunch, often not possible at even the best places.

Japanese Knife Company 8 Greek Street, W1D 4DG
020 3214 0066   www.japaneseknifecompany.com

If you want to be a serious chef or think you're of Michelin standard when cooking at home, you've got to have the very best kitchen knives. This bijou shop specializing in Japan's finest blades is a must-visit, and they have wonderful, classic designs (TC). For over 1,000 years Japan has been at the cutting edge of kitchen knives and the culmination of this experience can be purchased here. They also sharpen your knives and run courses on how to use them.

J Sheekey 28–34 St Martin's Court, WC2N 4AL
020 7240 2565   www.j-sheekey.co.uk

The service at this fish and seafood restaurant is really very good – grown-up and perceptive in manner, with seasoned waiting staff practising non-verbal communication with an 'I've seen it all before' confidence. Sometimes service is about more than just delivering food and drink to diners' tables – an important point fully appreciated by the front-of-house team at J Sheekey. You can also be sure that the kitchen will do a great job for you. The menu is a delight, with all manner of piscine pleasures, from a small selection of caviar (for absolute decadence, showing off or just the flavour) to a full array of fresh fish, crustaceans and bivalves from British shores and seas, plus a few from more distant waters. The fish pie is a perennial favourite, together with serious Dover sole, lobster thermidor and dressed crab. J Sheekey has recently expanded next door to include a proper horseshoe-shaped oyster bar. Enjoying a *plateau de fruits de mer* while seated at the bar and watching the chefs at work is one of the most pleasurable dining experiences in London.

196

NOPI 21–2 Warwick Street, W1B 5NE
020 7494 9584   www.nopi-restaurant.com

A soft blend of strong flavours from the sunny Mediterranean, Middle East and Asia has been carefully and eruditely brought together at NOPI. The menu is divided into four key sections – Veg, Fish, Meat and Sweets, and has been designed for sharing with friends (although it does work equally well when not sharing). Each section includes a choice of about six items, and they recommend three savoury dishes per person. It all works rather well.

NOPI (an acronym of 'north of Piccadilly') is the brainchild of Yotam Ottolenghi. Don't expect the trademark meringues in the window and the beautifully presented food displays that you find in his mini-chain of London delis and cafés, however. This is an all-day brasserie, but not in the traditional sense. There is a fresh and modern approach to everything here. The interior is a happy and unusual combination of white and brass that feels fresh and uplifting, with great attention to detail and some charming elements, such as the mirrors in the toilets, the large brass flower vases with pretty blooms and the brass 1920s-style doors that originally graced the portals of Harvey Nichols.

Sitting at either of the two large communal tables in the basement is a more informal experience and great fun: you can watch the kitchen staff toil away and admire the shelves of ingredients. The space doubles up as a dry store for the kitchen, and given the style of food they serve, there is lots to see and admire.

Layo Paskin

"

I live only five minutes' walk from Broadway Market – I'm there every Saturday, either with a full food mission or just to buy a fried mackerel sandwich or catfish banh mi – so it's hands down, my favourite, and luckily local, food market.

Co-owner, The Palomar

Above **The ground-floor dining room at NOPI, with brass detailing on a plain all-white backdrop.** Right **The basement tables at NOPI look directly into the kitchen.**

The Palomar 34 Rupert Street, W1D 6DN

020 7439 8777   www.thepalomar.co.uk

If you're looking for a dining experience that involves a fantastic atmosphere and pumping vibe, plus some of the most exciting food in London, you've got to head to The Palomar. Just reading about their food makes you hungry. They say that the menu is all about modern-day Jerusalem, inspired by Spain, North Africa and the Levant – a wonderful cultural mix and total YUM. On both occasions that I've visited, I perched at the rather cramped bar, directly overlooking the kitchen. Somehow, the elbow wrestling and balancing of each of your plates and drinks in a such small space all add to the frisson. The lack of space extends to the kitchen, which seems impossibly small, given the calibre of the food that they are producing. The kitchen includes a fantastic Josper oven. We have a few of these internal BBQ-style ovens that reach over 400°C (752°F) in some of our kitchens. They are amazing at speed-cooking ingredients while also imparting a lovely smokiness. At Palomar, they cook octopus in the Josper – to amazing effect, especially when it is served with chickpea masabacha and burnt aubergine. Thanks to the inspirational Yotam Ottolenghi, we are all now familiar with za'atar, sumac, labneh, tahini, harissa and the like and they are elevated to a new stratospheric level in the hands of the Palomar chefs. Even simple things like a *fattoush* salad become sublime in their hands. And make sure that you try their *shakshukit*, their deconstructed kebab with minced beef and lamb, yogurt, cured lemon and harissa. The other wonderful feature about Palomar is their fun and characterful management and staff. They all seem to be loving their workplace and are a key ingredient in making this such a lively place to be (PP).

Above **Dine while watching the chefs in their extremely cramped open kitchen at The Palomar.** Left **The menu is also the place setting at The Palomar.**

Above, left and right **The bar and kitchen at The Palomar merge together and diners at the counter can enjoy the banter behind it.**

Left **The atmosphere among the staff at The Palomar is infectious.** Right **Head chef Tomer Amedi.**

Octo-hummus

Serves 6

For the octopus

800g–1kg (1lb 12oz–2lb 4oz) octopus, inside cleaned (Spanish ones are great)
2 small onions, cut in half
1 tomato, cut into quarters
1 tsp black peppercorns
1 small unwaxed orange, cut into quarters
2 bay leaves
2 sprigs of thyme
1 unwaxed lemon, cut in half
1 unwaxed lime, cut in half (optional)
generous glug of red wine (optional)
1 leek, sliced (optional)
a few leafy celery sticks (optional)

For the tomato confit

18 cherry tomatoes
1 garlic clove, peeled
½ green chilli
125ml (4fl oz) olive oil
sea salt flakes and freshly ground black pepper

For the parsley dressing

½ bunch of parsley
1 tablespoon cured lemon paste (optional)
1 garlic clove, peeled
3 tablespoons lemon juice
pinch of toasted and ground cumin seeds
50ml (2fl oz) olive oil
50ml (2fl oz) rapeseed oil

For the chickpea masabacha

200g (7oz) dried chickpeas, soaked in 2 litres (3½ pints) cold water overnight
½ teaspoon bicarbonate of soda
1 garlic clove, peeled
½ green chilli, tail trimmed but left whole
handful of chopped parsley
handful of chopped coriander
squeeze of lemon juice
1 tablespoon Parsley Dressing (see above)

For the garnish

baba ganoush
1 small onion, cut into 8 wedges
4 tablespoons olive oil

For the octopus, first freeze your sea creature for 24 hours, then defrost it, which will help to tenderize it. Preheat your oven to 150°C (300°F), Gas Mark 2. Put the octopus in a baking tray and add the rest of the ingredients except the red wine. Cover the baking tray with baking parchment and then foil. Bake the octopus for 1½ hours. Increase the oven temperature to 160°C (325°F), Gas Mark 3 and cook for another 1½ hours – don't add any liquid. When you unveil the octopus, you will see that it's swimming in its own juices.

If, however, you want an octopus with a dark red colour, add some red wine for the last 20 minutes of the cooking time. Take the beast out of the tray and leave it to cool.

If you are going for steaks, make sure you work with a warmish octopus. Place a double layer of clingfilm on a chopping board, but leave the clingfilm attached to the roll.

Separate the tentacles from the head (discard the inside of the head and the beak). Place 4 tentacles in a row, thick part on your left hand side. Slice up the head and lay the slices on top of the tentacles. On top of this, lay the other 4 tentacles, thick part on your right hand side. Start rolling up the octopus tightly in the clingfilm into a sausage shape, using as much clingfilm as you need. With each rolling motion, squeeze the air out to the sides (imagine you're stretching the tentacles). Once it is all tightly rolled up, poke a few holes in the clingfilm with a skewer — we need all the air to be released from the sausage so that it will be nice and tight. Wipe the sausage with damp kitchen paper to clean it, then wrap again with more clingfilm. Chill in the fridge overnight, then cut into 6 steaks and remove the clingfilm. Alternatively, go freestyle and just roughly chop the octopus.

To make the tomato confit, preheat the oven to 140°C (275°F), Gas Mark 1. Place all the ingredients in a deep but small baking tray (make sure your tomatoes are nicely submerged in the oil) and bake for 2–3 hours. Remove from the oven and leave to cool. You can store the confit in the fridge for up to a week — transfer to a sterilized airtight container or jar and keep covered with oil.

To make the parsley dressing, blend all the ingredients except the oils together in a blender until well blended. While continuing to blend, add the oils gradually. Check the seasoning. This dressing is excellent with grilled fish and seafood.

To make the masabacha, drain and rinse the soaked chickpeas well, then place them in a saucepan with twice their volume of water. Simmer for 1 hour, skimming off any foam from time to time. Add the bicarbonate of soda, garlic and chilli, and cook for another 30 minutes to 1 hour, continuing to skim. The chickpeas need to be soft but not overcooked and mushy. Strain, reserving 125ml (4fl oz) of the cooking liquid along with the garlic and the chilli. Chop the chilli roughly.

Place the chickpeas in a saucepan with the garlic, chilli and reserved cooking liquid. Bring to a simmer and roughly mush with a fork, then add the herbs, lemon juice and the spoonful of dressing. Check for seasoning (it needs to be sour, a bit hot and spicy), adding salt to taste, and set aside. (This also goes brilliantly simply with yogurt and some harissa.)

Preheat the grill to its highest setting. Meanwhile, place the octopus steaks or chopped octopus and onion wedges on a baking tray, season with the olive oil, salt and pepper and bring to room temperature. Grill for 2–3 minutes on each side until nice and golden brown (the onion should be a bit charred), then remove from the oven and dress with the rest of the parsley dressing.

To serve, divide the baba ganoush between 6 serving plates and top up with a couple of spoonfuls of masabacha. Place 3 confit cherry tomatoes on each plate, divide the octopus and onions between the plates and, finally, garnish with the parsley dressing.

Recipe featured in *The Palomar Cookbook*, published by Mitchell Beazley

Malabi

Serves 6

For the malabi

500ml (18fl oz) milk
150ml (5fl oz/¼ pint) whipping cream
50g (1¾oz) granulated sugar
40g (1½oz) cornflour
4 teaspoons good-quality rosewater

For the raspberry coulis

150g (5½oz) raspberries, plus an extra 15–20 to garnish
40g (1½oz) icing sugar

For the pistachio brittle (can be replaced with 40g/1½oz toasted and chopped pistachio nuts)

25g (1oz) pistachio nuts
50g (1¾oz) caster sugar

For the coconut meringue (can be replaced with 20g/¾oz toasted desiccated coconut)

2 egg whites
2 tablespoons water
100g (3½oz) granulated sugar
50g (1¾oz) desiccated coconut

For the crispy kataifi

100g (3½oz) kataifi pastry, shredded baklava pastry fingers or similar
25g (1oz) icing sugar, sifted
50g (1¾oz) unsalted butter, melted
2 tablespoons rosewater

To make the malabi, set aside 125ml (4fl oz) of the milk. Pour the rest into a heavy-based saucepan with the cream and sugar, and simmer, stirring gently, until the sugar has dissolved. Add the cornflour to the milk you have set aside along with the rosewater, and stir until thoroughly blended and there are no lumps of cornflour left – the best tool to use here is your fingers, as it's the only way to ensure that the malabi has a smooth texture. When the creamy milk boils, give the cornflour a final stir before adding it to the saucepan of creamy milk. Simmer over a low heat until the mixture begins to thicken, stirring constantly to make sure there are no lumps – this should take no longer than 2 minutes.

Once thickened, pour the mixture either into 4 individual ramekins, or a large bowl if you're going family style. Cover with clingfilm and leave to cool to room temperature, then chill in the fridge for a couple of hours. The malabi can be kept in the fridge for up to 3 days. Now make the toppings.

To make the raspberry coulis, stir the raspberries and sugar together in a bain-marie – a heatproof bowl or pan set over a pan of barely simmering water – and cook until soft. This can also be done in a microwave-proof bowl in the microwave on a low heat, but make sure you cover the bowl with clingfilm so that you don't have a raspberry explosion in your microwave. Pass through a fine sieve or, if you prefer it chunkier, you can leave it as is. The coulis will keep in an airtight container in the fridge for up to 5 days.

To make the pistachio brittle, preheat the oven to 180°C (350°F), Gas Mark 4. Spread the pistachios out on a baking tray and toast in the oven for 7 minutes. To make the caramel for the pistachio brittle, heat a heavy-based nonstick pan over a low heat and add the sugar in an even layer. The most important thing here is not to stir: if you're worried about burning, add a couple of drops of water, but otherwise let it be. Once all the sugar has melted and you have a golden caramel, taken the pan off the heat, stir in the toasted pistachios and then transfer to a tray lined with baking parchment. Leave to cool completely, then chop finely. (This makes an amazing ice cream topping, too.) The pistachio brittle can be kept in an airtight container for up to 2 weeks.

To make the coconut meringue, preheat your oven to 140°C (275°F), Gas Mark 1 and line a baking tray with baking parchment. Place the egg whites in the bowl of an electric mixer fitted with a whisk attachment and beat to soft peaks. Put the measured water and the sugar in a saucepan and heat until you have a syrup that reaches 121°C (250°F) on a cooking thermometer, then pour into the egg whites in a slow, steady stream while beating on a high speed. Once combined, spoon the mixture into a piping bag fitted with a 1cm (½-inch) plain piping nozzle.

Scatter the desiccated coconut in an even layer on a tray. Now pipe 1cm (½in) spheres of the meringue mixture on to the tray, rolling the balls to coat them in the lovely coconut shards. Transfer the coconut balls to the lined baking tray and bake for 1½ hours until nice and dry (every oven is different, so you may need another 30 minutes, just make sure the meringues are completely dry). You'll have rather more meringues than you need here, but whisking a smaller quantity of egg whites is tricky, and besides, you're going to be nibbling them anyway… or you can use them as a fairly unbeatable ice cream topping. The meringues will keep in an airtight container for up to 2 weeks.

To make the crispy kataifi, preheat the oven to 200°C (400°F), Gas Mark 6. Using your fingers, crumble the kataifi into a mixing bowl, add the icing sugar and mix to coat well. Pour in the melted butter and rosewater and mix again. Spread the mixture on to a baking sheet and bake for 12–15 minutes until it's a lovely golden colour and is nice and crispy. The nibbling risk factor is high with this, too, so I'd recommend you make it in double or triple quantities.

To assemble the dish, grab your malabi from the fridge, pour over some of the raspberry coulis, scatter with your toppings at whim, top with the extra raspberries and enjoy the explosion of flavours and textures.

Recipe featured in *The Palomar Cookbook*, published by Mitchell Beazley

Polpetto 11 Berwick Street, W1F 0PL

020 7439 8627 www.polpetto.co.uk

The little sister to Polpo (see below) started out with just 28 seats and was originally located above The French House, Soho's most iconic pub. However, it outgrew its first location and moved to new premises in Berwick Street, where there are 60 seats and a chef's table. Russell Norman continues to feed Soho nighthawks here with his version of Venetian osteria dishes. Think *cicchetti*, *pizzette* and so on – everything is small, from the plates to the prices, and add this to a massively good atmosphere, you've got a great night out.

Polpo 41 Beak Street, W1F 9SB

020 7734 4479 www.polpo.co.uk

Russell Norman is the new king of Soho. He boasts an unimpeachable résumé, having managed a range of impressive restaurants, including Zuma, and also held the top front-of-house job in the capital when he was operations director for Caprice Holdings. But all that is behind him, and he is now Soho's leading restaurateur. Russell and his business partner have launched a completely new style of eatery for London: a bacaro, a type of wine bar on the Venetian model, specializing in *cicchetti*, or easy to eat snacks. At Polpo this means anchovy and chickpea *crostino*, artichoke and prosciutto, chopped chicken liver *crostino*, *arancini* or potato and Parmesan *crochetta*. All are great, and ideal with either a Bellini or an Aperol or Campari spritz. You can follow them with a range of *pizzette*, *piadina* and *panino*, then cheese, *fritto misto*, prawn and monk's beard risotto, calamari, then cotechino sausage, calf's liver or maybe a simple plate of cold meats. Finish with an *affogato* or maybe *tiramisu*.

One of the key reasons why Russell and his Polpo brand, now at several locations across London, reign supreme is that he delivers two main attractive features at his dining rooms: a great atmosphere that is based on informality and fun, plus great value for money. His menus are structured so that you don't need to spend a lot but could easily do so if you wanted.

One of Russell's original touches is the style and look of his restaurants. They are all stripped back to basics, with exposed walls and beams, tiled ceilings and no fuss or bother, save for one or two fancy lights, he has mastered the blessed speakeasy style that so many try and so few get right.

The 18th-century building on Beak Street was once home to Giovanni Antonio Canal (1697–1768), better known as the painter Canaletto, celebrated for his *vedute* of Venice. You couldn't make it up.

201

Above left **The cosy dining room in Polpetto.**
Left **Spinach, chickpea and chilli bruschetta at Polpetto.**

Portrait Restaurant at the National Portrait Gallery

St Martin's Place, WC2H 0HE 020 7312 2490 www.npg.org.uk

The recent arrival of Matthew Harris, formerly of Bibendum, as the chef at this restaurant with a fantastic view has given it a fillip that encourages a return visit, as well as a rather special gallery next door.

Princi 135 Wardour Street, W1F 0UT

020 7478 8888 www.princi.co.uk

This truly impressive Italian bakery and café is a joint venture by a famous Milanese bakery and Alan Yau. We can assure you that you won't be disappointed. The vast food displays set the pulse racing and the wood-oven-cooked pizza and endless other baked delights are perfect at any time of the day. Unmissable.

Savoy Grill Savoy Hotel, Strand, WC2R 0EU

020 7592 1600 www.gordonramsay.com/thesavoygrill

The Ramsay team have returned the menu to something quite sensible, a 'proper' grill menu – going back to the good old days, as many might say. It includes an extensive selection of steaks and meats cooked on the wood-charcoal grill, with over a dozen options – everything from rib-eye to lamb cutlets, and pork chop to a mixed grill – simply grilled and offered with a choice of sauces. The fancy Ramsay hallmarks have been dropped in favour of some good hearty food, with all the ingredients displaying exceptional provenance and conditioning.

Social Eating House 58 Poland Street, W1F 7NS

020 7993 3251 www.socialeatinghouse.com/

This is another one of (new) super-chef Jason Atherton's joints that proves to be a good location for a lively night out, with some more than decent food and great service. On the first floor, The Blind Pig bar cocktails all include a twist or quirk. On the ground floor, it is informal dining in a very dark and moody setting. You must try their wild mushrooms on toast, served in a plastic bag that is cut open at the table. The umami flavours of the mushrooms are properly extenuated, which proves to be a wonderful improvement on an already very good dish.

Best for... solid & reliable

Chez Bruce – worth the journey to Wandsworth

The Ivy – go to the original one on West Street, definitely not others; the service is super proficient

Spring – a proper grown-up restaurant with confident food, and similarly minded clientele

Left **The distinctive uniforms at Spring.** Right **Interior wall detail from one of the garden-themed private dining rooms at Spring.** Below left **Spring is favourably located in the majestic rooms of the now fully restored 19th-century Somerset House.**

Spring Somerset House, Lancaster Place, WC2R 1LA
020 3011 0115   www.springrestaurant.co.uk

This has got to be one of London's most elegant and sophisticated restaurants, and beautifully designed (TC). Everything about the setting (part of the wonderful 19th-century Somerset House) – the dining room, the furniture, the tableware, the people, the menu, the drinks list, the flowers and, of course, the culinary pedigree of its inspiration – is sheer class. Among those that know a thing or two about food and restaurants, Skye Gyngell (formerly head chef at Petersham Nurseries) is a highly admired chef and her menus at Spring are a joy to read and, of course, to dine from. They are highly seasonal, as you would expect, and also promote some of the finest ingredients that can be sourced from land and sea. These luxuries come at a price – wow, it is an expensive restaurant – but you can confidently walk away saying that you have enjoyed some form of value for money. It seems that this combination of sky(e)-high prices and an exercise in good taste is much in demand among a certain elements of London's cultured elite. On the two occasions I have dined at Spring there have been more than a few renowned 'faces' from London's arts and architecture scene also dining there. From talking with friends and customers at our own establishments, it's clear that Spring is recognized as the restaurant of choice for the unusual City types – those revelling in restrained quality. This is the place to entertain those with more than an wavering interest in the arts. Anyway, whatever the appeal, when you arrive, you'll be served by warm and friendly staff, and enjoy some delicious and perfectly judged food (PP).

Left **The fantastic scale of the various rooms at Spring makes it extra appealing.**

Andy Oliver

"It is the diversity that makes London so special – the choice and quality you can get now across a whole range of cuisines. Maybe it's partly to do with British cuisine not being as strong historically, so it gives more of a platform for other food cultures.

Chef patron, Som Saa

Above **High ceilings, commanding light, marble counters and stylish furniture at Spring help make it such an elegant dining room.**
Right **The garden-themed private dining room at Spring.**

Spuntino 61 Rupert Street, W1D 7PW

No telephone, no reservations

Moving away from the Venetian theme of Polpo and Polpetto (see page 201), Spuntino is all about New York's Lower East Side diner culture. While the food is different from that at Russell Norman's other joints, the speakeasy style is not. The entrance would be easy to miss if it weren't for the queues, and the inside is all about exposed tiles and bare filament lights without shades. The louche character of the surroundings all adds to the drama.

The menu includes 'sliders' – of-the-moment tiny burgers, mac and cheese, fried soft-shell crab; grits; a peanut butter sandwich and the much-talked-about truffled egg toast. Not exactly gourmet treats, but that's not the point: this den-like space is all about great cocktails, with food to soak up the booze.

There's no telephone and you can't make a reservation, but don't be deterred. There are just 27 bar stools and a popcorn machine. Go off peak: it's great fun.

Peter Gordon

"

When it comes to eating out, I love the tea room and dim sum at Yauatcha, the rice and wasabi tobiko hot pot at ROKA, and the Kiwiburger at GBK.

Head chef, The Providores

Above **The ultra-discreet Spuntino entrance.**
Left **Man about Soho: Russell Norman.**

This page **Inside Terroirs with its reclaimed French poster art and street signs.**

Terroirs 5 William VI Street, WC2N 4DW

020 7036 0660   www.terroirswinebar.com

One of the first and finest of the new-style wine bars (with great food, unlike their predecessors) that have become very popular in London over recent years, Terroirs is all about wine and food produced by artisans. All the key buzz words and beliefs are high on the agenda, with all the wines sustainably produced, organic, biodynamic, with minimal intervention and low or no sulphur dioxide, and many of them are unfiltered or unrefined.

There are two bars and two dining rooms to choose from, upstairs and downstairs, both pleasant in their own way. The menus are dominated by delicious French and Italian ingredients and recipes of renown. There is always a desirable selection of charcuterie, from the cured hams of the Pyrenees and Tuscany, via Lyon, to terrines and rillettes made in the Terroirs kitchens. The small plates selection offers a range of dishes from steak tartare to globe artichoke vinaigrette, salads, snails, smoked eel and much more. The main course *plats du jour* all complement the extensive wine list perfectly: try a bavette steak, confit de canard or maybe just a simple roast Landais chicken. The winter cassoulet is a full-on treat, and the boudin noir with a fried duck egg ambrosial. Cheese is taken very seriously, naturally, with perfectly conditioned specimens provided by Androuet of Spitalfields (see page 80).

As you would expect, the wine list – particularly the selection by the glass – is extensive and engaging. Doug Wregg, one of the directors of Les Caves de Pyrene, the wine merchants behind Terroirs, is an excellent writer, and his synopsis for each of the wines is a joy to read, offering insights into everything from the character of the wine maker to little history lessons and some humour, with a huge serving of savoir-faire.

Yauatcha 15–17 Broadwick Street, W1F 0DL

020 7494 8888   www.yauatcha.com

Another masterpiece created by Alan Yau, and now sold to the international Hakkasan group: an all-day contemporary Chinese teahouse and restaurant that has been a success since day one back in 2004. All manner of rumours circulated at the time about how the client had asked designer Christian Liaigre to change and adjust everything after it was already completed, but now this hardly matters, as the whole operation is such a complete and utter success in a very sexy setting. Upstairs is delightful, and the staff must surely wear the best uniforms in London, designed by Tim Yip, art director on the film *Crouching Tiger, Hidden Dragon*.

More places to visit in the area

Arigato Japanese Supermarket
48–50 Brewer Street, W1F 9TG
020 7287 1722
A great source for all manner of Japanese and Asian ingredients, from wasabi to special rice and vinegars, plus a decent range of sake. They also have a small in-store sushi bar.

Cây Tre
42–3 Dean Street, W1D 4QA
020 7317 9118
The best pho in Soho, plus the design of this French-Vietnamese cafe and cocktail bar is very cool.

Fernandez & Wells
43 Lexington Street, W1F 9AL
020 7734 1546 www.fernandezandwells.com
A mini-chain of three premises dotted around Soho, including an espresso bar and a simple café. Ultra-cool, great coffee.

Hummus Bros
88 Wardour Street, W1F OTJ
020 7734 1311 www.hbros.co.uk
We like Hummus Bros because Christian Mouysset and Ronen Givon, the two friends (not brothers) who set up the business, are devoted to fresh ingredients, flavour and simplicity. With an added dash of humour, the whole concept is slightly eccentric. 'Hummusychology' (their terminology) proffers interesting observations on ways of scooping your hummus with a choice of pitta and various toppings.

Kiln
58 Brewer Street, W1F 9TL
www.kilnsoho.com
A recently opened modern Thai joint that blends native UK ingredients with recipes from Yunnan, Burma and Bangkok.

Above **Thanks to the great food and drink, there's always a buzz around Fernandez & Wells.**

Lina Stores
18 Brewer Street, W1F 0SH
020 7437 6482   www.linastores.co.uk
It's been around for decades and is still one of
the best traditional Italian delis in the heart
of Soho, much loved by the community and
foodies alike. They don't come much better
than this.

Quo Vadis
6–9 Dean Street, W1D 3LL
020 7437 9585   www.quovadissoho.co.uk
Home to one of London's brightest
personalities in the form of Jeremy Lee. His
menus are a delight and his presence makes
every meal a special moment.

Randall & Aubin
16 Brewer Street, W1F 0SQ
020 7287 4447   www.randallandaubin.com
Housed in a former butcher's shop and
surrounded by sex shops and peep shows, this
atmospheric Champagne and oyster bar serves
great lobster and chips.

Rules
35 Maiden Lane, WC2E 7LB
020 7836 5314   www.rules.co.uk
Opened in 1798, Rules is the oldest restaurant
in London. They serve traditional British food,
with great game, hand-raised pigs, aged beef
and a hearty steak-and-kidney pudding. The
ornate interiors are worth a visit, too.

Whole Foods
20 Glasshouse Street, W1B 5AR
020 7406 3100   www.wholefoodsmarket.com/
stores/piccadilly
A massive food store and excellent resource for
those who are devoted to healthy, seasonal and
organic foods.

Wright Brothers Soho Oyster House
13 Kingly Street and G7/G8 Kingly Court,
W1B 5PW
020 7324 7731   www.thewrightbrothers.co.uk
Sister to the acclaimed oyster bar opposite
Borough Market (see page 300), this place is
much larger and laid out over several floors. It
may be slightly less atmospheric, but still offers
the full range of shellfish and oysters, plus
excellent fresh fish from Cornish dayboats.

Above left and right
**Lina Stores has stood
the test of time and
is one of the oldest
food businesses in
Soho and still one
of the best.**

Dalston
Hackney
Hoxton

Hackney was once considered the suburbs of London – wealthy lawyers in the 18th century might keep a country house there for weekend use and take refuge from the fug of the city. Despite the widespread industrialization that occurred in the 1800s, the area retains a huge amount of green space, repurposed for young people having barbecues at the weekends and walking designer dogs in this now very fashionable borough.

Anyone venturing further east than Shoreditch as recently as 15 years ago would have struggled to find much of culinary interest, save Dalston's many Turkish mangals, or grills, serving up plump meats seared over an open flame, and dishing them up with a simple salad and a plastic fork. With the centre of London moving east, so many of Shoreditch's creatives and entrepreneurs migrated further into Hackney in search of disused railway arches and warehouse spaces to call their own. Now the borough is home to the capital's most cutting-edge bars and a burgeoning group of start-up chefs and restaurateurs. The area seems to be the home for those wanting to put their first foot on the ladder of success. Destined to be glittering stars in the future, these guys are focused, innovative and driven. There has also been an explosion of artisan bakeries in the area and deadly serious coffee makers. You won't find a tube station here (although it's well served by the rapidly improving overground) or a department store, but you will find the pulse of the city – its most creative and enterprising people and places. That said, it's still Hackney at heart – the stylishly refurbished warehouses and boutique coffee houses sit cheek by jowl with tower blocks, and tend to be unostentatious in their attitude and menus. Watch out for the new Hackney Walk development down Morning Lane; at the planning stage, it promised lots in terms of giving young fashion entrepreneurs a place to manufacture and sell their wares, but early signals suggest that it is a different end of the apparel spectrum, with the big Bond Street brands flogging their end-of-season stock. Not very well suited, we think. The borough wears its new wealth, like most of its inhabitants, dressed right down.

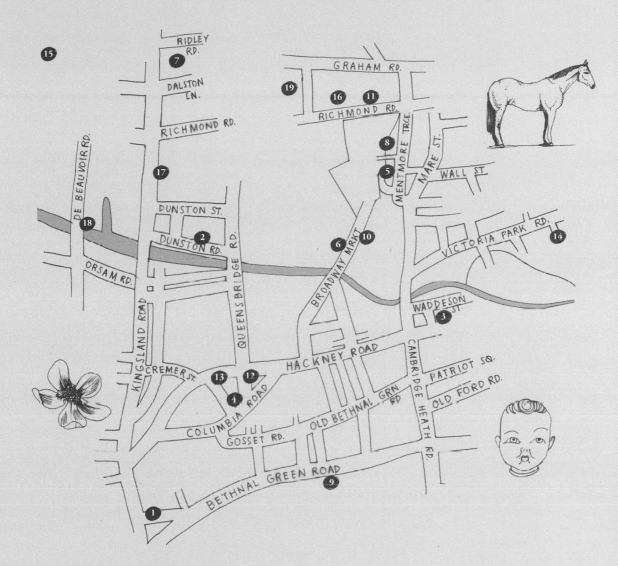

1 Allpress	**9** E Pellicci
2 Berber & Q	**10** Hill & Szrok
3 Bistrotheque	**11** Lardo
4 Brawn	**12** The Marksman
5 The Bread Station	**13** Morito
6 Broadway Market	**14** Pavilion Café
7 The Dusty Knuckle Bakery	**15** Primeur
8 E5 Bakehouse	**16** Rawduck

17 Rotorino
18 Towpath Café
19 Violet

uk.allpressespresso.com

Right and below
**Raw coffee beans
arriving at the
roastery.**

Allpress has a bit of a cult following, especially in east London and among our antipodean friends searching for a taste of back home. When Allpress had its roastery and café on Redchurch Street in Shoreditch, the place was always packed out and soon became a hub for like-minded groups. The atmosphere transcended the brilliant coffee, which is quite an achievement. The café was superbly run, with many of the staff soon becoming close friends with their customers. It was clear in 2014 that they had outgrown their premises, both in terms of the café space and the on-site roastery. A move to a former joinery workshop in Dalston gave them fantastic new premises. They've retained a small espresso bar in Shoreditch, where it all started, but this ambitious new outpost is very special indeed. Just the scale of the space makes it worth a visit and then you add the lovely garden at the front of the building and, of course, their very particular coffee and delicious food. Knowing the team at Allpress, I've got to focus a large part of the credit on Tony Papas, their visionary leader in the UK. Originally founded by Michael Allpress in New Zealand back in 1986, the partnership with Tony, already a well-known Sydney restaurateur in his own right, led to a move to Australia in 2000 and then their move to the UK in 2010. Now, their coffee is loved in Auckland, Dunedin, Sydney, Melbourne and Tokyo, and in more than 1,000 independent cafés and restaurants, so you can often find their distinctive beans in cups all over London.

Below **A perfect
Allpress flat white
with a lovely slice
of toast.**

Above and right
Relaxing in the garden outside Allpress.
Below **Enjoying a simple breakfast of boiled eggs and tall soldiers at Allpress.**

Below **The Allpress terrace is the perfect morning hangout on a sunny morning.**

Right **The menu at Allpress is very simple, but exactly what is appropriate.**

214   **Berber & Q** Arch 338 Acton Mews, E8 4EA

020 7923 0829   www.berberandq.com

You can be assured of some really very strong flavours and proper modern Turkish food at this place. The brunch is particularly good. I had some amazing Turkish eggs with a side of delicious *sucuk* sausages – a bit like *merguez*, but perhaps better – a *fattoush* salad and their delicious version of a Bloody Mary made with smoked vodka and rose harissa. It's a very atmospheric place and great for a group of friends to enjoy a fantastic night out. I keep wanting to go back (PP).

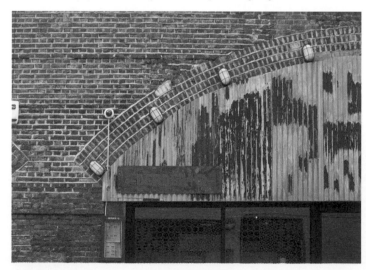

Above **The long dining tables are virtually inside the kitchen at Berber & Q.**
Above right **Cauliflower shawarma.**
Left **Berber & Q is located in a railway arch under the new East London Line.**

Bistrotheque 23–7 Wadeson Street, E2 9DR

020 8983 7900   www.bistrotheque.com

The owners have a previous life in the fashion world that has clearly influenced the whole operation. Bistrotheque has been included in all editions of *Eat London* and has remained super-cool over the last ten years – just like its owners. Lying on a dark cobbled street, with no obvious sign to indicate its discreet entrance, this restaurant is not easy to find. The area is still rather gritty and now boasts some edgy galleries and workshops that have moved from Shoreditch. As you ascend the concrete staircase, you may wonder if you have taken a wrong turn into a fire exit or staff area, but continue walking and you will discover a really enlightening space. The dining room is set in the eaves of this old East End sweatshop, and over the years has seen a few tweaks to its format – each time it seems to get better. The current layout includes a great island bar, and they have thankfully retained the polished white-tiled walls, nautical pendant lamps and steel-frame windows with mottled glass. This is the perfect location for dating couples. I should know – this is where my wife and I had our first proper dinner date (PP).

Right **The old ground-floor bar at Bistrotheque – it has since been refurbished.**

Michael Sager

"

I love a place with a great drinks offering even during brunch. Bistrotheque nails it every single time with simple aesthetics and good service.

Co-owner, Sager + Wilde

Right **Chefs preparing caramelized chicory at Bistrotheque.**
Left **The industrial-style interior at Bistrotheque.**

Caramelized Chicory with Roquefort Gratin

Serves 2

2 thick slices sourdough bread, crusts removed
2 garlic cloves
5g (¼ oz) or a few stems of parsley
5g (¼ oz) or a few stems of chives
10g (½ oz) nibbed almonds
160g (3 oz) chicory (2 small heads)
10g (½ oz) butter
vegetable oil
pinch of demerara sugar
¼ head of celeriac, peeled
2 sprigs of thyme, leaves chopped
40g (1½ oz) spinach leaves,
roughly chopped
6 g (3 oz) Roquefort cheese
Maldon sea salt and cracked black pepper

Make a herb crust by blending the sourdough with garlic, parsley and chives in a food processor or blender. Turn out into a bowl, stir in the nibbed almonds and set aside.

Cut the chicory in half lengthwise. Heat a large ovenproof frying pan over a high heat.

Add a quarter of the butter, a little oil and the chicory halves. Once the chicory begins to take on some colour, turn it over and add another quarter of the butter, the demerara sugar, and season with salt and pepper. Place in a preheated oven at 200°C (400°F), Gas Mark 6, for 10–15 minutes or until tender. Set aside.

Meanwhile slice the celeriac very finely into large roughly-shaped discs. Heat half the remaining butter in a saucepan over a medium heat and add the celeriac, thyme leaves, salt and pepper, and cook for about 4 minutes or until the celeriac is cooked.

To assemble the dish, warm the chicory and celeriac through in 1 saucepan with the remaining butter, add the chopped spinach and stir until the leaves wilt. Divide the chicory, celeriac and spinach neatly in the middle of 2 small heatproof serving plates and pour over any juices from the pan. Arrange slices of Roquefort on top of the vegetables, and sprinkle over the herb crust. Place under a preheated hot grill until golden brown. Serve immediately.

Brawn 49 Columbia Road, E2 7RG

020 7729 5692 www.brawn.co

We should always be wary about describing any restaurant as the 'best'. We all have different views on what makes the *best* gourmet experience or all-round restaurant. But there can be little doubt that this small neighbourhood wine bar and bistro is the apotheosis of its type. All this talk of the 'best' is prompted by the controversy generated by this charming offering when it received a (rare) maximum score from the long-established restaurant critic of the London's *Evening Standard*. Brawn is a great place to visit, but the *ES* accolade was surprising for a number of reasons, and ignited an interesting debate on Twitter. Notwithstanding, almost all the national newspaper reviews have also been very positive.

Whatever the case, Brawn is certainly a very, very good example of a friendly and welcoming local restaurant. There is much to admire, and it manages to deliver its own inventiveness without being too gimmicky.

The wine list at Brawn includes many natural, biodynamic and organic wines, all at quite reasonable prices. Instead of being listed by geographical location, they are grouped under headings such as 'Stones, Shells and Sea', 'Clean Lines' and 'Aromatics From Eastern France'. Some of my favourites come under the heading 'Vins de Soif' ('wines for thirsty drinkers' – a highly apt description for wines that make the perfect accompaniment to much of the menu at Brawn).

Ed Wilson, formerly of some of London's top restaurants, including The Wolseley, is the owner and head chef and even the DJ. The menu also has its own unique approach. Forget first course, mains and puddings. Brawn is all about Taste Ticklers (from oysters to brandade), Raw & Cured (Italian-style steak tartare, smoked eel and salads), Pig (from excellent *saucisson* to pork *rillettes*), Plancha (from foie gras and clams to artichokes and quail, all cooked directly on a very hot metal surface) and Slow Cook (think *choucroute*, baked vacherin mont d'or and gratins). As these ingredients indicate, there is a strong French influence to the menu, which also includes treats from Italy and Spain, as well as from British fields, farms and waters.

All in all, Brawn is a fine example of simple, delicious food paired with excellent wines in a relaxed setting – probably London's best little neighbourhood restaurant.

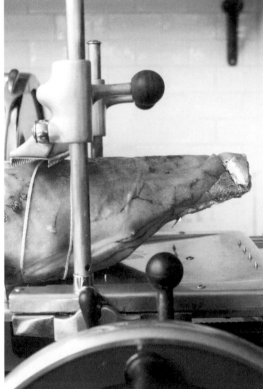

Above **A wonderful hand-operated Berkel slicer.** Opposite **White-washed walls and poster art at Brawn provide a modest backdrop for brilliant food.**

Cervelle de Canut

Makes 500 g (1 lb)

500 g (1 lb) fromage blanc or quark
1 shallot, very finely diced
1 tablespoon chopped chives
1 tablespoon chopped tarragon
1 tabelspoon chopped chervil
3 tablespoons cider vinegar
2 tablespoons walnut oil (plus extra to serve)
salt (optional)

Put the fromage blanc into a bowl and add
the diced shallot, chopped herbs and vinegar.
Mix together thoroughly, then add the walnut
oil. Taste. The vinegar should bring enough
acidity to enliven the fromage blanc but should
not mask the flavours of the herbs and shallot.
The walnut oil should bring a little depth of
flavour. You may also want to add a little salt.
An artisan fromage blanc will also add flavour.

To finish, drizzle a little extra walnut oil
over the top and serve with bread with aperitifs
or as a starter.

This page **Broadway Market is extensive with stalls offering all manner of products, from fresh fruit and fish to cheese and doughnuts, there's something to sate every shopper.**

Left **Unlike some other markets, Broadway still attracts genuine shoppers.**

Below **While Broadway is busiest on market day (Saturday), the restaurants are often bustling all week in this enviable corner of east London.**

Right **Claire Ptak's Violet bakery was one of the first stalls at the reinvented Broadway Market.**

The Bread Station Arch 373 Hemsley Place, E8 3SB
020 7254 7388 www.thebreadstation.co.uk

Over the last few years the number of bakeries in this corner of east London has exploded and we are now blessed with a healthy supply. Unlike yesteryear, they are not based on the high street but, instead, almost always in railway arches. This usually allows a little space for a few tables and chairs for the owners to fashion a small adjoining café. It also means that the bakers are not banished to overnight work and can instead go about their craft in full view of those chomping on their handiwork. This is a wonderful development, in so many ways, from a greater appreciation of the art of the baker to the enjoyment of some fresh-out-of-the-oven buns. These bakeries have also stretched the range of treats one can expect. No longer is it just tin loaves and formulaic breads, each place is seeking its own distinctive range of sweet, savoury and sour creations.

In the case of The Bread Station, its USP is the Danish guys behind the business. First, you've got Christoffer Hruskova, he of Michelin star status, thanks to his now closed North Road restaurant, who has teamed up with Danish master baker Per Brun. The focus is on traditional Danish baking skills. Their unique formula is based on three key components: 1. Cold rise – the dough is mixed thoroughly and then real salt added before they cold-rise the dough at 5°C (41°F). This gives the dough more time to prove and that means more flavour. 2. Yeast free – dough without added yeast, where all the bread is made the natural way, without any mother dough, giving the bread a longer shelf life. 3. Stone mill – all of the flour they use is ground in their own stone mill, making all of the dough completely wholegrain with the grains and husks. This helps with fermentation and again adds to the flavour profile.

Broadway Market Broadway Market, E8 4QJ
Saturdays 9am–5pm www.broadwaymarket.co.uk

There have been barrow boys at Broadway Market since 1890, but it was in 2004 that the market was re-established in its present form. Every Saturday, a narrow road between the oft-forgotten greenery of London Fields and Goldsmiths Row comes to life. Broadway is not a farmers' market, but rather welcomes all styles of food, as long as it's good. Ghanaian fast food or fried wild mushrooms on toasted sourdough with a hefty slug of garlic are both great. You could have traditional Indian street food from Gujarati Rasoi to buttermilk-fried chicken or some of the best smoked salmon to be had in London from Hansen & Lydersen. There is even the odd fancy boutique, plus the wonderful Aesop and a few fashion, music and small *objets* stalls. Nestling among a few galleries, a florist and a couple of great bookshops, artisanal food retailers offer an ideal excuse to avoid ghastly supermarket fare and a great opportunity to shop locally in the community.

The crowd here is quite modish, but you will also see many cheerful young families in this evolving corner of Hackney. Its location and the lack of major transport links nearby mean that this food market is thankfully mainly for locals.

Although the market is only open on Saturday, there is also a happy buzz here on Sundays, especially over the summer months.

This is my favourite London food market, for many reasons.

Above **F Cooke is one of only a few remaining pie and mash shops in London.**
Left **Sticky doughnuts from Crosstown,** one of the stalls at Broadway Market.

The Dusty Knuckle Bakery Abbot Street Car Park, 3 Abbot Street, E8 3DP

www.thedustyknuckle.com

What a great name! Once you've found this place, which isn't easy, you'll discover a disused shipping container converted into a mini bakery. They've formed a big window with the bakers kneading their dough facing outward towards the yard – a former goods depot now adorned with raised beds full of flowers, veg and herbs. It's not exactly Petersham Nurseries, but this is East London, don't forget, and everything is a bit scruffy but well hearted, especially given that this is an award-winning social enterprise. They work with young people facing social barriers, young offenders, early school leavers and the long-term unemployed, to help them build financial independence, and offer a range of baking and cooking programmes.

I happened to visit this bakery with my two-year-old son on the first morning that they were serving brunch – it was all a bit haphazard but we had a wonderful time. My son was fascinated when peering through the window watching the bakers rolling and kneading the dough (PP).

Below **A large window in the container allows light for the bakers and lots of interest for visitors.**

Israeli Roast Aubergine, Green Sauce, Tahini and Summer Herb Sandwich

Serves 2–3

For the aubergine, egg and bread

1 aubergine
olive oil
1 egg, at room temperature
4–6 slices of good-quality sourdough bread
salt and pepper

For the green sauce

½ garlic clove
½ bunch of coriander
½ bunch of flat leaf parsley
1 teaspoon cumin seeds, freshly toasted and ground
½ long green chilli (ideally Turkish), deseeded
good glug of extra virgin olive oil
1 tablespoon moscatel vinegar, sherry vinegar or white wine vinegar

For the tahini

½ garlic clove
2 tablespoons tahini
2 tablespoons Greek yogurt
juice of ½ lemon
2–3 tablespoons water

For the lemon dressing

juice of ½ lemon
2 tablespoons extra virgin olive oil
glug of moscatel vinegar, or sherry vinegar, or white wine vinegar

For the salad

4 cherry tomatoes
½ baby cucumber, deseeded
3 radishes
1 spring onion
3 purslane sprigs or rocket sprigs
small bunch of coriander
small bunch of flat leaf parsley
small bunch of mint
1 teaspoon za'atar (or 2 parts toasted sesame seeds mixed with 1 part dried thyme and 1 part sumac)

Cut the aubergine into fat finger-thick rounds. Rub a small amount of salt on each side and leave to drain in a colander for 20 minutes. Preheat the oven to 240°C (475°F), Gas Mark 9.

Meanwhile, make the green sauce. Put all the ingredients – except half the oil and the vinegar – in a blender, add salt and pepper and blitz until it looks like a pesto. (You can use a mortar and pestle if you don't have a blender, or want to be more authentic. If you are doing this, crush the garlic with a pinch of salt first, then crush in the roughly chopped herbs before adding the remaining ingredients.) Then add the other half of the olive oil and the vinegar.

For the tahini, crush the garlic with a pinch of salt using a mortar and pestle, then stir in the tahini and yogurt. Add the lemon juice – the mixture will thicken – then loosen it with the measured water, using as much as necessary to give it the consistency you prefer.

Brush the salt off the aubergine slices, the rub olive oil on each side and place on a roasting tray so that they are not touching. Roast for 20 minutes, turning halfway through. They should be dark brown by the end.

Make the lemon dressing by placing all the ingredients in a bowl and whisking, or place in a clean jam jar with a lid and shake up and until emulsified. Season well.

Bring a pan of water to the boil, then place in the egg and boil for 7 minutes. Place in cold water to cool, then shell the egg, and slice.

Meanwhile, make the salad. Chop the tomatoes, cucumber, radishes and spring onion into similar-sized small chunks, roughly 1cm (½ inch) cubes. Roughly chop the herbs. Mix the salad vegetables, herbs and dressing, then season with the za'atar, salt and pepper.

Now assemble your sandwich. For each sandwich, cut 2 chunky slices of bread, place aubergine slices on the bread, top with green sauce, dressed salad, egg, then tahini dressing, top with the second piece of bread and eat with haste!

For all gluten pessimists, leave off the second slice of bread and serve as a tartine, or ditch the carbs completely and serve the filling ingredients as a delicious salad.

Bruno Loubet

"

The dynamic young generation of chefs coming through is what's most exciting about the London food scene for me. They are essential in ensuring London's enduring feature as one of the most exciting food capitals of the world.

Chef patron, Grain Store

Dalston / Hackney / Hoxton

223

Left **Inside the diminutive E Pellicci with its Formica tables and happy locals.**

E5 Bakehouse Arch 395, Mentmore Terrace, E8 3PH

020 8986 9600 www.e5bakehouse.com

Elsewhere in this chapter we've talked about the welcome increase in the number of bakeries in east London and it is worth saying that E5 was one of the first. In the early days, this new project was attracting attention because its founder didn't come from a baking background – Ben Mackinnon was frustrated by his office job and took a leap of faith in the baking world. We haven't got space in this book to tell the full story but do visit their very informative website where you'll find a whole host of information on the early days and how they have developed in a very short time. They now occupy three railway arches and the business is thriving, with everything from baking classes to cakes, pizzas and much more. Visit at the weekend and you'll find a great community atmosphere and, like every other new bakery, a brilliant barista.

E Pellicci Bethnal Green Road, E2 0AG

020 7739 4873 www.epellicci.com

We love Pellicci's because it's a family business and an east London institution, housed in premises partly listed by English Heritage. The English breakfast will satisfy all comers, from locals on a budget to tourists and those in search of a hint of 1950s Italian Formica café nostalgia.

Hill & Szrok 60 Broadway Market, E8 4QJ

020 7254 8805 www.hillandszrok.co.uk

According to their website, they call themselves a cookshop based on the 15th century idea of a shop and a place to cook and eat, although it has all been updated for the 21st century. In this case, by day it is an exceptionally good master butcher specializing in free-range and organic meats from small farms, and by night the space is transformed into a communal dining table seating just 25 at a push, where you can select the actual piece of meat you want, not just the cut. And they do also have some unusual and under-utilized delicious cuts. The whole experience is fun and very connected to the whole idea of quality meat. Vegetarians stay away!

Above **Lardo has some of the best pizzas in east London.**

Lardo 197–201 Richmond Road, E8 3NJ
020 8985 2683 www.lardo.co.uk

With so many different pizza joints in London, each supposedly with their own particular style or method of cooking, you start to form favourites. For me, I think the thickness/thinness of the base at Lardo is just perfect. Not too thin, but easy to fold and enjoy a mouthful without it being too chewy or doughy. Plus, compared to most others, I think the toppings are more gourmet and interesting. My current favourite is porcini, Taleggio, thyme and parmigiano. In fact, I generally find it hard to order as I want to choose several of their pizzas (PP).

The menu offers much more than pizza. There is a lovely selection of antipasti from fritto misto and salt cod croquettes to baked ricotta and contechino with Puy lentils – the pickled endive is also yum. There's a good selection of cured meats, as the restaurants name suggests. There are a few delicious main courses such as risotto, gnocchi and daily homemade egg pasta, as well as good examples of the classic Italian desserts: *affogato*, *pannacotta*, *tiramisu* and so on.

I've had a great many meals here and can't say that I've ever been disappointed. This isn't top-end dining but it is a reliably good place with a changeable menu, lovely staff and an outside terrace when the weather is fine, and it's good value for money. It's a place where you can enjoy an Aperol spritz and then a glass or two of Italian wines, in a relaxed and jolly environment. It's a perfect neighbourhood restaurant and fortunately it's in my neighbourhood (PP).

Above **The mirror tile-clad pizza oven at Lardo.**
Right **Pizza fresh from the oven at Lardo.**

The Marksman 254 Hackney Road, E2 7SJ

020 7739 7393 www.marksmanpublichouse.com

Below **The curved marble bar and dining counter at Morito.**

This place is heartily recommended for two reasons. First, on the ground floor, it still has many of the charms of an old East End boozer, although it's been cleaned up a bit and the food is much, much better. They've still got the wood panelling and old furniture, a good choice of local beers on tap and a juke box, making the old-guard regulars feel at home. Upstairs, Martino Gamper, the London-based Italian designer of note, has created an interesting small space that has the benefit of a little roof terrace. Overseeing it all is Tom Harris, formerly of St John, and Jon Rotheram, formerly of Fifteen. I've also heard a whisper that (Saint) Jamie Oliver is also involved. I've visited a few times and enjoyed varied dishes, from a very good and well-judged roast lunch on a Sunday to a goat curry on the roof terrace. However, I've not yet tried their famous beef and barley buns – others have and loved them.

You should also try to attend some of their events, such as Cookbook Dinners where famous chefs cook up some of their signature and loved dishes.

This page **Marianna Leivaditaki (with the headscarf), the impressive head chef at Morito, surrounded by her team.**

Morito 195 Hackney Road, E2 8JL

020 7613 0754 www.moritohackneyroad.co.uk

There have been lots of mixed views about the design of this place, which is probably rather unfair. Yes, it is a little awkward, the lighting is harsh and the concrete floor and ceiling mean that the acoustics aren't very comfortable. However, let's put things into context. I think the estimable owners are trying to re-create a basic Spanish diner-meets-tapas bar that you might find in a provincial Spanish setting. And it is the food that matters here. It's all about simple small plates of food with strong-flavour ingredients. I particularly like seeing lots of different ingredients on the table – on a recent visit we had a wide range of tastes, from grilled octopus to lamb chops with paprika and anchovy, plus some very hot peppers, labneh with chillies and charred corn, and plenty of flat breads with dukkah. All washed down with a few glasses of verdejo. As you might expect, they encourage you to enjoy their selection of sherries or a glass of the easy-going cava (PP).

Fried Aubergines, Whipped Feta and Date Syrup

Serves 4

2 aubergines
150g (5½oz) feta cheese
1 tablespoon olive oil
2 tablespoons water, plus extra if needed
pinch of caster sugar
150g (5½oz) fine or medium semolina flour
50g (1¾oz) plain flour
500ml (18fl oz) olive, sunflower or rapeseed oil, or a mixture, for frying
4 tablespoons date syrup, nectar or molasses (from Middle Eastern stores or large supermarkets), or equal parts of clear honey and black treacle
2 tablespoons mint, shredded just before serving so the leaves do not go black
salt

Cut the aubergines into chunky chips and soak in salty water for 30 minutes, until you are ready to cook.

Meanwhile, make the whipped feta. Cut the feta into small pieces and place in a food processor with the 1 tablespoon of olive oil and the 2 tablespoons of water. Blitz until the mixture is smooth and silky; this may take a few minutes. The mix should resemble double cream in texture, so add more water if you need it. Usually no extra salt is needed as the feta is salty enough, however the sugar is sometimes good to balance the acidity so taste and it a pinch of caster sugar if you think it needs it. Cover and set aside in the fridge.

Dry the aubergine chips thoroughly between 2 tea towels. Put the semolina and flour in a bowl and mix it with ½ teaspoon of salt. Toss the aubergines in the mix and shake off any excess.

Put the oil in a large saucepan, ensuring the level of the oil is about halfway or less, and place over a medium heat. When the oil is hot but not smoking – around 180°C (350°F) on a sugar thermometer – gently lower the aubergine chips into the oil and fry until golden and crispy outside and soft within. Remove from the oil with a slotted spoon and place in a bowl lined with kitchen paper to absorb excess oil. Sprinkle over some salt, toss gently and keep hot.

To serve, place the aubergines on a plate, give the whipped feta a good stir, then drizzle it over the chips followed by the date syrup and finally a scattering of the mint. Eat immediately.

Lamb Chops with Anchovy and Paprika Butter

Serves 4

2 teaspoons cumin seeds, freshly ground
1 teaspoon sea salt flakes
sprinkling of sweet smoked paprika

For the anchovy and paprika butter
75g (2¾oz) unsalted butter
8 good-quality salted anchovy fillets
(we use Ortiz)
1 tablespoon very finely chopped rosemary
leaves
2 teaspoons hot smoked paprika
juice of ½ lemon

For the chops and marinade
2 garlic cloves
½ teaspoon salt
¼ onion, finely grated
1 teaspoon sweet smoked paprika
2 teaspoons freshly ground cumin seeds
2 tablespoons olive oil
2 tablespoons lemon juice
8–12 lamb chops, depending on size

To make the anchovy butter, place all the
ingredients in a food processor and blitz until
smooth. Transfer to a bowl and refrigerate.

For the chops, crush the garlic with the
salt using a pestle and mortar, then mix with
the onion, spices, oil and lemon juice in a
bowl. Add the chops and turn to coat really
well. Cover and leave for 1 hour at room
temperature, or overnight in the fridge.

When you are ready to cook, return
the meat to room temperature, if necessary.
Sprinkle the lamb liberally with half the
ground cumin and a good pinch of the salt.
Preheat a grill to hot, or heat a griddle pan
until smoking-hot, or bring a barbecue to
cooking temperature with white-hot coals.

Place the chops under the hot grill, on the
smoking-hot griddle or barbecue, and cook
for 5–8 minutes on each side for pink meat,
turning once or twice.

Remove from the heat, sprinkle with the
remaining cumin and salt and the paprika
and serve immediately, with a dollop of the
anchovy butter smeared on each chop. These
are delicious with Turkish chopped salad,
flatbread and seasoned yogurt, or anything
else you fancy.

Dalston / Hoxton / Hackney

229

From left to right
**Fried okra, walnuts,
pomegranates and
yogurt; lamb chops
with anchovy and
paprika butter, and
fried aubergine,
whipped feta and date
syrup (see recipe on
page 227).**

Pavilion Café Corner Old Ford Road, Victoria Park, E9 7DE

There can be few lovelier spots to eat an egg in the capital than this no-frills café, where you take your breakfast overlooking the pond at glorious Victoria Park. In summer, you'll have pedalos and rowboats for people-watching purposes, the rest of the year you'll have joggers, swans, cyclists and pram-pushers enjoying the 44 acres of greenery that make up London's oldest public park, and provide the backdrop to your bacon. There is a theory that the seating at McDonald's is designed to keep its patrons comfortable for just long enough to eat their food, and then become so uncomfortable they quickly move on and free up their place for others. It is possible the Pavilion keeps its clientele moving on, despite the linger-worthy view, in the same way: food is served up, picnic-style, on rickety fold-up benches and tables, which quickly lose their appeal. But if it wasn't, would anyone ever leave?

The café was taken over by Brett Redman and Rob Green of Elliot's in Borough Market in 2007. The pair took a typical British park pavilion, with its average line-up of limp sandwiches and fizzy drinks, and turned it into one of London's best-loved brunch spots – baking their own sourdough, sourcing bacon and sausages from nearby Ginger Pig, and putting the great back into the Full English. Redman retreated in 2014 to concentrate on new ventures (including The Richmond), but the café lives on with a new Sri Lankan menu on offer alongside its more traditional breakfast options. If you like to mix cuisines, that means you can have crispy egg hoppers, a fragrant curry and a pinch of coconut sambal served with a side of portly Cumberland sausage.

Primeur 116 Petherton Road, N5 2RT

020 7226 5271 www.primeurn5.co.uk

There's been a lot of talk in the restaurant world about the Paris bistronomy movement and this little dining room seems to suggest that it is of the same ilk, but with a London slant, obviously. The location isn't exactly easy but it is worth making the trip. Jump on the tube to Highbury & Islington and it's just a 12-minute walk – just don't go when there is an Arsenal game. While you are in the area, do make a point to visit Stoke Newington High Street and also Clissold Park. Like the dining room, which is set in a former car repair garage, with lovely bifold doors, it is all a lot better when the weather is fine. One of the essential parts of a place like this is the natural wines, those wines made with minimal intervention and no/low added chemicals. In itself, that is a good reason to visit Primeur but I would also say that the food is also rather good. I was impressed to see that they didn't have any core line spirits, but they did have the wonderful vieille prune, a plum *eau de vie* made in Souillac in the Lot *département* in south-west France (PP).

Best for... family friendly

Albion – at the weekend and during school holidays, Albion provide free meals for children under six, all day, until bedtime

Balthazar – the size of this place and its menu makes it a place to please everybody

Pavilion Café – Victoria Park is one of the best green spaces in London, and this brilliant café at its heart provides the icing on the cake

Above **Pickling and fermenting are a key part of the Rawduck identity.**
Left **The long communal table at Rawduck adorned with plants.**

Left **Cherry, raspberry and melon drinking vinegars at Rawduck.** Right **Seeded oat and nut granola, Greek yogurt and plum compote at Rawduck.** Below **Rawduck's roast aubergine, labneh, mint and cumin on toast.**

Rawduck 197 Richmond Road, E8 3NJ
020 8986 6534 www.rawduckhackney.co.uk

Weekend brunch is best here! Of course, it is good during the week, but this place seems to get a new life at the weekend. And, we're not talking about your typical eggs Benedict and Bloody Marys. Instead, the menu and drinks list here is far more global and creative. From eggs with shiitake dashi, buckwheat soba and spinach to tarka dhal with brown rice and harissa eggs on charred sourdough with Greek yogurt and coriander. You should also try their pickles and cured things. The drinks menu is also worth making the trip to this corner of Hackney, just at the edge of the busy London Fields park.

I particularly like the drinking vinegars, nut milks, ferments, sodas and their 'brews', as they call them. And Clare Lattin, the owner, is a bit of an evangelist when it comes to natural and biodynamic wines.

Yes, the location is a little inconvenient for some – the Hackney Empire is just around the corner, so perhaps try to make a night of it, but not for me – as it is only about half a mile from home. However, sadly, due to my work commitments, I don't get to visit as often as I would like – my wife does visit regularly and always sends back very favourable reports.

If you don't get a chance to visit Rawduck, or its sister restaurant Ducksoup in Soho (see www.ducksoupsoho.co.uk), do try to get a copy of the book *Ducksoup Cookbook*, which includes favourite recipes from their menus. I find it to be very much in tune with modern London life and it is beautifully styled (PP).

Rotorino 434 Kingsland Road, E8 4AA

020 7249 9081 www.rotorino.com

In terms of quality, Rotorino is probably a little out of place in Dalston. This is a modestly priced offering in a cool neighbourhood with an interior that does in fact suit the area. The denizens of E8 have peripatetic chef Stevie Parle to thank for his southern Italian menus. You can enjoy well-sourced cured meats, simple pasta dishes or something delicious from the wood grill. The short but interesting wine list by Ruth Spivey, of Wine Car Boot and Street Vin, also deserves a mention.

Above **The interior of Rotorino suits its Dalston setting.**
Right **One of the young chefs just outside Rotorino in Dalston.**
Opposite **Stevie Parle now owns a string of restaurants in London.**

Pea Gnudi

Serves 4

500g (1lb 2oz) fresh ricotta, ideally from buffalo or sheeps' milk
200g (7oz) podded fresh peas
75g (2¾oz) finely grated Parmesan cheese
500g (1lb 2oz) fine semolina for pasta
good olive oil
salt and pepper

Put the ricotta into a sieve or colander and leave to drain for 1 hour, or longer if you have time.

In a small pan of well-salted boiling water, cook the peas until they are soft, then pulse-chop them in a blender, or roughly crush using a mortar and pestle. Mix the ricotta with the peas and Parmesan in a bowl, seasoning with salt and pepper to taste.

Pour the semolina into a large wide bowl or tray. Roll the ricotta into balls about 8cm (3¼ inches) in diameter. Gently place them into the semolina and turn to cover them. Let them sit for a few hours covered in semolina and they will form a delicate protective 'skin'.

When you are ready to eat, put a pan of well-salted water on to boil. Carefully add the gnudi and blanch gently for 2–3 minutes, or until the gnudi rise to the top of the pan. Carefully remove the gnudi from the pan with a slotted spoon and place into a large warm bowl, then generously pour over olive oil.

233

Flâneur Saturday in East London

Charles Baudelaire defined a *flâneur* (a stroller, lounger, saunterer or loafer, from the verb *flâner*, to stroll) as 'a person who walks the city in order to experience it'. Add a little shopping, sipping, snacking and dining, and you have the perfect weekend in east London. A bicycle would add more pace, but might detract from the relaxed state of mind savoured by the true *flâneur*.

A few suggested routes:
– Start at Victoria Park village and a peek at The Ginger Pig butchers getting ready for a busy day – if you love meat, you'll enjoy their fantastic meat vitrines. Once the warming delights of their sausage rolls have got the appetite rumbling, head to Pavilion Café in Victoria Park for a delicious breakfast – their scrambled eggs are fantastic or you could have a Sri Lankan hopper.
– After breakfast, you'll need a brisk walk around the park and then along the charming canal footpath to Broadway Market.
– Saunter around the market, probably the best in London, and revel in the amazing atmosphere.

Grab a coffee and perhaps some fancy gifts for friends or treats for yourself.
– Head across London Fields to Rawduck for brunch and start with a drinking vinegar or nut milk. Or perhaps you'd prefer a pizza at Lardo just next door.
– Don't have a dessert at the restaurant – instead head for a fancy little cake at Violet.
– Take a stroll to The Flour Station bakery and admire their craft. Then on to E5 Bakehouse and perhaps see if they have any bakery classes that day.
– As you start to tire, you need a good stiff cocktail and, for this, you have a brilliant choice of Peg + Patriot or Satan's Whiskers.
– Then, decide on dinner. Is it to a fantastic-tasting menu at the bijou Pidgin or a more gutsy affair at The Marksman, complete with a proper East End boozer spirit?
– If you've still got energy, head to Dalston for a bar and club crawl; there's lots to choose from.
– Fall to sleep in a comfy bed at Typing Room, or perhaps Boundary in Shoreditch.

234

Towpath Café 36 De Beauvoir Crescent, N1 5SB

020 7254 7606

An ideal stop-off and coffee injection with dainty carbs for anyone exploring east London. The patron has a smile and a positive outlook that are so rare (especially when the service is so chaotic). Watch out for joggers and cyclists – somebody's bound to fall in the canal one day. While you are in the area, you could also try The Bargehouse (46a De Beauvoir Crescent, N1 5RY) or Arepa (58A De Beauvoir Crescent, N1 5SB).

Violet 47 Wilton Way, E8 3ED

020 7275 8360 www.violetcakes.com

Claire Ptak is one of the most talented pastry chefs, bakers and food stylists working in London today. Having arrived in London in 2005 after serving as thepastry chef at Alice Waters' legendary Chez Panisse in California, Claire started baking from her flat in Hackney to supply her weekly stall at Broadway Market.

I used to live in the same building, and the pervading smells were glorious. Things have moved on since those early days. Claire is now a full-on London food personality. A visit to her cute little cake shop and café is a weekly ritual for many – a precious blessing for local residents.

Best for...
East End
cocktail bars

We heartily recommend a trip to Bethnal Green, where you will find three of the best cocktail bars – places where you can enjoy a pre-prandial drink of the highest order, whether a classic martini or a new creation, all within a short walk or stumble of each other. Each has its own personality and specialist area of the drinks world, and each delivers it with much style and a large dose of cool. Cheers!

Peg + Patriot

Satan's Whiskers

The Sun Tavern

Left **Violet is Claire Ptak's bijou cake shop and café on Wilton Road.**

Pear Crumble Muffins

Makes 12 muffins

More than anything else, these muffins are a vehicle for perfectly ripe pears. At Violet we change the fruit as new and wonderful types come into season. In the summer, strawberries, raspberries, cherries and then plums feature in the moist crumb of the muffin, topped with buttery crumble. Muffins are best when made by hand, as over-mixing ruins the texture. At Violet, we make all our muffins in small batches without the aid of electric mixers.

275g (9oz) plain flour
2½ teaspoons baking powder
½ teaspoon bicarbonate of soda
¼ teaspoon salt
2 eggs
175g (6oz) caster sugar
75g (3oz) unsalted butter, melted
140ml (4¾fl oz) buttermilk or natural yogurt
½ lemon
3 ripe pears such as Comice (or about 200g/ 7oz other fruits in season)

For the crumble topping

100g (3½oz) cold unsalted butter
150g (5oz) plain flour
4 tablespoons light brown sugar

Preheat the oven to 170°C (340°F), Gas Mark 3½, and line a 12-cup muffin tin with paper cases.

In a large bowl combine the flour, baking powder, bicarbonate of soda and salt and use a balloon whisk to mix it all together. We find this much easier than sifting, and it works in the same way to distribute the baking powder and bicarbonate of soda evenly through the flour. Set aside.

In another bowl, whisk together the eggs and caster sugar. Gradually drizzle in the melted butter and, finally, whisk in the buttermilk or plain yogurt. Zest the lemon straight into the bowl so that you catch the aromatic oils that are released. Pour the liquid into the dry ingredients and stir together until the dry ingredients are only just incorporated into the liquid so as not to over mix – the batter will be quite thick.

Spoon the batter into the paper cases. Quarter and core the pears and cut each quarter into bite-sized pieces. Push about a quarter of a pear into each paper case.

Quickly mash all the crumble ingredients together and sprinkle generously over the muffins. The topping can be made in advance and kept in the refrigerator for up to a week or in the freezer for up to a month.

Bake the muffins for 25–30 minutes or until a skewer inserted into the middle comes out clean. Serve warm with a pot of fresh coffee.

235

Above **All the cakes and biscuits at Violet are baked on the premises. If you visit, you don't need to be told this – you will smell it.**

More places to visit in the area

Beagle
397–400 Geffrye Street, E2 8HZ
020 7613 2967 www.beaglelondon.co.uk
There is something very appealing about the simplicity of Beagle's menu and the chef's confidence in his ingredients and light-touch cooking. Nothing fancy, just great seasonal ingredients sensitively cooked. Great for Sunday lunch.

Brooksby's Walk
77 Brooksby's Walk, E9 6DA
www.brooksbyswalk.com
Creative and solid cooking on a small, lightly weatherproofed rooftop above an old public convenience. A very unusual experience, but worth a trip in the summer.

Draughts
337 Acton Mews, E8 4EA
www.draughtslondon.com
Something a bit different; play a board game while enjoying brunch.

Ellory
Netil House, 1 Westgate Street, E8 3RL
0203 095 9455 www.ellorylondon.com
Another place in deepest Hackney to win a Michelin star recently – definitely a signal that Michelin are changing for the better and Hackney is now the rising star in the culinary world.

Fabrique Bakery
Arch 385, Geffrye Street, E2 8HZ
020 7033 0268 www.fabrique.co.uk
Another, yes another, excellent bakery in this part of London. My son loves the cinnamon buns and I don't blame him.

Ginger Pig
99 Lauriston Road, E9 7HJ
020 8986 6911 www.thegingerpig.co.uk
If you find yourself near the splendid Victoria Park, don't leave before exploring the nearby Lauriston Road 'village', where you'll find the excellent Ginger Pig butchers – you really must have one of their decadent sausage rolls. Next door you'll find Bottle Apostle, a great little wine and craft beer shop; Jonathan Norris, the fishmonger, is across the way and Broadway Market is just up the road.

Above **A heavily veined marble dining counter hosting a simple lunch of pâté, toasted sourdough and cornichons at Ellory.**

Above, below
and below right
**Viennoiserie and
cookies straight from
the oven at Fabrique
bakery. East London
now boast a fine
selection of excellent
artisan bakeries.**

Jim's Café
59 Chatsworth Rd, Clapton E5 0LH
020 3026 4465
A superb new all-day café from Nuno Mendes,
he of Chiltern Firehouse fame. He's sensitively
refurbished an old caff and made it into a new
caff with great food. I recently enjoyed one of
the best breakfasts ever: an open omelette with
eel and foraged sea herbs.

P Franco
107 Lower Clapton Road, E5 0NP
020 8533 4660 www.pfranco.co.uk
Don't get confused by the big sign above the
entrance; it actually says The Great Wall (of
China restaurant) and quite obviously relates
to the previous tenants and the new guys
simply haven't had the volition or cash to
change it. Inside, you'll find a combination of
wine shop, bar, tasting event space, supper club
and some brilliant food. I'm not sure how long
this will continue so enjoy it while you can as
part of their supper clubs.

Peg + Patriot
Patriot Square, E2 9NF
020 8709 4528 www.talentedmrfox.com/
pegandpatriot
Whimsical craft cocktails.

Pidgin
52 Wilton Way, E8 1BG
020 7254 8311 www.pidginlondon.com
This tiny place with a set four-course,
weekly changing tasting menu has just
won a Michelin star.

Ridley Road Market
Dalston, E8 www.ridleyroad.co.uk
Monday to Wednesday 9 am–3 pm, Thursday
9 am–12 pm, Friday and Saturday 9 am–5 pm
Hackney is a melting pot of different ethnicities,
and one of the best examples must be this
market. Jewish immigrants, followed by Asian,
Greek, Turkish and West Indian communities
(hence the reggae music), have dominated the
stalls over the years. All can rub shoulders here
in this loud and raw vibe.

Satan's Whiskers
343 Cambridge Heath Road, E2 9RA
020 7739 8362
A compact cocktail bar with a hip-hop
soundtrack.

Sun Tavern
441 Bethnal Green Road
020 7739 4097 www.thesuntavern.co.uk
Punch cocktails and classic mixed drinks.

Tonkotsu
382 Mare Street, E8 1HR
020 8533 1840 www.tonkotsu.co.uk
Now a mini chain, this is the first location
that I visited with my son when he was
10 months old; he loved the noodles (PP).
They specialize in ramen, gyoza and *tonkotsu*
– a rich, sea-salt-based pork stock with thin
noodles, melt-in-the-mouth pork belly, a
soft-boiled egg, *menma*, beansprouts and
spring onions.

Typing Room
Town Hall Hotel, Patriot Square, E2 9NF
020 7871 0461 www.typingroom.com
Another Jason Atherton outpost. This one has
more of an independent spirit.

Fitzrovia
Marylebone

A few years ago, Marylebone was a quietly nice bit of London, home to a quietly stylish high street, Sherlock Holmes enthusiasts and one of the Monopoly railway stations. Now it is home to Chiltern Street, and the Chiltern Street Firehouse – where paparazzi photographers go on a quiet night to take home a picture of a celebrity. In fact, the queue of tourists snaking down Marylebone Road from Madame Tussauds might save themselves a few hours by pitching up outside André Balazs' hotel and restaurant to see the real thing. However, it's been possible to eat well in Marylebone for a long time – its farmers' market, La Fromagerie, the Ginger Pig, The Providores and other boutique restaurants have been a good sanctuary for those wanting to eat in town, near to the thundering of shoppers' feet on Oxford Street, but feeling a world away. Marylebone High Street is the much admired model of the perfect up-market high street and now the tributary streets are providing a buzz, with some great restaurants.

Fitzrovia has its own claim on the hotel *du jour* title – The Edition, with its Berner's Tavern, is doing its own bit for central London glamour, and already had the feel of one of London's great old dining institutions when the paint was still drying. With Europe's longest shopping street carved through it, it's hard to believe that Fitzrovia was once a bohemian quarter. In fact, it is said to have been given its name by Welsh *bon viveurs* Augustus John and Dylan Thomas, who used to frequent the Fitzroy Tavern on Charlotte Street. The pub is still standing and worth a visit in December, when its firmly more-is-more approach to Christmas decorations makes it one of the most gleefully gaudy spots in the capital. The name Fitzrovia only appeared on Ordnance Survey maps in 1994, and has since seen off attempts by developers to rebrand the area as Noho. Long may it continue to do so.

1 Bonnie Gull Seafood Shack	9 Honey & Smoke	17 Riding House Café
2 Bubble Dogs/Kitchen Table	10 Honey & Spice	18 ROKA
3 Chiltern Firehouse	11 Kaffeine	19 Selfridges Food Hall
4 La Fromagerie	12 Locanda Locatelli	20 Texture Restaurant
5 Galvin	13 Marylebone Farmers' Market	
6 The Ginger Pig	14 Orrery	
7 Hakkasan	15 Portland	
8 Honey & Co	16 The Providores	

Right **Simple white bistro chairs add to the charm of Bonnie Gull's terrace.**

Bonnie Gull Seafood Shack 21A Foley Street, W1W 6DS

020 7436 0921   www.bonniegull.com

The owners call it 'a seaside restaurant in the city'. Just starting with that makes me hungry. I absolutely love a good fish and seafood restaurant and dream of opening one some day. You'd think they'd be everywhere, but they aren't and it is even harder to find a good one like Bonnie Gull. Of course, the first expectation is spankingly fresh seafood, and then the knowledge and confidence of the kitchen to cook things to perfection, have the ability to keep things simple and only combine ingredients for the overall good of the dish. Last summer, I had the joy of visiting this restaurant on a hot day and sat outside in the sun, imagining I was by the sea, with a cold glass of wine in hand and a lovely tray of oysters about to be devoured (PP).

Best for... fish & seafood

Bonnie Gull – great fresh fish in a charming setting, especially in the summer

Scott's – seriously high-end, with a sprinkling of celebs

Bentley's – also one of the best oyster bars in London, all within an historic setting. Quite an experience.

Above left **On a sunny day the outside terrace is extended and is one of the best urban spots to enjoy incredibly fresh seafood.**

Smoked Mackerel, Horseradish and Pickled Cucumber Pâté

Serves 10 as a starter

3½ tablespoons white wine vinegar
2 tablespoons water
10g (¼oz) granulated sugar
½ cucumber, seeds removed, finely chopped
400g (14oz) smoked mackerel fillets, skinned
200g (7oz) crème fraîche
100g (3½oz) creamed horseradish
finely grated zest and juice of 1 lemon
toast, to serve

First, mix the vinegar, measured water and sugar in a saucepan and bring to the boil. Meanwhile, halve the cucumber lengthways and remove the seeds by running a teaspoon down the centre and discard. Add the chopped cucumber to the boiling vinegar mixture, then take the pan off the heat. Allow to cool.

Put the mackerel fillets, crème fraîche, horseradish and lemon zest and juice into a food processor and process to bring them all together. Do not process for too long: the pâté should retain texture.

Drain the pickled cucumber and pat it dry with kitchen paper. Fold into the pâté, cover and chill for at least 2 hours. (It will keep in the fridge for 3 days.)

Make some toast and serve it with the pâté, with a glass of nice wine.

Bouillabaisse

Serves 12

For the soup

2 small red mullet, gutted and gills removed
1kg (2lb 4oz) gurnard, gutted and gills removed
500g (1lb 2oz) plum tomatoes, sliced
1 large onion, finely sliced
1 fennel bulb, finely sliced
1 garlic bulb, cloves peeled and sliced
1 leek, finely sliced
100ml (3½fl oz) extra virgin olive oil, plus extra for cooking
25g (1oz) sea salt
15g (½oz) basil
10g (¼oz) parsley sprigs
2 thyme sprigs
10 peppercorns
1 teaspoon coriander seeds
1 teaspoon fennel seeds
a few saffron threads
1 clove
pinch of cayenne pepper
150ml (¼ pint) good-quality white wine
50g (1¾oz) tomato purée
500g (1lb 2oz) chopped tomatoes
3 litres (5¼ pints) good fish stock or water
sea salt and freshly ground black pepper

For the garnish

2 leeks, washed
600g (1lb 5oz) Maris Piper potatoes, peeled
1kg (2lb 3oz) whole monkfish fillet, trimmed
olive oil
12 large langoustines
12 scallops

For the soup, slice the fish into 3cm (1¼ inch) pieces, keeping the heads and tails attached, and mix well in a large bowl with all the other ingredients except the wine, tomato purée, chopped tomatoes and fish stock. Marinate for 24 hours, turning the contents every 4 hours.

After 24 hours separate the fish from the rest of the mix, reserving any liquid as well as the vegetables, herbs and spices left in the bowl. Pan-fry the fish well in a large frying pan until golden brown, using a splash more olive oil if needed. At the same time, in another saucepan large enough to hold all the contents of the soup, begin to sweat the vegetables, herbs and spices left in the bowl in a little olive oil, but don't let them change colour. Add any juices from the bowl and salt and pepper. When all the fish is coloured and the vegetables are soft, remove the fish from the frying pan, deglaze the pan with a splash of the white wine, stirring to collect all the flavour from the pan, then add them both to the vegetables with the tomato purée and cook for 5 minutes. Now add the chopped tomatoes and remaining wine, bring to the boil, then reduce the heat to a steady simmer and reduce the liquid in the saucepan for 10 minutes.

Add the fish stock, bring to the boil rapidly, then reduce the heat to a simmer and cook for 20 minutes.

Working in batches, blend the soup until very smooth – bones, heads, tails and all – then pass through a fine sieve. Return it to a clean large saucepan and place over a medium-low heat, to warm through.

Meanwhile, start on the garnish. Bring 3 saucepans of well-salted water to the boil. Drop the leeks into a pan and blanch for 2 minutes, then drain and refresh in cold water, to stop the cooking. Slice them into 1cm (½ inch) rounds. Drop the potatoes into another pan, reduce the heat to a simmer and cook for 20 minutes, or until tender but still holding their shape. Drain and, when cool enough to handle, cut into bite-sized pieces.

Sear the monkfish tail in olive oil in a hot frying pan until golden, about 5 minutes, turning to cook on all sides. Do not cook all the way through. Take out of the pan, slice into 24 slices and add to the soup to cook through.

Blanch the langoustines in the salted water in the last saucepan for 1 minute, then drain.

Sear the seasoned scallops in the same pan you used for the monkfish, this time cooking them all the way through.

Add the leeks, potatoes, langoustines and scallops to the soup and serve.

Bubbledogs / Kitchen Table 70 Charlotte Street, W1T 4QG

020 7637 7770 (Bubbledogs) www.bubbledogs.co.uk
www.kitchentablelondon.co.uk

Hard to believe but this is a restaurant that specializes in Champagne and hot dogs. The Champagnes are not your usual Moët or Laurent Perrier but those much more beloved of sommeliers: Grower Champagnes. These are produced by the same estate that owns the vineyards from which the grapes come. Generally, it is said that they have more character and personality. All this paired with hot dogs? We'll leave you to make your own mind up about that.

Tucked away at the back of Bubbledogs is Kitchen Table, run by an excellent chef called James Knappett. James has worked in some of the finest modern kitchens, such as Per Se, The Ledbury and Noma, to mention a few. There are just 19 seats at a horseshoe-shaped dining counter that overlooks the kitchen. The menu changes daily and the restaurant has already won a Michelin star.

Right **Chiltern Street is now a very smart retail destination.**

Above **Previously those large black doors were portals for Marylebone's fire engines, but now they open on to the super-chic Chiltern Firehouse dining room.**

Chiltern Firehouse 1 Chiltern Street, W1U 7PA

020 7073 7676 www.chilternfirehouse.com

The brainchild of mega hotelier and socialite André Balazs, Chiltern immediately became a celebrity hotspot when it opened. It was one of the biggest openings London had ever seen and there was lots of talk about Chiltern stealing The Ivy's crown. When the project was first announced, it was, at that time, a relatively unappealing location for this type of star attracting operation and the prospect of dining in a former fire station certainly didn't excite too many people. That was before Mr Balazs went about town recruiting the best and most expensive front-of-house people in the business and creating one of the most understated but most stylish interiors in London.

So, what is it really like? Well, I would say brilliant, and, having been a number of times now, I would also say consistently so. In the early days, almost nothing was said about the food but it is in fact very good. This is mainly thanks to Nuno Mendes (previously of Viajante and The Loft Project, possibly the first supper club in London). And now Nuno also has his own little Portuguese place next to Spitalfields Market. His food at Chiltern is more international, with an American accent, and you can expect the finest ingredients – they say it is all about reimagined classics and bold new flavours, with an emphasis on seasonality (PP).

If you're not of a mind to dine at Chiltern, then I would also recommend the very cool and sexy bars. The cocktails are totally brilliant and some of the best examples of the classics you can find in London. The bar experts, in their smart white dinner jackets, seem to find just the right balance between the taste, alcohol and viscosity that a good drink has to have. And the bar food is totally delicious – you must try the crab doughnuts and the bacon cornbread. In the summer, the garden is also a very pleasant place to quaff a dozen oysters and a bottle of Chablis.

When Chiltern first opened, I was very angry with Mr Balazs as he took two of my best staff and appointed them as head sommelier and restaurant general manager. My anger has subsequently subsided, not least because it's now very easy for me to reserve a table and I also receive brilliant service (PP).

Finally, if you like a late-night drink, don't forget to visit the club underneath the pavement, accessed through a secret door at the back of the lavatories.

Left **The cheese room at the superlative La Fromagerie is one of the best food destinations in all of London.**

Above and below **Purple garlic and packets of grains, from the brilliant deli selection at La Fromagerie.**

Left **The communal dining table at La Fromagerie is surrounded by delicious food.**

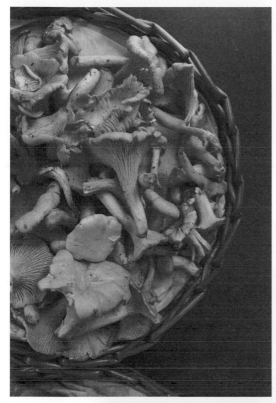

La Fromagerie 2–6 Moxon Street, W1U 4 EW

020 7935 0341 www.lafromagerie.co.uk

In the second edition of *Eat London*, there was a catastrophic error in that we mistakenly edited out La Fromagerie. It was in the first edition and we included the Highbury branch but not, by cruel omission, the Marylebone store. This was a massive oversight, as La Fromagerie is possibly my all-time favourite food destination in all of London. And Patricia Michelson, the founder, is one of my food heroes. I'm now extremely pleased to see it back in the book and encourage everybody to visit without delay. As the name suggests, the main attraction is cheese. As you step inside the sliding door to the dedicated temperature-controlled cheese room, you soon realize that you've entered some form of heavenly space. The choice of cheeses is nonpareil and when you add to this that they only offer cheese of the finest quality and condition, all served by individual experts in the subject, you'll soon be in awe. Over the years, La Fromagerie has expanded and now includes much more, with good wines, fine groceries, fruit and vegetables, plus a lovely place to dine. I really cannot recommend it enough (PP).

Right **Patricia Michelson, one** of London's most-respected and admired food personalities.

Top, left and right **La Fromagerie isn't** just about cheese. It also has an exceptional range of fresh fruit and vegetables, plus some fine groceries and wines.

246

Galvin 66 Baker Street, W1U 7DJ

020 7935 4007   www.galvinrestaurants.com

Sibling success is the key ingredient at Galvin. Chris Galvin has more than 30 years' experience in top kitchens, having gained a Michelin star at Orrery and launching The Wolseley as head chef. Jeff Galvin has cooked at The Savoy, with Marco Pierre White and Nico Ladenis. They now cook simple bistro food, to a chorus of approval throughout London. The brothers call it a *bistrot de luxe*, and we wouldn't demur. The menu is full of simple classics such as snails, oysters, steak tartare, calf's liver with bacon and crème brûlée and the *prix fixe* menu is a great deal. The tarte au citron is the best I have ever tasted. The brothers have gone on to open other restaurants, but this remains our first choice.

The Ginger Pig 8–10 Moxon Street, W1U 4EW

020 7935 7788   www.thegingerpig.co.uk

This meat-lover's paradise is how the archetypal local butcher's shop should look, smell and sound. Tim Wilson presides over one of the best food retail experiences in London with a huge walk-in cold room with countless carcasses awaiting the knife, and the smell of game pies baking in the oven. Longhorn cattle (the oldest domestic beef cattle breed in Britain), Dorset and Swaledale sheep and several rare-breed pigs, including Tamworths (the original ginger pig), all come from Tim's organic farms (he has three) on the Yorkshire moors. Free-range geese, chickens and turkeys are sourced from the 500-acre Belvoir Estate in Rutland, and game is from the most reputable shoots. The selection of sausages, bacon, hams, terrines and pies is not cheap, but the value lies in the flavour. Do try the epic sausage roll.

Best for... Asian & Fusion

Hakkasan – two restaurants to choose from, both dark and sexy, and the food is pretty good too

HKK – a true Cantonese banquet

Hutong – a glamorous setting near the top of The Shard

Above **The Galvin bistrot de luxe tart au citron.**

Above **Subterranean decadence, masses of teak and seriously considered mood lighting at Hakkasan.**

Hakkasan 8 Hanway Place, Hanway Street, W1T 1HD

020 7927 7000 www.hakkasan.com

Seminal Hong Kong meets Chinese cuisine in glamorous surroundings. Tong Chee Hwee, the original chef and master of the Hakkasan kitchens, deserves a very special mention: this restaurant won a Michelin star in 2003 and has retained it ever since. If you can't get a table, try the Ling Ling bar for an extensive menu of great cocktails. The interior is sleek and atmospheric, so sit back and admire the design details, especially the evocative lighting scheme by light designer Arnold Chan.

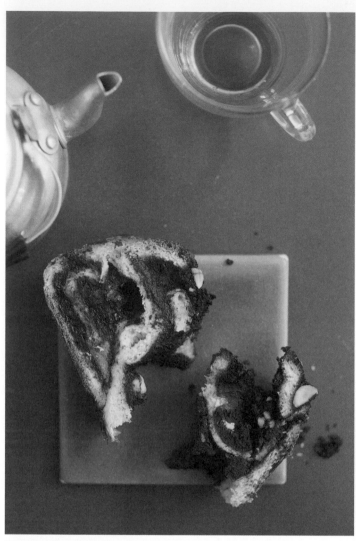

Left **Chocolate, hazelnut and cinnamon krantz loaf cake.**
Right **Lemons are a key ingredient at Honey & Co.**

Below, from top **Baba ganoush with pomegranate seeds; hummous; muhamra (pepper and walnut), and labneh dips.**

Honey & Co 25 Warren Street, W1T 5LZ 020 7388 6175

Honey & Smoke 216 Great Portland Street, W1W 5QW 020 7388 6175

Honey & Spice 52 Warren Street, W1T 5NJ 020 7388 6175

www.honeyandco.co.uk

These three places are all about two people: Sarit Packer and Itamar Srulovich. They are a married couple, with Sarit looking after everything pastry and bakery orientated and Itamar running the other corners of a restaurant kitchen. Their food is that of the Middle East, with lots of bold flavours, and is deliciously tasty. When recently dining at Honey & Grill, their latest place, the whole table said immediately that this was the best food that we'd all had for a very long time. They seem to bring out the best in ingredients and combine flavours perfectly.

Left and right **Freshly baked cakes in the window display at Honey & Co.**

Left and right **One-pan dishes such as lamb siniya (right) with flatbread and a salad are a popular choice at Honey & Co.**

Left **A salad of peaches and goats' cheese with roasted almonds at Honey & Co.**
Right **Outside seating at Honey & Co.**

This page **Kaffeine offers more than just excellent coffee.**

Kaffeine 66 Great Titchfield Street, W1W 7QJ

020 7580 6755 www.kaffeine.co.uk

Another independent antipodean coffee bar where the bean is worshipped and cherished: the influx of these coffee entrepreneurs from Australia and New Zealand has given a welcome fillip to the scene and provides an excellent counterblast to the proliferation of the big chains. It lies directly opposite the Riding House Café (see page 256), where the coffee is good but not as good as at Kaffeine, so cross the road for a post-lunch espresso.

Right **Skilled baristas are the backbone of London's coffee culture.**

Locanda Locatelli 8 Seymour Street, W1H 7JZ
020 7935 9088 www.locandalocatelli.com

Following his achievement at Zafferano, it was inevitable that Giorgio Locatelli's own little inn, or *locanda*, would be a great success when it first opened in 2002. The diaries seemed to be full even as the paint was drying on the David Collins-designed modern and elegant dining room, and have remained so. Along with The River Café in Hammersmith, Locanda Locatelli is definitely our top Italian eatery, with Locatelli certainly being the more refined version.

You start with a generous basket of beautiful homemade bread, as you'd expect, from a deliciously moist focaccia to wafer-thin *pane*, and the tables are also laid with 60cm (2-ft-long) *grissini*. Go with an appetite: it would be a shame to have anything less than four courses. The menu is vast, starting with an exceptional selection of antipasti, then about a dozen different pasta dishes, followed by a fine selection of meat and fish dishes, and you cannot visit without a little *dolci*.

The front of house is also close to perfect, marked by an almost uncanny blend of intuition and anticipation. The specials are recommended with such passion, and you feel that while every member of the team is the ultimate in professionalism, they also live and dine together as a happy family.

Above **The bread at the start of a meal at Locanda Locatelli says a great deal about the quality that you are about to experience.**

Marylebone Farmers' Market Cramer Street Car Park,
off Marylebone High Street, W1U 4DB

Sunday 10am–2pm

Marylebone High Street and its environs already have their full complement of fine retail food outlets, but when the market comes to town on Sunday, the vast choice is enough to sate any foodie's deepest desires. The Marylebone market is London's largest *exclusively* farmers' market, with between 30 and 40 stalls; Borough Market is significantly larger, but it doesn't follow the strict rules set down by the London Farmers' Market Association, whose website, www.lfm.org.uk gives information about other London markets.

It's always enjoyable to visit these markets and talk with the farmers, growers, fishermen and producers themselves. Over time, I have learned to focus my purchasing on meat, game, fruit, vegetables and salad leaves. The cheese is eclipsed by the selection at nearby La Fromagerie or Neal's Yard Dairy (see pages 244–5 and 295), and the cakes are better from other specialist shops.

Orrery 55 Marylebone High Street, W1U 5RB
020 7616 8000 www.orrery-restaurant.co.uk

Named after the mechanical device that illustrates the relative positions of the planets in the solar system and also the name of the second Conran restaurant in 1954, as it happens), Orrery has several noteworthy features. The restaurant space – long, narrow and very elegant – sits above The Conran Shop as part of a converted stable building, with large arched windows overlooking the carefully tended grounds of the churchyard opposite and a row of banquette seating on the facing wall. This really lovely dining room is at its best at lunch. It is also complemented by the unique summer terrace upstairs, which not too many people know about. Orrery delivers on several levels; most exciting, however, is its award-winning cheese trolley. If you are serious about cheese (and we are – very), this is the place to dine. There is also a blockbuster wine list.

Left and below
Hard work behind the scenes at Locanda Locatelli.

Spaghetti 'Latini' alla Vongole

Serves 4

75ml (3fl oz) extra-virgin olive oil
3 garlic cloves, peeled and finely chopped
1 chilli, finely chopped
1kg (2lb) veraci clams (palourdes or carpetshell)
½ wineglass of dry white wine
400g (13oz) spaghetti 'Latini'
1 handful of parsley, finely chopped

Place a large pan of lightly salted water over a high heat and bring it to the boil. Meanwhile, heat half of the olive oil in a large sauté pan over a medium heat. The aim is to cook the garlic (so that it is digestible) but not burn it (or it will be bitter), so it is a good idea to tilt the pan a little. This way, the oil flows to one spot. Place the garlic and chilli into the oil so they can cook in this depth and will be less likely to burn. Cook gently for a few minutes until they start to colour.

Place the pan back down fully onto the stove and add the clams. Cook them for about 30 seconds and then add the white wine. Cover the pan with a lid to allow the clams to steam open. After about one minute or up to 90 seconds, remove the lid and discard any clams that haven't opened.

Leave around one-quarter of the clams in their shells, but scrape out the rest, discarding the shells. Turn off the heat.

Once the large pan of salted water has come to the boil, place the pasta into it and let it boil for about a minute less than the time given on the packet (usually 5–6 minutes), until al dente. Drain the pasta, reserving the cooking water.

Add the pasta to the clams along with the remaining oil and toss thoroughly for about a minute to let the pasta absorb the flavours and allow the starch to thicken the sauce.

If you need to loosen it slightly, add a little cooking water from the pasta. You will see that the sauce starts to cling to the pasta, so that when you serve it the pasta it will stay coated. Sprinkle with chopped parsley and serve straight away.

Giorgio Locatelli – one of London's greatest chefs and restaurateurs.

Left and below
**Lots of happy diners
and a busy kitchen
at Portland.**

Above **A blowtorch is
now an essential part
of the chefs *batterie
de cuisine*.**

Portland 113 Great Portland Street, W1W 6QQ

020 7436 3261 www.portlandrestaurant.co.uk

Portland achieved brilliant reviews when it first opened, including a five-star score from the late A A Gill. However, I wasn't really loving what I was reading about the restaurant, so it slipped down my to-do list. When I did actually visit, it jumped to the top of the must-go-again list. The menu is pleasingly straightforward, with each course based on a choice of three dishes: vegetables, meat and fish. You start with a selection of little snacks and they usually offer some excellent daily specials. It's rather difficult to pigeon-hole this restaurant, but I would probably say that it is a modern British approach to professional restaurant keeping. If you are a wine lover, you'll also enjoy this place. The team have been very passionate and informative about everything vinous. The main wine list has been excellently curated and offers first a tasting note, then the name of the wine, for example: *Lemon & ginger dominate this wine* Domaine Dirler-Cadé, Riesling Saering, Alsace. The owners have recently opened a second restaurant nearby called Clipstone. I've not been yet but all of the reviews that I have read have been very positive (PP).

Right **Professional,
well-informaed staff
at Portland.**

Left **The brilliantly
talented Kiwi Peter
Gordon.**
Right **Wild strawberry
sorbet with
gooseberry espresso
compote, vanilla
cream, hazelnut
praline and a torta
de aceite biscuit at
The Providores.**

The Providores 109 Marylebone High Street, W1U 4RX

020 7935 6175 www.theprovidores.co.uk

Originally, this was known as a pioneering fusion restaurant led by the brilliant
New Zealander Peter Gordon, probably the first and best chef cooking this type
of food at this (high) level. This was at a time when in the hands of less skilled
chefs the whole idea of fusion food was much maligned. Opinions have changed
and we are now more accustomed to menus that combine a wide range of
flavours and ingredients. Now, the fusion word is hardly mentioned and instead
this is simply known as an excellent restaurant led by a pioneering chef. If you
like quality New Zealand wines, you might be interested to note that this
restaurant boasts the largest selection in Europe.

The ground-floor Tapa Room, named after a wood-fibre ceremonial cloth
used throughout the Pacific for celebratory feasts, offers probably the most
innovative breakfast-brunch menu in London. Dishes include French toast with
banana and pecans with grilled smoked streaky bacon and vanilla verjus syrup;
and kumara, caramelized red onion, kawakawa and feta tortilla with Turkish
yogurt, piquillo peppers and rocket.

Right **Pan-fried
halibut on a
kawakawa potato
cake with morel,
shiitake and edamame
ragout and samphire
at The Providores.**

changa Turkish Eggs

Serves 4

The Providores have worked with changa restaurant in Istanbul since 1999. This is a dish we have eaten many times in Turkey and it is one of our most popular dishes at breakfast time in the restaurant. In Turkey the yoghurt has raw garlic beaten into it but we've found that's a bit too much for the English breakfast palate.

300 g (10 oz) thick yogurt
½ teaspoon fine sea salt
1 garlic clove, peeled and finely chopped (optional)
75 ml (3 fl oz) extra virgin olive oil
75 ml (3 fl oz) white vinegar
8 medium or large eggs
50 g (2 oz) butter
1 teaspoon kirmizi biber (dried Turkish chilli flakes)
2 tablespoons roughly chopped parsley
wholewheat sourdough toast

Beat the yogurt with the salt, garlic and half the oil and divide two-thirds of it among 4 bowls.

Bring a deep pot (about 3 litres/6 pints in capacity) of water to the boil. Reduce the temperature so the water just simmers and add the vinegar. Crack the eggs in one by one and poach them until the whites are set but the yolks are still runny. This should take about 5–7 minutes.

Meanwhile, heat the butter in a small pan until it turns pale nut-brown. Add the chilli flakes and let them sizzle. Then remove them from the heat, add the remaining olive oil and set aside.

Carefully lift the eggs out of the pot with a slotted spoon and place 2 in each bowl, on top of the yogurt. Spoon the remaining yoghurt on top of the eggs. Give the chilli butter a good stir and spoon this on top.

Scatter with the parsley and serve the toast on a separate plate.

Riding House Café 43–51 Great Titchfield Street, W1W 7PQ

020 7927 0840   www.ridinghousecafe.co.uk

The cheeseburger is brilliant, excellent value and the epitome of the place.
The whole ensemble, from the design details to the attitude of the staff, seems
to be trying so terribly hard to be New York-esque, and in the main it works.
It's a great meeting point and informal gathering place for the ad agency and
design kids on the block. We recommend this place highly for a weekend
breakfast, brunch or late lunch, or maybe an early evening drink on a first date.

Above **The dining
area at the Riding
House Café.**
Right **A very
professionally
prepared waiter
station at Riding
House Café.**

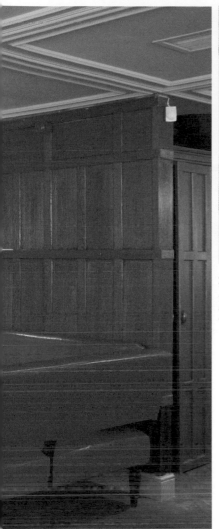

Above and below left
The bar with some of the most comfortable swivel bar stools you could expect.

Right **The communal table featuring salvaged and repurposed theatre seats.**

ROKA 37 Charlotte Street, W1T 1RR

020 7580 6464 www.rokarestaurant.com

Launched after its renowned sibling Zuma in Knightsbridge (see page 72), ROKA is generally perceived as a less serious offering, but in our view it is much better and we prefer the ambience and interior at ROKA. Japan's esteemed Super Potato and Noriyoshi Muramatsu collaborated on the architecture and design. Light floods through the windows during the day, creating perfect conditions in which to admire the food. An abundance of natural materials, especially timber, combined with pickling jars on shelves, completes the interior design. The principal feature is the central Robata grill, a type of Japanese barbecue. This open kitchen allows guests to observe the chef preparing lamb cutlets with Korean spices, tiger prawns with ginger, yuzu and mirin or scallop skewers with wasabi and shiso. The menu includes sashimi, nigiri and much more. The desserts are particularly good and the presentation is inspired.

Named after the Japanese spirit, the Shochu Lounge in the basement is sexy and cool. Unlike sake, which is brewed, shochu is distilled to produce an alcohol content of about 25 per cent. The cocktail list has elevated the drink to new heights; expertly devised and perfectly executed, a drink downstairs before or after your meal upstairs is a must.

Selfridges Food Hall Selfridges, 400 Oxford Street, W1A 2LR

0800 123 400 www.selfridges.com

Every possible gourmet comestible is to be found at Selfridges, now one of the best department-store food halls in London. If you want it, they've got it. The individual counters are as good, if not better, than you might find at your local baker's, butcher's, fishmonger's, cheese monger's and greengrocer's. Alongside this fine selection of ingredients, there are some very interesting concessions that seem to change on a regular basis, making sure that the food hall is always on trend and in tune with what is happening in the London food bubble. Currently, they include a Hemsley + Hemsley Café and they are welcoming Dan Barber from New York State's Blue Hill restaurant with a thought-provoking initiative all about food waste. They also operate other pop-up bars and restaurants on the roof.

Texture 34 Portman Street, W1H 7BY

020 7224 0028 www.texture-restaurant.co.uk

I really wasn't expecting to like this restaurant, but it did that difficult thing and changed my views on Nordic cuisine. Aggi Sverrisson, the chef patron, is Icelandic and clearly very talented. The wine list is also very good (PP).

Above and above right
Fine dining at Texture.

More places to visit in the area

Above right **The BT Tower – in the 1960's it housed a restaurant on the top floor that rotated completely every 22 minutes.**

28°–50°
15–17 Marylebone Lane, W1U 2NE
020 7486 7922 www.2850.co.uk
An imaginative and modern wine bar with very good food.

BAO Fitzrovia
31 Windmill Street, W1T 2JN
020 3011 1632 www.baolondon.com
If you can't be bothered with the queues at the Soho branch then it's usually a little easier to snag a space at this location.

Berners Tavern
10 Berners Street, W1T 3NP
020 7908 7979 www.editionhotels.com/london/restaurants-and-bars/berners-tavern
Another Jason Atherton outpost, this time in partnership with a big hotel group, which seems to reduce some of the appeal. But it is glamorous enough for a big night out.

Comptoir Libanais
65 Wigmore Street, W1U 1PZ
020 7935 1110 www.lecomptoir.co.uk
Lebanese-style canteen cooking and deli at very affordable prices in a funky modern setting. Lots to like, not least the flavours. Now part of a larger group.

Ethos
48 Eastcastle Street, W1W 8DX
020 3581 1538 www.ethosfoods.com
This is quite different from most other establishments listed in this book in that it is a self-service restaurant that offers meat-free menus. The pricing is Pay by Weight.

Mac & Wild
65 Great Titchfield Street, W1W 7PS
020 7637 0510 www.macandwild.com
A new restaurant aiming to promote excellent produce from Scotland – great game, in season.

Pied à Terre
34 Charlotte Street, W1T 2NH
020 7636 1178 www.pied-a-terre.co.uk
A good example of what some might call highfalutin fine dining.

Royal China Club
40–2 Baker Street, W1U 7AJ 020 7486 3898
24–26 Baker Street, W1U 3BZ
020 7487 4688 www.theroyalchina.co.uk
Authentic Chinese food and dim sum from the best exponents of this style of food in the capital. Both offer suitably flash and shiny settings.

The Sea Shell
49–51 Lisson Grove, NW1 6UH
020 7224 9000 www.seashellrestaurant.co.uk
The world's most Michelin-starred chef, Alain Ducasse, says this offers the best battered fish and chips in London.

Trishna
5–17 Blandford Street, W1U 3DG
020 7935 5624 www.trishnalondon.com
A small but excellent restaurant specializing in coastal Indian food, with an impressive wine list.

Vinoteca
15 Seymour Place, W1H 5BD
020 7724 7288 www.vinoteca.co.uk
Sister of the original Vinoteca near Smithfield.

Mayfair
Piccadilly
St James's
Westminster

For a taste of reassuring, chocolate-box Britishness in London, we'll always have Piccadilly. This sweep of Regency architecture takes in The Wolseley, The Ritz, The Royal Academy, Fortnum & Mason – all institutions that change gratifyingly little and serve consistently well regardless of the passage of time and advent of cultural revolutions. The Tudor edifice of St James's Palace, built by Henry VIII on the site of a leper hospital, is the oldest building in what is otherwise a predominantly Georgian area. Interestingly, it is said to feature a secret tunnel that runs directly to Berry Bros & Rudd, the UK's first wine merchant. It's a fascinating place, built on the site of the King's tennis court, and with a rich history of harbouring ne'er-do-wells and eminences up to no good. The tunnel from St James's allowed philandering royals access to extra-marital liaisons, while its basement rooms have sheltered a Napoleon III on the run, as well as a thirsty Lord Byron, William Pitt the Younger and serious oenophiles for the past 300 years. I doubt our current, comparatively boring, royal family would even dream of such bacchanalian fun. The 'mad, bad and dangerous to know' Byron (the expression was coined for him) would find plenty to recognize in today's Piccadilly and St James's. He could still buy a bespoke suit on Savile Row or the ready-to-wear variety on Jermyn Street (known to many as Bloke Street, as until recently it catered almost exclusively for the sartorial needs of the gentleman class). Byron would still be able to drink the day and night away in any number of gentlemen's clubs, and he would also be able to smoke a cigar in James J Fox – the 229-year-old smoking shop has a special, extremely rare, exemption from the UK-wide smoking ban. Churchill, arguably the world's most famous cigar smoker and James J Fox patron, would have approved.

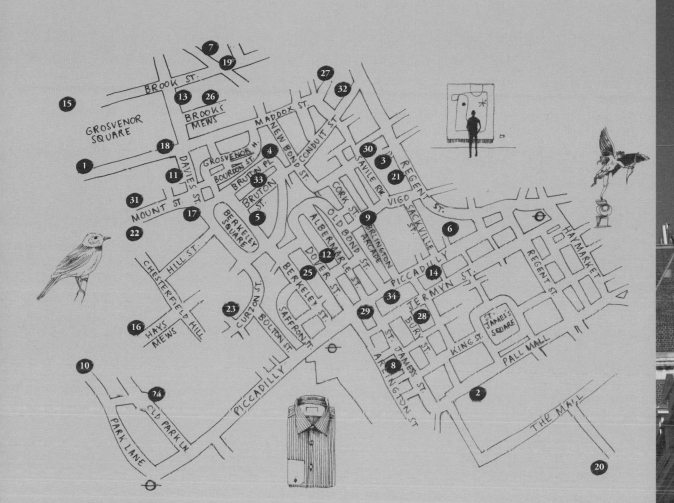

If Scott's is Mayfair's fish restaurant of choice (see page 279), then 34 is
the steak house where its denizens flock; both are owned by Richard Caring.
Much has been said about Mr Caring, but ultimately it is now over ten
years since he bought, at a great price, his entry into the restaurant world,
having acquired three of London's top restaurants: The Ivy, J Sheekey
and Le Caprice (see pages 195 and 264). He's gone on to create new
restaurants and constantly injects huge amounts of cash into his restaurant
empire. As a result, it would be disingenuous to deny his place as one of the
titans of the London restaurant world. At 34, it is clear that he has invested
in the finest materials and equipment. Front of house, the banquette seating
and proper dining chairs are clad in striking burnt-orange leather; there is fine
metal detailing all around you, and underfoot there is a beautiful oak parquet
floor. In the kitchen, they've got a massive parrilla grill. Having visited kitchens
in Argentina to look at these amazing fires, I have much praise for the chefs
who work with these magnificent heat boxes. Unlike with other grills, the
cooking is done over very, very hot coals but with very limited flames. This
tends to mean that you taste more of the meat and less of the carbonized
effects of the flames. The menu at 34 offers several different cuts from four
types of beef: USDA Prime, Wagyu and some excellent grass-fed beef from
Yorkshire and Scotland.

The art at 34 should also be mentioned, and upstairs there is the
Tracey Emin private dining room, with a collection of specially commissioned
art by one of Britain's most celebrated artists.

67 Pall Mall 67 Pall Mall, SW1Y 5EZ
020 3000 6767 www.67pallmall.co.uk

Access to this Grade II listed Lutyens building might be a little difficult
due to 67, as it is simply known in the wine trade, actually being a private
members' club. However, they regularly host wine tastings and various
wine-related events that can make access possible. If not, you might need
to ask your local wine shop if they know any members and try to blag
access by becoming their wine-loving friend. I'm not a member, yet, but
have actually been to 67 several times. It is paradise for any serious
oenophile. They offer over 500 wines by the glass, thanks to the Coravin
system, and have a massive list of other wines to choose from. This is all
wonderful, but then you add the fact that the mark-ups at 67 are some
of the lowest I've ever known at any restaurant or bar – ever. Lots of
restaurateurs and sommeliers talk about low margins at the top end of
their wine list and even when they do actually do what they say, the
mark-ups are still pretty staggering in actual hard cash terms. At 67,
it is almost impossible to accept that they offer such low margins.
As an example, most restaurants that buy a bottle of wine at £100 will
have it on their wine list at around £350, whereas at 67, they might
charge something in the region of £140. So, without any hesitation,
it has got to be declared that 67 is by far the best location for those that
appreciate fine wine (PP).

Francesco Mazzei

"London represented my first work
experience abroad – I left Calabria to
learn English and landed a job at The
Dorchester in the '90s. And eventually,
over the years, it became my home base
and my children have been growing
up here. I feel so attached to this
wonderful city and I'm so grateful for
all the opportunities it has sent my way.
Chef patron, Sartoria

Above **Hanover
Square on a sunny
summer's day.**

The Araki Unit 4, 12 New Burlington Street, W1S 3BF

020 7287 2481 www.the-araki.com

Possibly London's most expensive restaurant at £300 *sans* grog and service. Wow! With just nine seats you can possibly appreciate that they have to cover their costs by charging high prices but this is also dining at a higher level. Saying all that, the food on offer is also to the highest possible standard. Sushi master Mitsuhiro Araki has closed his three-Michelin star restaurant in Tokyo to open this new London *omakase*-style dining experience. They only serve sushi, nothing else, and the website makes it clear that they do not accommodate dietery requirements. Araki-san, we salute your brave and adventurous decisions, not to mention your skill and technique.

Bellamy's 18–18a Bruton Place, W1J 6LY

020 7491 2727 www.bellamysrestaurant.co.uk

Simple Anglo-French menus delivered with poise and a certain *je ne sais quoi*. Incongruously among otherwise humble ingredients, the centrepiece of the menu card is a selection of caviar – a pointer to the old-school society clientele that this restaurant attracts. Owner Gavin Rankin was previously involved in various private members' clubs and many of the clientele have followed him. The adjoining shop sells the finest comestibles that the grand homes of Mayfair cannot afford to be without.

Benares 12a Berkeley Square House, Berkeley Square, W1J 6BS

020 7629 8886 www.benaresrestaurant.com

Atul Kochhar's subtly spiced Indian recipes are perfectly executed, with a menu that includes a large proportion of premium ingredients. Alongside high-quality meats are lobster, bass, scallops and turbot, none of which is ever overwhelmed by the Indian seasonings and accompanying ingredients. This prestigious Berkeley Square address is one of the country's best modern Indian restaurateurs. Many top restaurant critics believe that Atul Kochhar is the best Indian chef in London.

Bentley's Oyster Bar & Grill 11–15 Swallow Street, W1B 4DG

020 7734 4756 www.bentleys.org

Bentley's is a civilized restaurant serving mainly fish and crustacea, conveniently positioned on a narrow street between Regent Street and Piccadilly. The ground-floor oyster bar menu features a fine selection of bi-valves. You can also find really good smoked salmon from Ireland, smoked eel or kippers, fried squid, crubeens (pigs' trotters cooked in traditional Irish fashion), posh fish and chips with mushy peas and tartare sauce good enough to eat on its own, and noble Dover sole. The fish pie is very luxurious, and pricey. Sit at the marble bar and chat with the shuckers, dressed in traditional white coats, while sipping a chilled Chablis grand cru. To finish, the brown sugar meringue with strawberries and Jersey cream is celestial.

The upstairs Grill and Rib Room offers a more extensive menu, including both fish and meat. Meat main-course highlights include a mixed grill featuring a pork and sage sausage, sirloin of beef, belly of pork and lamb chops. The grilled West Cork beef with béarnaise and chips is also very tempting. The outside terrace is also worth a visit on a hot summer's day.

Bonhams 7 Haunch of Venison Yard, W1K 5ES

020 7468 5868 www.bonhamsrestaurant.com

The term 'hidden gem' is often used by marketing people to help overcome a difficult location, especially in regard to restaurants. In the case of Bonhams, the world-famous auction house, their restaurant is accurately described as just that. Thanks to the peerless cooking of Tom Kebble, formerly of Fäviken and Hedone, they've won a Michelin star and deliver some really excellent cooking. The service is also rather good, and Master of Wine Richard Harvey, head of Bonhams wine department, oversees the wine list, which is quite special.

Le Caprice Arlington House, Arlington Street, SW1A 1RJ

020 7629 2239 www.le-caprice.co.uk

Located behind The Ritz, Le Caprice is a sister restaurant to The Ivy, J Sheekey and Scott's among others in Richard Caring's group of restaurants (see pages 195 and 279). Legendary maître d' Jesus Adorno oversees the unflappable service, as he has done since the restaurant opened in 1981. The Sunday brunch is a favourite: Bloody May, followed by a proper Eggs Arlington and Caesar salad.

Cecconi's 5a Burlington Gardens, W1S 3EP

020 7434 1500 www.cecconis.co.uk

If Curzon Street is hedge fund alley, this is the fund managers' dining room, especially at breakfast time. The alluring dining room and bar in this easy-on-the-eye setting were designed by Ilse Crawford in partnership with Nick Jones and his Soho House group: the marble floor and lush green leather chairs are particularly stylish. In the 1980s this was *the* socialite restaurant, then it lost its way in the 1990s. Now Nick Jones has worked his magic, and it is again one of the hottest destinations for those with very deep pockets.

They make a great Negroni cocktail, as you might expect at a Venetian-inspired restaurant, and I would also rate the excellent lobster spaghetti. On a previous visit, the waiter brought some white truffles to the table and kept shaving and shaving and shaving. I hope the chef didn't find out.

Best for... a special occasion or birthday

When you are treating somebody or wanting them to feel special, your selection of the appropriate restaurant is all-important. You'll need to think about booking in advance.

China Tang

The Ritz

Zuma

Left and far left **Dishes from Cecconi's** including a spring vegetable salad and cheesecake with poached rhubarb. Above **The busy reception desk at Cecconi's.**

Top **The dining room at China Tang, designed by Sir David Tang.**
Above **Special equipment was imported from China to meet the demanding requirements of the chefs at China Tang.**
Right **Distinctive and classy staff uniforms at China Tang.**

China Tang at The Dorchester Hotel 53 Park Lane, W1K 1QA
020 7629 9988 www.thedorchester.com/china-tang

There are some horrible places within the Dorchester Hotel (particularly the hideous bar). China Tang is the arch-opposite and a beacon of good taste. it offers an enchanting blend of chinoiserie and 1930s art deco. Having worked with Sir David Tang, we can say that he is enormously talented in every aspect of life. The Cantonese food here is excellent and the Peking duck is essential.

C London 23–5 Davies Street, W1K 3DE
020 7399 0500 www.crestaurant.co.uk

When this restaurant opened in 2004 it was called Cipriani, but a High Court judgment in 2010 forced it to change its name (we're not making this up). This is one of those restaurants that you should make an effort to try just once. I've visited the London restaurant a couple of times as well as those in New York and Hong Kong; all the dining rooms are very elegant, and the waiters' gallant white uniforms set the tone to a tee. Order the beef carpaccio – you will be eating a piece of culinary history (PP).

The English Tea Room at Brown's Hotel Albemarle Street, W1S 4BP
020 7518 4155 www.roccofortehotels.com

If you don't fancy The Ritz, this is a great and less touristy place to enjoy a classic English afternoon tea. Comfortable armchairs, pressed linen, silver multilayer cake stands and ornate teapots – all very cosseting while you enjoy your finger sandwiches and dainty cakes, not forgetting the quintessential scones.

Left **Raphael Rodriguez, the sommelier at Fera.**

Right **Some of the kitchen wizardry equipment at Fera.** Opposite, above **The dining room at Fera designed by Guy Oliver.** Opposite, below **Head Chef Daniel Cox.**

Fera Claridge's, 49 Brook Street, W1K 4HR

020 7107 8888 www.feraatclaridges.co.uk

Set within the majestic halls of Claridge's, this is mega-chef Simon Rogan's London outpost. Known for his seminal restaurant in the Lake District, Simon applies his ingenuity and creativity to bring highly seasonal dishes to the table. Having dined at Fera with a few mates that were expecting a proper *dégustation* menu experience, we all left a little disappointed, and more than a little hungry. However, I think we all missed the point and our expectations were wrongly collated. You need to understand Fera's aims before you dine there. They seek to impress through more than just taste. I would also say that Simon's commitment to his suppliers and his own farm growing much of the produce for Fera is very admirable. A visit to Fera is also likely to introduce you to some new and unusual, often foraged, vegetables and herbs, plus all manner of other flora and fauna.

Fera means wild in Latin and it is the link between nature and the restaurant that the use of the word is trying to convey.

268

Fortnum & Mason 181 Piccadilly, W1A 1ER

020 7734 8040 www.fortnumandmason.com

In 1707, William Fortnum and Hugh Mason founded a grocery store that has become an iconic British institution. Fortnum's is probably even more renowned in the eyes of overseas visitors than it is for Londoners. The Scotch egg was invented here in 1851, apparently, and in 1886 this was the first place in Britain to sell Heinz baked beans. Today it is grocer to Her Majesty, and is more commonly associated with its loose-leaf teas, its confectionery and its amazing collection of hampers, ranging from the picnic variety that are the envy of all at Glyndebourne and Henley to luxury Christmas gift versions. In 2007 the store received a revamp and introduced a few new concepts, including a new wine bar, where you can order wine from the adjacent wine department and pay a fixed £15 corkage charge. Most recently, they have installed Ewan Venters as the impressive chief executive and he is dramatically shaking up this great institution. He's also recently introduced a new restaurant called 45 Jermyn Street.

Above **Cloches – the epitome of old-school fine dining on the pass at Le Gavroche.**

Best for... business entertaining

Le Gavroche – negotiate the best deal while enjoying one of the best meal deals in London. The fixed price lunch menu offers great value for money

The Greenhouse – super-high end, with one of the world's best wine lists and a Mayfair address to impress

Lutyens – vying for the best dining room in the Square Mile; certainly the wine list is hard to beat

Pétrus – the name says it all

Left **Preparing the soufflé suissesse in the kitchen at Le Gavroche.**

Le Gavroche 43 Upper Brook Street, W1K 7QR
020 7408 0881 www.le-gavroche.co.uk

No restaurant has won more awards than Le Gavroche, and we don't just mean from the Michelin man – although it is worth noting that in 1982 Le Gavroche became the first restaurant in the UK to be awarded three Michelin stars. Most of the awards it receives are voted for by industry peers, as testament to their admiration for the kitchen and front-of-house teams. More to the point, the restaurant is one of the best in London.

First established in Lower Sloane Street in 1967 by brothers Michel and Albert Roux, the restaurant moved to its current location in 1981. When Albert's son, Michel Jr, took over the kitchen in 1991, he subtly modernized the menus and gradually ushered in lighter elements. The rich cheese soufflé recipe is not of the latter variety, however.

Silvano Giraldin, the front-of-house maestro, has also been a major contributor to the restaurant's success. He has been with the Roux brothers since 1971 and is now a director of the company, though he has now stepped back a little.

Another admirable feature of Le Gavroche is the attractively priced all-inclusive lunch menu, including three courses, mineral water, wine, coffee and petits fours.

The Greenhouse 27a Hay's Mews, W1X 7RJ
020 7499 3331 www.greenhouserestaurant.co.uk

This is serious fine dining where no expense is spared. They've got two Michelin stars and serve some of the most intricate food you can imagine. The restaurant's head sommelier appears to have an even bigger budget and more lavish expenditure, however. The Greenhouse has one of the most extensive wine lists in the world and in 2005 won the Wine Spectator's Grand Award, one of only four restaurants in the world to have done so.

Hedonism Wines 3–7 Davies Street, W1K 3LD
020 7290 7870 www.hedonism.co.uk

If 67 Pall Mall is the best place in London to enjoy a glass or two of very fine wine (see page 262), then Hedonism is the best place to buy the most pre-eminent wines on the planet. They've got everything you can ever imagine from the world of wines and spirits, from a staggering collection of 100-point Robert Parker wines to a room dedicated to just Château d'Yquem. Walking around Hedonism gives wine lovers goosebumps; the vast array covers everything from Krug to the largest and oldest wine bottles available anywhere in the world. If you've got a wine-loving friend with a special birthday on the horizon, this is the place to visit. Mercifully, they have an army of former sommeliers patrolling the shop to help and guide you to the best wine, while also offering a wealth of information and advice. Cheers!

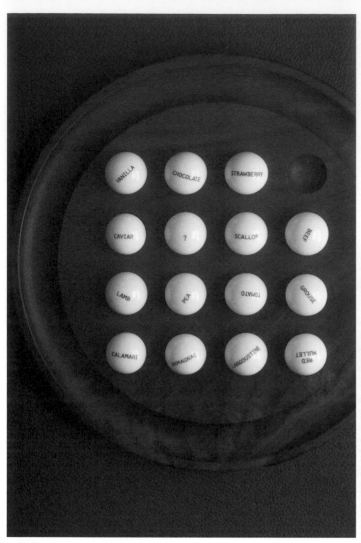

Hélène Darroze at The Connaught Carlos Place, W1K 2AL

020 3147 7200   www.the-connaught.co.uk

Hélène hails from south-west France where her family are renowned restaurateurs and also produce one of the best Armagnacs on the market, so there is naturally a large selection on display here. Also on display in the restaurant as you enter is a table piled with brilliant butter in large, churn-size blocks, alongside cured hams and cheese truckles – an unusual feature for a dining room of this calibre, and something to be applauded. A visit must involve sampling the food from her native Gascony, including duck foie gras followed by Landais chicken.

The old Connaught dining experiences are long gone. This new version may not be to everybody's liking, but it is much invigorated and opens a new chapter in the illustrious history of this once noblest of hotels.

If you are meeting an important client or trying to clinch a major deal, you'd be advised to start with a pre-dinner glass of champagne or a Dry Martini at The Connaught bar. It was designed by the late David Collins and is probably one of the most distinguished bars in Mayfair, which is saying a lot.

Left **A lighting detail from the bar at The Connaught.** Opposite **The bar at The Connaught designed by the David Collins Studio.**

Ikeda 30 Brook Street, W1K 5DJ

020 7629 2730   www.ikedarestaurant.com/

Back in the early 1990s, this was one of the first serious Japanese restaurants
I visited. Within six months of my first visit, Mr Ikeda and I worked together
on a special event for the Japanese royal family, plus a memorable wedding
attended by a number of British and European royals. The sushi is that good.
Ikeda is a traditional Japanese restaurant with a great deal to offer, even if
you don't fancy sushi and especially if you want a substantial lunch at very
reasonable prices. Ask for the *omakase* menu, which translates loosely as
'I'll leave it to the chef to decide' (PP).

Inn The Park St James's Park, SW1A 2BJ

020 7451 9999   www.peytonandbyrne.co.uk

The royal parks of London are among the capital's greatest assets, and
the addition of a restaurant in St James's Park has increased their value
enormously. What was once a dreary park café, with poor-quality ice cream,
bad snacks and not much else, has undergone a complete transformation.
The architect Michael Hopkins has created a timber building with a
turfed roof, with fittings from Tom Dixon, and the food is the best of British,
as befits the location.

Right **Few things say
British summertime
more than a stripey
deck chair.**

Below **The tree-lined
lake in St James's Park
is often busy with
waterfowl, including
a resident colony of
pelicans.**

Momo Restaurant Familial / Mo Tearoom and Bazaar

25 Heddon Street, W1B 4BH

020 7434 4040   www.momoresto.com

Mourad 'Momo' Mazouz has re-created the Maghreb in a small cul-de-sac off Regent Street. The cuisine and culture of this atmospheric collection of North African nations are combined here with beautiful staff, electro world music and souk-like interiors. Endless artefacts, antiquities and objects collide with a lively, sometimes loud, evening crowd to create an eclectic ambience. The menu displays the fruits of energetic research, with a broad and judiciously applied range of herbs and spices. It may not be strictly authentic, but some would say it is all the better for that, as it benefits from superior ingredients.

Next door, the Mo Tearoom and Bazaar is always busy with fashionistas sucking on shisha pipes or tucking into *kemia* (Arab tapas).

The Mount Street Deli 100 Mount Street, W1K 2TG

020 7499 6843   www.themountstreetdeli.co.uk

If you can't get a table at one of Richard Caring's group of eternally modish restaurants, then you can taste a little of what you are missing at his deli. The Mount Street Deli stocks sushi from Sexy Fish, shepherd's pie from The Ivy, J Sheekey's fish pie, Mark's Club Scotch eggs, Annabel's club chocolate cake and Scott's carrot cake. Mr Caring is rapidly becoming the Blofeld of the food world, aiming at nothing less than world domination. Whatever next?

Murano 20 Queen Street, W1J 5PP

020 7495 1127   www.muranolondon.com

Angela Hartnett spent the early part of her career working with Gordon Ramsay, and it has often been said that she was the star of a nebulous bunch. Since leaving the GR group, Angela's reputation has grown exponentially and she is now one of the country's most admired female chefs. This is her flagship restaurant, which offers refined Italian cuisine.

Mayfair / Piccadilly / St James's / Westminster

Best for...
Indian/
Subcontinent

Gunpowder – no reservations but they do operate an innovative text alert system while you wait for a table in a nearby drinking hole

Gymkhana – extremely difficult to get a table but worth the effort

Trishna – a sister to Gymkhana with a perfectly suited wine list

Right **An apposite message on the staff uniforms at Inn The Park.**

Nobu 19 Old Park Lane, W1K 1LB

020 447 4747 www.noburestaurants.com

This is the restaurant that put black cod on the culinary map in the UK. The illustrious Nobu Matsuhisa opened the first European branch of his now global empire on the first floor of the sophisticated Metropolitan Hotel in 1997, since when it has been a perpetual success. I remember visiting in the early days when the staff were exclusively models dressed in designer clothes – it was revolutionary. Over 20 years on it's still a challenge to secure a table, and the paparazzi are regularly camped out on the doorstep. The interior design is quite dry (they call it minimalist), and don't be swayed by the hype surrounding tables with 'views over Hyde Park': firstly, it's actually a view over the traffic of Park Lane and, secondly it's much better to sit at the sushi bar or the chef's table at the far end of the restaurant. Here you are away from the noise and posturing of the main restaurant – where so many of the diners spend the evening checking out their fellow diners – and you get a chance to watch the sushi masters at work. There is a second Nobu just off Berkeley Square, where they also have a great cocktail bar. A Nobu hotel near Shoreditch in east London is due to open in 2017.

Park Chinois 17 Berkeley Street, W1J 8EA

020 3327 8888 www.parkchinois.com

This place makes The Dorchester hotel look like a down-at-heel youth hostel. I was almost blinded by the acres of gold leaf, silks and ornate detailing. Apparently, the inspiration for the creators, Jacques Garcia, über-designer, and Alan Yau, über-restaurateur, was the 1930s big-band dinner dance setting, the Cotton Club era, with all the old-school luxury and decadence you could ever imagine. It's all about fine chinoiserie – a louche blend of French elegance and the mystique of the East (PP).

We've been told by some very well-informed people connected with Park Chinois that it cost almost £40 million to develop this restaurant – that's got to be some kind of special achievement.

Park Chinois is clearly orientated toward a night-time experience with music and fun. It is, however, also open during the day – they need to recover some of the investment, I guess, and it is at lunch that I happen to have visited twice. Sadly, it is completely devoid of any atmosphere, other than that of ostentatious expense bloated on the dining room. Despite this, the food and service are really very, very good, especially if you aren't paying the bill. It must be a bitter-sweet experience if you have to pick up the tab here. This is possibly the most expensive dim sum in the whole of London, but it is extremely good and the duck de Chine is unbelievably sumptuous.

Top **Phenomenal and dazzling gilding in the downstairs bar at Park Chinois suggests decadence and indulgence.** Left and right **Inside Park Chinois.**

Best for... Japanese

The Araki – probably the most expensive fixed-menu dining in London

Dinings – sitting at the sushi bar is a must

Nobu – two locations to choose from. The food – and the bling factor – are equally good at each. They are also due to open an hotel in Shoreditch

Sushi Tetsu – you need to book a long way in advance

Umu – no expense spared brilliant Kyoto-inspired cuisine with two Michelin stars to boot

La Petite Maison 53–54 Brook's Mews, W1K 4EG
020 7493 4774   www.lpmlondon.co.uk

Beautiful tomatoes, artichokes, peppers, baby courgettes, aubergines, olives and their oil, soft herbes de Provence, tapenade and pissaladière all speak of the brilliant cuisine of Nice and its region. The full range of Mediterranean seafood is also available at this charming dining room, and whole roast Black Leg chicken with foie gras is another highlight (cooked to order, so be sure to let your waiter know the moment you are seated).

Pollen Street Social 8–10 Pollen Street, W1S 1NQ
020 7290 7600   www.pollenstreetsocial.com

This is not generally my style of restaurant, but some of the food is very good. Its quirks, twists and gimmicks can be intense, but underneath them all lies the good intention of providing an interesting meal experience. Although a little annoying sometimes, the food on the plate does still involve a great deal of technique and skill. And, they seem to properly champion some really excellent British produce. Jason Atherton is renowned as the first British chef to work at elBulli, the high temple of molecular gastronomy in Roses on the Costa Brava, and this is his first solo venture after a long period working under Gordon Ramsay. The interior is pleasingly simple, with some interesting details, though it can get a little loud. Jason also claims to have created London's first dessert bar, seating just six.

Quaglino's 16 Bury Street, SW1Y 6AJ

020 7930 6767   www.quaglinos-restaurant.co.uk

Quaglino's opened on Valentine's Day 1993 with a jaw-dropping new design by Sir Terence Conran. This new incarnation was loosely based on the earlier version opened in 1929 by Giovanni Quaglino, combined with the scale of La Coupole in Paris and the spirit of other famous Parisian brasseries, but with an entirely new approach to a restaurant and an entirely new style of restaurant management. The 1993 opening sent shock waves across London: this was the first of a new breed of restaurant, on a scale that eclipsed anything London had seen before. Quaglino's was the most sought-after restaurant in London when it opened, thrilling hundreds of people every night. Along the way it seemed to become *de rigueur* for its customers to 'acquire' one of its famous ashtrays. Now managed by a company called D&D London, Quaglino's is trying to regain some of its past glamour.

The Ritz 150 Piccadilly, W1J 9BR

020 7493 8181   www.theritzlondon.com

'Gentlemen are required to wear a jacket and tie... jeans and sport shoes are not permitted': a few short words that tell you everything you need to know about The Ritz.

The restaurant is a magnificently regal dining room with furnishings reminiscent of the Palace of Versailles. The food is grand-palace-style cooking by John Williams, a veteran of Claridge's and the Savoy Group. Service is by would-be footmen. The Palm Court is eternally popular for afternoon tea, and is a destination for many overseas visitors so you need to book several months in advance. Before touring the restaurants of Russia, I would have said that The Ritz restaurant is one of the most impressive in the world – but that was before I saw Turandot in Moscow, a £50 million restoration masterpiece (PP).

After a great campaign by many of London's top food personalities, The Ritz dining room recently achieved Michelin star status for the first time – a great credit to John Williams.

Left **Impressive flower displays at Quaglino's.**
Right **The epic-scale Quaglino's has been redesigned by Russell Sage.**

Left **David d'Almada has undertaken a major redecoration of Sartoria.**
Right **The dishes at Sartoria are inspired by chef Francesco Mazzei's home region of Calabria.**

Below **Head bar man Gaetano Chiavetta at the Libare Bar at Sartoria.**

Sartoria 20 Savile Row, W1S 3PR

020 7534 7000 www.sartoria-restaurant.co.uk

This restaurant is all about one person: Francesco Mazzei, the chef patron.
If you focus on Francesco's cooking and ignore almost everything else, you
are going to have a really fabulous meal, strong on flavour and generously
giving in every sense. However, allow a little time: the service can be on the
slow side and certainly isn't suitable for quick business lunches. If you happen
to be a well-heeled Italian and appreciate a luxuriant setting, this is where
you belong. The pasta seems to take inspiration from the dining room
upholstery – lush and silky, and the beef tagliata with cured marrow bone
is equally plush. You also might bump into some spicy 'nduja thanks to
Francesco's Calabrian heritage – it is said that Francesco is the person
responsible for adding this spreadable pork salumi to every pizza in every
corner of London over the last couple of years.

Left **The outside terrace at Scott's is now infamous thanks to its connection with Charles Saatchi and Nigella Lawson.**

Right **Scott's has literally got everything – from a brilliant menu and wine list to a very elegant interior and a very desirable art collection.**

Scott's 20 Mount Street, W1K 2HE

020 7495 7309 www.scotts-restaurant.com

Scott's is now one of the most distinguished restaurants in Mayfair. It is superb for celeb spotting or discreet meetings, fantastic for oysters and seafood. The menu is now very upmarket, and the service is always immaculate. The interior looks ravishing and is also comfortable, the art is engaging, the cocktails spot-on, and the wine list caters to all tastes. In fact just about everything is present and correct. This could well be the definitive model for success, in every way.

Left **Bakewell tart and almond ice cream at Scott's.**

Sketch Lecture Room & Library 9 Conduit Street, W1S 2XG

020 7659 4500 www.sketch.uk.com

No other restaurant in London polarizes like Sketch. You either love it or hate it. Generally, though, everybody has enormous respect for the project's ambition and creativity. The brainchild of Mourad 'Momo' Mazouz, who is also responsible for the equally admirable Momo restaurant (see page 273), this project is brave and daring and regularly changes its themes and directions, bringing together the avant-garde from the worlds of art, music, design and food. Pierre Gagnaire, another hugely creative figure, oversees all of the menus, and his experimental food is at its best in the Lecture Room & Library – also known as one of London's most expensive restaurants.

Umu 14–16 Bruton Place, W1J 6LX

020 7499 8881 www.umurestaurant.com

This is London's only Kyoto restaurant, serving exquisite food and stocking the largest sake collection in the capital. When the restaurant opened in 2004, its £200 kaiseki menu attracted some negative publicity, which sadly seemed to have an impact on the number of diners, initially. However, they have gone on to win two Michelin stars and become possibly the best Japanese restaurant in London. The standards across every aspect are nothing short of excellent.

The Wolseley 160 Piccadilly, W1J 9EB

020 7499 6996 www.thewolseley.com

Behind the listed façade and doorman, you enter a world with star-studded clientele, and seating positions are all important; the inner horseshoe is reserved for the London 'faces' one should immediately recognize. The Wolseley calls itself a Grand Café–Restaurant, and follows the tradition of the great European (chiefly Parisian and Viennese) cafés of the 19th century. One of its key characteristics is an extensive selection of menus to choose from – a chef's nightmare, but a diner's dream. You can have anything here, from an all-day menu, lunch, dinner and afternoon tea to hot breakfasts, grills and crustacea, all based on what people want to eat (and not always what the chef wants to serve).

Above **Yoshinori Ishii, the super-talented executive chef at Umu.**

More places to visit in the area

Above **A glimpse of Sexy Fish. It is rumoured that this restaurant cost almost £20 million to create.** Above right **A patriotic scene in Mayfair.**

Le Boudin Blanc
5 Trebeck Street, W1J 7LT
020 7499 3292 www.boudinblanc.co.uk
A decent French restaurant with a lovely atmosphere.

Corrigan's Mayfair
28 Upper Grosvenor Street, W1K 7EH
020 7499 9943 www.corrigansmayfair.com
Richard Corrigan's flagship dining room.

Gymkhana
42 Albemarle Street, W1S 4JH
020 3011 5900 www.gymkhanalondon.com
One of the best upmarket Indian restaurants in Mayfair, and as a result it's impossibly difficult to snag a table.

Hakkasan
17 Bruton Street, W1J 6QB
020 7907 1888 www.hakkasan.com
With this sister to the original in Hanway Place in Fitzrovia, the Hakkasan brand has launched in a location that is probably more suited to its expensive modern chinoiserie style. This place is great for celebrity spotting, if that's your thing. The menu is massive, from abalone and ostrich to dim sum and sweet and sour pork. Ask the waiter to recommend the house specialities and you will have a great meal. The wine lists at both London Hakkasans should not be underestimated: the utmost care and attention have been given to the selection, and the choice by the glass is ideal. They also make a great martini.

Maze Grill
10–13 Grosvenor Square, W1K 6JP
020 7495 2211
www.gordonramsayrestaurants.com/maze-grill-mayfair
A Gordon Ramsay-owned upmarket grill restaurant with grass-fed, grain-fed, corn-fed and Wagyu beef, and much more. The grilled fish and several other items on the menu are also very good.

Sexy Fish
Berkeley Square House,
Berkeley Square, W1J 6BR
020 3764 2000 www.sexyfish.com
No comment on the name – it speaks for itself. A very lavish Asian fusion restaurant for lavish people.

Wild Honey
12 St George Street, Mayfair, London W1S 2FB
020 7758 9160
www.wildhoneyrestaurant.co.uk
With elegant wood panelling and ornate plasterwork, this is a comfortable dining room with some solid cooking by a very experienced chef in Anthony Demetre.

Southwark

This area has gone by many names – until the 1900s, it was known in civic offices as *The Ward of Bridge Without*, which has a ring to it. But Borough is one that has stuck, referring to its position outside, or below, the city of London – and it still has a feeling of otherness about it, despite being just a trot over the bridge from the City, and in the shadow of The Shard. It was desperately poor and overcrowded following industrialization – so much so that an early precursor of the NHS was opened here in 1926 by a philanthropic doctor, Alfred Salter, who was desperate to alleviate the hardships of the Bermondsey poor. His public health centre, which treated the needy for free, predated the NHS by at least 20 years. But through prosperity and poverty, the area has always had an association with food trading – there are references to the 'market town' of Southwark in literature from 1014, making Borough Market more than 1,000 years old. Proximity to London's docks meant that in the 1800s the area became known as 'London's larder', and canneries opened up to process the butter, cheese and meats that landed from the boats. Even so, this part of London has really blossomed as a foodie destination once more over the last 20 years. Borough Market has been joined by Maltby Street on the foodie day-tripper's bucket list of destinations. While Borough has spawned a network of excellent restaurants and food sellers in its perimeter, Maltby Street, or rather the railway arches that rub along it, has taken only five years to transform itself from derelict to *de rigueur*. This is the first of many reasons to visit Bermondsey (the new White Cube Gallery is also here – a sure sign that the area has made it), and you can comfortably cover that and a visit to the extended Tate Modern by foot, if you don't get distracted by the vast foodie offering available en route.

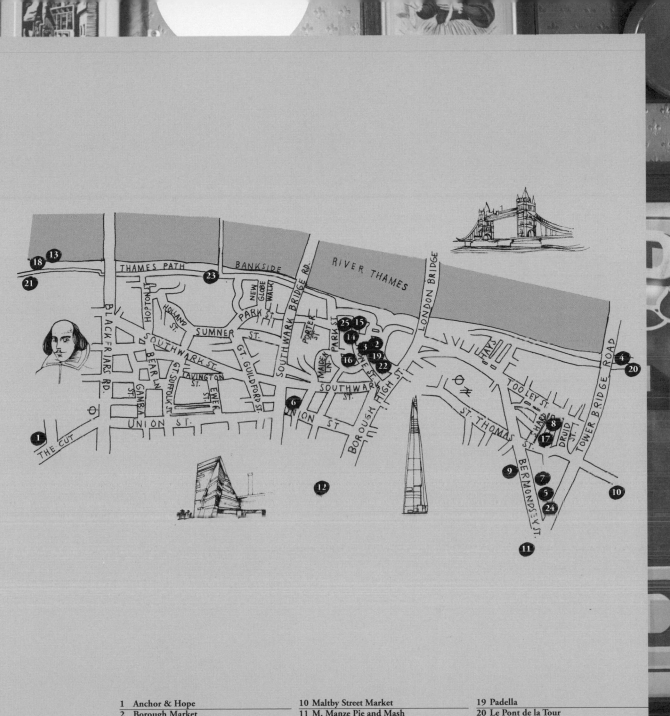

1 Anchor & Hope
2 Borough Market
3 Bread Ahead
4 Butlers Wharf Chop House
5 Casse-Croûte
6 Flat Iron Square
7 The Garrison
8 Hutong
9 José
10 Maltby Street Market
11 M. Manze Pie and Mash
12 Mercato Metropolitano
13 The Mondrian
14 Monmouth Coffee Company
15 Mrs King's Pork Pies
16 Neal's Yard Dairy
17 Oblix
18 Oxo Tower Restaurant and Brasserie
19 Padella
20 Le Pont de la Tour
21 Skylon
22 Tapas Brindisa
23 Tate Modern
24 Village East
25 Wright Brothers Oyster
   and Porter House

Anchor & Hope 36 The Cut, SE1 8LP

020 7928 9898 www.anchorandhopepub.co.uk

Unprepossessing portals lead to some of the best-tasting food in London – just don't expect comfortable surroundings or fawning service. The no-reservations policy (except for Sunday lunch) means there is sometimes a delay before you are seated, and you often have to share a table with other diners in the rather poky and ear-splittingly noisy dining room. Service is relaxed, but once you get to know the staff, perspicacious recommendations are sure to follow.

The menu focuses on earthy and robust flavours and excellent ingredients, cooked with skill but without unnecessary garniture. The dish descriptions may be laconic, but you can be assured of first-class provenance. Expect hearty British favourites, with the occasional French, Spanish or Italian influence. The sharing dishes and large cuts of meat for two, three or four are perfect for this type of setting. Go with friends, maybe after a performance at The Old Vic or the Young Vic, ignore the place's imperfections and just tuck in to some really gutsy food.

Above **Whole roast Sasso chicken and Caesar salad at Anchor & Hope.**

Best for...
food markets

Borough – this place was the catalyst for almost every other new street market

Broadway – a perfect example of a reinvented east London market that's now one of the best food experiences in London

Maltby Street – a challenger to Borough, this has a bigger following among London's fooderati

Marylebone – a more upmarket clientele than most other London markets

Above **Roast is a restaurant located above the salvaged and restored portico at Borough Market,** formerly at the entrance of the Royal Opera House in Covent Graden. Right Scenes from around Borough Market.

Borough Market 8 Southwark Street, SE1 1TL

020 7407 1002 www.boroughmarket.org.uk

Wednesday & Thursday 10–5; Friday 10–6; Saturday 8–5

More than 10,000 visitors flock to Borough Market every weekend to enjoy one of the best food experiences in the country, if not the world. Not only is the food and drink selection excellent, the feel-good factor of seeing small artisan producers in such atmospheric surroundings is palpable.

Historically focused around a wholesale fruit and vegetable market, the weekend fine-foods market has more than 70 stalls. Between them they offer delights ranging from olive oils, herbs, spices, dried fruits and pâtisserie to regional British dairy products and the best fish, shellfish, aged beef, rare-breed pork and game birds, as well as specialist beers and wines. All manner of lovingly prepared foods are to be found here. Many stalls sell only one product, such as Isle of Wight tomatoes or single cheeses. As you stroll along the cramped and crowded walkways, you might find yourself bumping into a whole deer, straight from the fields, hanging on a railing awaiting the knife. Pheasants in full plumage, huge monkfish, mounds of oysters, truckles of cheese: all these and much more are to be found at Borough Market in a very raw and tempting state.

The market also makes a great brunch or lunch destination, with plenty of excellent stalls offering real meat burgers, lamb koftas and proper pizza slices, or you can simply gorge on the many free tasters on offer. As Saturdays have now become so busy, more and more traders now operate earlier in the week, when many Londoners now prefer to go.

Southwark

285

Rillettes de Saumon

Serves 4

400g (14oz) fresh salmon
150g (5½oz) smoked salmon
50g (1¾oz) shallots, finely chopped
bunch of dill, leaves picked and chopped
300ml (½ pint) double cream
sea salt flakes and freshly ground black pepper

Put both types of fish in a steamer basket, then place over a saucepan of boiling water and steam for 6 minutes. Transfer to a bowl and leave to cool.

Mix in the shallots, dill, cream and salt and pepper, then pack into a dish, cover and chill for 24 hours.

To serve, spoon the rillettes on to serving plates and eat with hot toast and a dressed green salad.

Bread Ahead

Borough Market, Cathedral Street, SE1 9DE

020 7403 5444   www.breadahead.com

If you've got an afternoon free and want to do something really interesting, try to book one of the bakery school classes here (there are about 25 to choose from). The classes are open to beginners and those more experienced. I did the Complete French Baking Workshop, which involved making a fougasse, baguette and sourdough loaf (PP).

And do make sure you get one or possibly two or three of Bread Ahead's brilliant doughnuts – possibly the best in London.

Butlers Wharf Chop House

The Butlers Wharf Building, 36e Shad Thames, SE1 2YE

020 7403 3403   www.chophouse-restaurant.co.uk

Reminiscent of a cricket pavilion or boat shed, the Chop House sports walls, floors and a slatted ceiling of English oak. With heavy timber furniture and zinc and marble tops, it looks the same today as when it opened two decades ago, and we hope it will look the same for many years to come.

The cooking is the best of British. Steak and kidney pudding is one of their signature dishes, alongside fish and chips with mushy peas. The choice of steaks and chops from the charcoal grill is extensive.

Casse-Croûte 109 Bermondsey Street, SE1 3XB

020 7407 2140   www.cassecroute.co.uk

This has got to be the most beguiling French bistro in London. It's a tiny room but it just oozes a certain Frenchness. There are red leather banquettes, a black-and-white tiled floor, old French posters and copper pans on the wall, red-and-white gingham undercloths and paper table tops. The service is friendly – not very French – and the daily changing blackboard menu is a dream. Nothing new or innovative, nothing challenging or quirky, just well-known classics. Thankfully, there are no attempts to modernize. Instead, you've got a sincere and knowledgeable interpretation of pure Gallic charm.

Above **The modest exterior of Casse-Croûte.** Right and far right **A black-and-white tiled floor, bentwood chairs, gingham undercloths, paper table tops, Parisian goblets and French signage all signal the archetypal bistro.**

Hervé Durochat

"

Comptoir Gourmand in Maltby Street is where I go to get breakfast – great croissants/pains au chocolat and great coffee. I try to get some croissants twice a week early in the morning for the staff at Casse-Croûte.

Co-owner, Casse-Croûte

Above and above right
The clichéd dining room at Casse-Croûte is also considered to be chic and of the moment.

Left **Hervé Durochat at his restaurant Casse-Croûte** on fashionable **Bermondsey Street.**

Flat Iron Square 68 Union Street, SE1 1TD

020 3179 9800   www.flatironsquare.co.uk

At the time of writing, this place had just opened – I went to the opening night party and had a stonking burrito, and then went back a few days later for a yum buttermilk pancake. It's a massive undertaking, just a hop, skip and a jump away from the already buzzing Borough Market. It will consist of seven food vendors, three restaurants, three food trucks, five bars, a little general retail and a live music venue – it's going to be massive in every sense of the word, all spread across seven railways arches and the Grade II listed Devonshire House (PP).

Flat Iron Square is the first point on London's Low Line, a long-planned and exciting initiative that sees the reopening of the walkway through Borough, based on the original railway viaducts. When complete you will be able to walk down the Low Line as far as Waterloo, taking in different projects along the way.

The Garrison 99–101 Bermondsey Street, SE1 3XB

020 7089 9355 www.thegarrison.co.uk

A lovely neighbourhood public house with a menu that outdoes most other attempts at gastropub grub. The prices are competitive and the dishes are prepared with some skill. The space is decorated in an eclectic fashion with mostly reclaimed and intentionally distressed furniture, sensitively juxtaposed with a few modern pieces. The basement houses a mini-cinema, available for private hire and ideal for birthdays.

Hutong The Shard, 31 St Thomas Street SE1 9RY

020 3011 1257 www.hutong.co.uk

I dined in the original Hutong in Hong Kong (also up a skyscraper) and thought it amazing – I had a pig's oesophagus for my main course, although I would add that this was rather extreme and that most of the other dishes and the dim sum were far more normal in concept, but extraordinary in taste. When we heard it was coming to London, we knew it would be wildly popular, especially as it is located on the 33rd floor of The Shard (PP).

José Tapas Bar 104 Bermondsey Street, SE1 3UB
020 7403 4902 www.josepizarro.com

This bustling sherry and tapas bar – another welcome addition to the Bermondsey Street scene – is brought to you by José Pizarro. Just like the Andalucian versions, it is standing or bar-stool dining, while you watch the chefs work the plancha grill. The only problem with these places is that you just can't stop ordering and eating. You start with a few Padrón peppers, croquetas, calamares and a glass or two of something, then the enthusiasm takes over and the next thing you know you've had four glasses of wine and about a dozen different small plates – all delicious. If you do visit, try to save yourself for the chocolate, sea salt and olive oil pot or the torta de Santiago.

Further down Bermondsey Street, José also has a proper restaurant called Pizarro, which, incidentally, he named after his grandfather.

Right **One of the many tapas at José.**
Right below **A plate of jamon and a glass of sherry are essential at José.**

Best for... tapas

There's been an explosion in the number of excellent modern-style tapas bars, the below is just a short selection.

| Barrafina |
| Duende |
| José |
| Morito |

Left, above **A chef carefully carving the jamon at José** – each slice has to be wafer-thin and the size of your tongue.
Left **The excellent tapas at José.**
Right **Tarta de Santiago** at the end of good meal at José.

Left **Ropewalk now provides the home for Maltby Street Market.** Below left **One of the cheese stalls in a railway arch at Maltby Street Market.**

Right **Ole Hansen carving his exceptionally high-quality Hansen & Lydersen smoked salmon.**

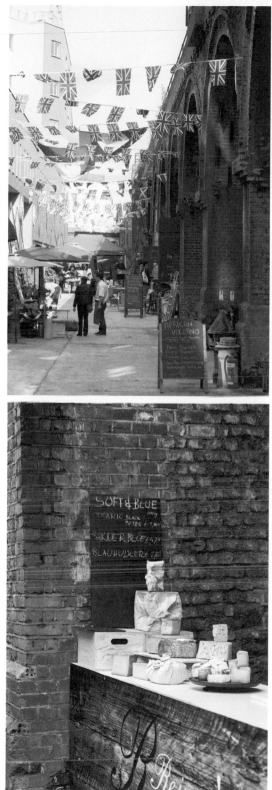

Maltby Street Market

Ropewalk, London SE1 3PA

www.maltby.st Saturday 9–4; Sunday 11–4

In the previous edition of *Eat London* we talked about a nascent market just down the road from the massively popular Borough Market. Back in 2010 this was all about quality food merchants and producers that had been priced out of Borough and wanted to start up their own market. Initially, it was just a few arches, but from the outset it included a stellar group. One of these was the excellent St John bakery proffering their magnificent custard doughnuts. I'm not really a doughnut lover but these creations are game-changers. Another one of the early group was the supremely good Tayshaw greengrocer's. Even if I wasn't in need of some of the best vegetables in London, I would make a point to visit and admire the amazing array of produce. Via their wholesale arm, we work with Tayshaw to provide our restaurants with excellent wild mushrooms and the occasional truffle or two. Now, the market has extended further and Ropewalk, the alleyway alongside the brilliant LASSCO architectural salvage specialist, is full of street-food traders. When you visit, you must include a tour around the LASSCO showrooms – it is sure to inspire you, and at the heart of the space, among all of the antiques and *objets trouvés*, there is a fun cocktail bar.

St John have also opened another little dining room here, with their particular brand of British brunch and supper creations, among them the bloody good blood cake with duck egg and brown sauce.

The good thing about Maltby Street is that it is equally vibrant on Sunday as it is on Saturday, when Borough Market is closed.

There's plenty to see, eat and drink at Maltby Street, and if you are a fan of natural wines, those with limited chemicals and pesticides, then you should head to 40 Maltby Street, where you will also find some very good food with equally admirable ethics at its centre. And I must mention Maltby & Greek, where you can buy the finest Greek produce in London (PP).

292

M. Manze Pie and Mash 87 Tower Bridge Road, SE1 4TW

020 7407 2985   www.manze.co.uk

Only a few pie and mash shops survive in London; Manze's is one of the best.

Mercato Metropolitano 42 Newington Causeway, SE1 6DR

020 7403 0930   www.mercatometropolitano.co.uk

This is another massively positive development for south London and, specifically, the area close to Elephant and Castle. Previously an ugly, no-go zone, this
forthcoming development is great news. Helping to kick-start things is the
Mercato Metropolitano social movement from Turin. The development is
massive, with 4,200 sq m (45,000 sq ft) of space dedicated to the best regional
producers from all over Italy.

The Mondrian 20 Upper Ground, London SE1 9PD

020 3747 1000   www.morganshotelgroup.com/mondrian/

Housed in Sea Containers House, formerly one of the ugliest river-facing
façades in London before a recent revamp – the new manifestation is much
better. The design of The Mondrian hotel transports you on a nautical tour
in a 1920s cruise ship, courtesy of über-designer Tom Dixon's imagination and
his Design Research Studio. The massive copper-clad wall in the reception area,
designed to look like a ship's hull, is striking. There are two stunning bars to
choose from. Most people head to the rooftop Rumpus Room but, in fact,
the best cocktails are to be had at Dandelyan on the raised ground floor
on the river side.

Above **The copper-
clad nautical-themed
reception, designed
by Tom Dixon at The
Mondrian.**

Opposite above
**The Rumpus Room
on the top floor
overlooking the
Thames at The
Mondrian.**
Opposite below
**Sea Containers dining
room at The Mondrian,
inspired by the golden
period of transatlantic
cruise liners.**

Monmouth Coffee Company 2 Park Street, SE1 9AB

020 7232 3010   www.monmouthcoffee.co.uk

Southwark has two branches of this business, which is ultra-serious in its pursuit of excellent coffee. The Park Street coffee shop, adjacent to Borough Market, has lovely pastries and provides an ideal meeting point before setting off to explore the market, or a haven to which to repair after the onslaught. The second branch, part of the Maltby Street Market (see page 291), includes the roastery and is for the eager bean aficionado. There is also a shop on Monmouth Street in Covent Garden.

Mrs King's Pork Pies Borough Market, 8 Southwark Street, SE1 1TL

020 7407 1002   www.mrskingsporkpies.co.uk

Wednesday & Thursday 9–5; Friday 9–6; Saturday 8–5

It was in 1853 that Elizabeth King set up her family business in the village of Cotgrave near Nottingham, at the heart of Melton Mowbray country. The trio of brothers who have owned Mrs King's since the 1980s continue to champion her original recipes, and these authentic pies have now attained virtually cult status among the pie-lovers of London.

The meat comes only from the shoulder of pigs fed on whey from the nearby Stilton dairies, and the hot-water crust is formed without the assistance of a tin. Everything is hand-made, and the jelly is derived from boiled-down trotters (the head and spleen are no longer used for jelly since the BSE crisis of the late 1990s – much to the disappointment of Ian Hartland, who mans the market stall each week).

In 2008, Melton Mowbray pork pies were awarded Protected Geographical Indication, which means that only pie-makers who are situated within the designated area and who use the specified techniques can call their pies Melton Mowbray. Mrs King's now also offer a few variations on the original recipes, but our favourite is the simple pork pie, with its peppery back note, especially as part of a ploughman's lunch or partnered by good English ale.

Mrs King's pies are so good that we stock them in all of our Albion shops and cafés (see pages 78 and 160).

Best for... cheesemongers

Frankly, you must only visit these places if you want to buy cheese in London. Of course, there are plenty more to choose from, but don't bother – head for the best.

Androuet

La Fromagerie

Neal's Yard Dairy

Above **Monmouth Coffee, a stalwart in their premises near Borough Market, and Mrs Kings Pork Pies are just two of the great many food producers that have stalls at the market.**

Randolph Hodgson

My favourite restaurants include Clarke's (Sally Clarke was one of my first restaurant customers) and I like Anchor & Hope and St John for their no-nonsense approach and gutsy cooking.

Owner, Neal's Yard Dairy

Right **The Shard, by Renzo Piano, overshadows Borough Market, and on the upper floors includes Hutong, Aqua Shard and Oblix restaurants.** Far right **Cheese at Neal's Yard Diary.**

Neal's Yard Dairy 6 Park Street, SE1 9AB

020 7367 0799 www.nealsyarddairy.co.uk

Quite simply the best place in London to buy British cheeses, this shop is a retail experience of considerable note, where you can be assured of peerless cheese in perfect condition. Keen's, Montgomery, Isle of Mull, Westcombe and Daylesford seem to be the most popular Cheddar styles. The wealth of other cheeses – hard, soft, blue and washed rind, made from cows', goats' and sheep's milk – comes from 40 cheesemakers in Britain and Ireland. The big difference with NYD is that they select, mature and sell cheese – the latter only when it is in perfect condition. I've tasted the same cheese from other cheese retailers and they are never taste as good as the NYD-matured cheeses (PP).

Neal's Yard also operate a burgeoning wholesale arm and a worldwide mail-order service. They also sell a few other dairy and creamery offerings, such as good butter, cream, crème fraîche, eggs and milk.

Oblix The Shard, 31 St Thomas Street, SE1 9RY

020 7268 6700 www.oblixrestaurant.com

I've got mixed views on this restaurant on the 32nd floor of The Shard (not only the tallest building in the capital, but also now an emblem of new London, I certainly feel that the view is one of the best features. And what a view it is. When this restaurant first opened, I happened to visit three times in three weeks – not always my choice of venue. On each occasion, I couldn't quite work out why I didn't think it was appealing but on each occasion I felt it was worth a further visit – mainly for the view (PP).

Oxo Tower Restaurant and Brasserie 8th floor, Oxo Tower Wharf, Bargehouse Street, SE1 9PH

020 7803 3888 www.oxotower.co.uk

The Oxo Tower has attracted occasional criticism for its sky-high prices. Here, restaurant dining is all about occasions, special dates and the odd honourable proposal, while the brasserie offers simpler fare. But there is no doubt: the views across the river toward the architecture of the capital are amazing.

Left and below **A chef being precise with the pasta preparation at Padella.**

Above **Rolling large sheets of fresh hand-made pasta.**
Below **Fresh pasta at Padella.**

Padella 6 Southwark Street, SE1 1TQ

www.padella.co

This is such an obvious and simple concept – so much so that it is hard to believe that it hasn't already been done before to this level in London. The format is based on two main tenets, fresh daily hand-made pasta and very, very reasonable pricing. Chef Tim Siadatan is a product of Jamie Oliver's Fifteen restaurant, and he and his business partner Jordan Frieda have apparently had the desire to realize this project for over 10 years and have spent the intervening years tasting their way around Italy looking for ideas, ingredients and recipes. They already run the excellent Trullo in Islington, where you can also enjoy a fine plate of pasta (see page 120). The menu is very short, with just a small handful of antipasti to start and then just about seven or eight pasta dishes, mostly taglierini, tagliatelle, pappardelle and ravioli. And, two tarts for puddings, plus salted caramel ice cream – fortunately, my favourite (PP).

The interior, like everything else, is simple but effective. It's all white tiles and zinc counters, with a hint of 1950s Italian cafés. On the ground floor it is all about dining at the counter or ledges around the edges of the room. There is more comfortable dining downstairs. All of this combines to create a much-desired dining spot on the edge of Borough Market. You'll need to go off-peak if you want to avoid the queues.

Le Pont de la Tour 36D Shad Thames, SE1 2YE

020 7403 8403 www.lepontdelatour.co.uk

The South Bank is now blessed with many excellent restaurants, and one of the first of these was Le Pont de la Tour. In the 1980s, when Terence Conran was masterminding the Shad Thames redevelopment and turning derelict warehouses into cool riverside apartments, it was Le Pont de la Tour – with its bar, grill, deli, bakery, wine shop and 'posh' French brasserie – that lay at the heart of this transformation, the first Conran gastrodrome. Ownership of the restaurant is now with D&D London and they've altered the original ideas and design, but you can't deny that it is still an excellent spot for a decent dinner on a summer evening if you are able to secure one of the outside terrace tables looking towards majestic Tower Bridge. The current head chef is Frederick Forster, a Master of Culinary Arts, he's also won various other chef competitions and has one of the best CVs of a chef working in London today.

Skylon Royal Festival Hall, Belvedere Road, SE1 8XX

020 7654 7800 www.skylon-restaurant.co.uk

If you have a preference for mega-restaurants with a capacity topping a few hundred, Skylon is definitely for you. The ceilings are high, the dimensions wide and long, and the huge windows add further depth to this unique space. The designers have cleverly divided up the single room by creating three distinct offerings.

A central raised island bar serving expensive and creative cocktails, complemented by excellent table service from waiting staff wearing statement uniforms, makes an ideal meeting point before or after a concert, talk or dance performance in the vibrant Royal Festival Hall.

Skylon takes its name from the futuristic structure that was built alongside the Royal Festival Hall for the Festival of Britain in 1951: a fascinating event well worth reading up on.

Above **The window tables overlooking the Thames at Skylon, designed by Conran and Partners.** Right **Stylish interiors inside Skylon.**

Top right **The outside terrace at Le Pont de la Tour. Founded by Terence Conran, it was the first in a string of gastrodome-style destinations to open in London and beyond.**

Above and right **Scenes from London's South Bank.**

Housed in a converted potato warehouse on the edge of Borough Market,
this small bar and dining room delivers an authentic tapas experience.
The name Brindisa derives from the Spanish *brindis*, meaning a drink or
toast. In celebration of all things Spanish, we suggest you raise a small glass
of fino, manzanilla or oloroso over a simple plate of hand-carved Joselito ham.
You can stand in the bar and *jamoneria* (traditional ham-carving corner)
and enjoy grilled anchovies, salt cod or croquettes, or take a seat under the
shelves of specially imported products and order a range of small individual
plates of Montadito tapas.

Underneath Roast restaurant along Stoney Street, Brindisa also has a small
shop, open Tuesday to Saturday, selling an extensive range of Spanish tinned
fish, olive oils, hams and innumerable Iberian delicacies.

Left, above and below
**Some of the excellent
tapas at Brindisa.**

Left **The new £80 million Switch House extension to Tate Modern.**
Right **Professional staff are assured at the Tate Modern restaurant.**
Below left **The Foster + Partners-designed Millennium Bridge for pedestrians, crossing the Thames from Bankside to St Paul's in the City.**

Tate Modern Bankside, SE1 9TG
020 7887 8888 www.tate.org.uk

In the 1990s, the Victoria and Albert Museum press office proudly declared that it had an ace café with a good museum attached. Since then, dining in museums and galleries has been as good as on the high street, and in many cases significantly better. Certainly, all of the Tate cafés and restaurants are professionally managed.

The menus might not demonstrate creativity on a par with many of the Tate's esteemed artists, but they are good solid affairs none the less, and you certainly don't need to leave the gallery to enjoy a tasty meal or snack. It is also pleasing to see their patriotism, promoting British ingredients, farmers, growers and other esteemed food producers to their international visitors.

There is a wide selection of dining and drinking options in both the Boiler House building and the new Switch House extension. All perfect refuelling points before taking on Dali and Surrealism or Lichtenstein, Warhol and Pop Art. You can choose from espresso bars to cafés and bars to something smarter. The views across the River Thames and London from the dining rooms and the controversial viewing gallery also add to the allure. As a relatively new father, I would also say that they seem to be more family-friendly than other galleries across London. Beware, though, of the problems with the lifts in the Switch House – don't get in at the ground floor, instead go to the basement to avoid the queues (PP)

Village East 171–3 Bermondsey Street, SE1 3UW

020 7357 6082   www.villageeast.co.uk

Whether it is thanks to gentrification or simply its pleasant environment, Bermondsey Street – just a short walk from London Bridge or Butlers Wharf and the Thames – is a feel-good area. Like nearby Shad Thames, it has historic links with food warehousing, and Bermondsey is inextricably linked with chocolate. Many of the original warehouses are now trendy apartments or hip, creative design offices. Add a little green, a florist, some quirky retailers, the Zandra Rhodes' Fashion and Textile Museum and the most impressive White Cube Gallery, you have a magnet for serious urbanites.

Village East has certainly helped to put Bermondsey Street on the map of places to go. The owners of this style-led, multifaceted operation, who also run the nearby Garrison gastropub, describe Village East as a 'New York warehouse -style brasserie restaurant'.

Wright Brothers Oyster and Porter House 11 Stoney Street, SE1 9AD

020 7403 9554   www.thewrightbrothers.co.uk

From Cromer crabs, Poole Bay prawns, Dorset lobsters and the world's finest langoustines, fished from Scottish waters, to a fine range of oysters sourced from around the coastline, humble mussels, clams, shrimps, cockles and whelks, Wright Brothers Oyster and Porter House is a celebration of all British seafood.

Behind the business are Ben Wright and Robin Hancock, two family friends (not brothers) who share a passion for oysters and who have previously grown, imported and supplied oysters to London's top chefs.

The tiny dining space consists essentially of an L-shaped counter overlooking the oyster display and shucking activities, a few raised long tables with stools, and a tiny open kitchen for preparing the few cooked dishes on the menu. The exposed brick walls and electrics suggest a hint of Manhattan fused with the classic sign-writing of a Parisian zinc bar.

The choice of oysters is extensive, with a range including specialities such as French *spéciales de claire*, rocks from Cornwall and natives from Mersea Island in the Thames estuary near Colchester. You can enjoy your oysters *au naturel* or garnished by delights such as Kilpatrick (smoked bacon), New Orleans (deep-fried, tartare sauce), Spanish (chorizo) or Japanese (wasabi, soy and ginger).

The menu, written on the blackboard above the counter, also includes delicious oyster rarebit and a steak, oyster and Guinness pie.

There are now a few other Wright Brothers restaurants around London and they all serve great seafood, but this, the original, seems to be, by far, the most atmospheric.

Top **A platter of British shellfish at the outstanding Wright Brothers.** Right **The Wright Brothers oyster bar is located on the edge of Borough Market.**

More places to visit in the area

Albion
NEO Bankside, Pavillion B,
Holland Street, SE1 9FU
020 3764 5550 www.albion-uk.london
Immediately opposite Tate Modern, Albion
is open all day, seven days per week, serving
no-nonsense, modestly priced, seasonal British
food. Albion also has a small shop selling
British cheeses, meats, organic vegetables and
fruit, plus a few store-cupboard essentials.

Elliot's
12 Stoney Street, Borough Market, SE1 9AD
02074037436 www.elliotscafe.com
Cheek by jowl with Borough Market and
a menu inspired by the produce available
there. The Dexter beef sirloin wing-rib
sharing dishes cooked on the wood-fired
grill are worth the trip.

Hixter
16 Great Guildford Street, SE1 0HS
020 7921 9508 www.hixrestaurants.co.uk
A stylish and fun Mark Hix joint with great
cocktails, steaks and chicken.

Mar I Terra
14 Gambia Street, SE1 0XH
020 7928 7628 www.mariterra.co.uk
Not part of the newwave of tapas, this place
serves more authentic Spanish food and has
a massive menu.

O Ver
44–6 Southwark Street, SE1 1UN
020 7378 9933 www.overuk.com
They say they are the first UK restaurant to use
pure sea water as an ingredient for making
their healthy Neapolitan street food.

Restaurant Story
199 Tooley Street, SE1 2JX
020 7183 2117 www.restaurantstory.co.uk
Tom Sellers, the chef here, is ultra-confident
about himself, and so he should be with a
career that has included spells working with
Thomas Keller and René Redzepi at Noma.
Restaurant Story opened in 2013 and won a
Michelin star within five months – more
reasons for his confidence.

The Table Café
83 Southwark Street, SE1 0HX
020 7401 2760 www.thetablecafe.com
A great weekend brunch spot with waffles
and pancakes.

Above **Chicken and chips, Mark Hix-style, at Hixter.** Above right **The stylish bar at Hixter.**

Index

Index